Best Practice in Professional Supervision

Best Practice in
Professional Supervision

Second Edition

A GUIDE FOR THE
HELPING PROFESSIONS

Allyson Davys
and
Liz Beddoe

Jessica Kingsley Publishers
London and Philadelphia

First edition published in Great Britain in 2010 by Jessica Kingsley Publishers
This second edition published in Great Britain in 2021 by Jessica Kingsley Publishers
An Hachette Company

1

A CIP catalogue record for this title is available from the British Library and the Library of Congress

ISBN 978 1 78592 471 2
eISBN 978 1 78450 857 9

Printed and bound in Great Britain by Clays Ltd.

Jessica Kingsley Publishers' policy is to use papers that are natural, renewable and recyclable
products and made from wood grown in sustainable forests. The logging and manufacturing
processes are expected to conform to the environmental regulations of the country of origin.

Jessica Kingsley Publishers
Carmelite House
50 Victoria Embankment
London EC4Y 0DZ

www.jkp.com

Contents

Contents

Acknowledgments

We would like to acknowledge our past and present supervisors who have facilitated our professional reflection and growth and all the supervisees who have shared their journeys with us. Particularly, we thank the many practitioners who have attended our courses and who have contributed to our understanding and learning through their generous sharing of the challenges of, and excitement about, supervision. Finally, to our families, Harold, Caitlin, David, Genevieve, Mike and Sebastien, thank you for your encouragement, support and patience.

CHAPTER 1

The Context of Professional Supervision

It is an unfortunate reality that although it is relevant to all fields of human services and has become mandatory in many, the practice of professional supervision is contested and very differently understood and interpreted. Thus we began *Best Practice in Professional Supervision* (Davys and Beddoe 2010). Ten years later, at the start of this second edition, we again survey the territory of professional supervision. We note that the profile of professional supervision has continued to grow during this time through research, publication and practice. Supervision appears on the practice agenda of people from an increasing range of professional and occupational groups, many of whom do not have supervision as a tradition of practice. That being said, there remains a broad range of understanding about, and practice of, professional supervision (Kelly and Green 2019; Sewell 2018).

At the beginning of our involvement in supervisory education the literature rather unvaryingly focused on the rationale for supervision and the 'state' of supervision during a period of rapid change in health and human services. Students rightly criticized the traditional literature as assuming much more benign and well-resourced health and social care services than was a reality by the late 1980s. This situation has improved in subsequent years where many authors have contributed useful perspectives which acknowledge the impact of the organizational and political climates (Beddoe and Maidment 2015; Bond and Holland 1998; Brown and Bourne 1996; Hawkins and Shohet 1989; Hughes and Pengelly 1997; Noble, Gray and Johnston 2016). Since our 2010 publication of *Best Practice* Hawkins and Shohet have published their fourth edition and a raft of new books have appeared, for example: Edwards, (2012); Owen and Shohet (2012); Carroll (2014); Falender, Shafranske and Falicov (2014); Noble, Gray and Johnston, (2016); Hewson and Carroll (2016) and Beinart and Clohessy (2017). Publications addressing supervision have thus rapidly grown in both numbers and professional orientation. The publication of *The Wiley International Handbook of Clinical Supervision* (Watkins and Milne 2014) also represents an important occasion in the history of supervision scholarship. Our own second book, *Challenges in Professional Supervision: Current Themes and Models for Practice*, (Beddoe and Davys 2016), provided us with the opportunity to explore more recent developments in supervision and to expand on such topics as supervision ethics, difficult conversations in supervision, group supervision, interprofessional supervision and supervisor education.

Supervision, which is believed by some to have its early antecedents in the 17th and 18th centuries, developed into the practice we recognize today during the past 130 years (Grauel 2002). The growth and refinement of supervision have been accompanied by an associated complexity (and richness) of definition and practice as different professional and occupational groups have adopted supervision as one form of professional development and accountability. The result, 'a malleable concept in search of precise definition' (Grauel 2002, p.4), aptly captures one of the key dilemmas for today's practitioners who are faced with a form of professional practice which, for all its similarities, is differently positioned within separate professions, and indeed for some professions is differently positioned across international borders. Carroll (2014), reflecting on this range of understanding, comments that it has required him to consider what he personally believes to be supervision and to consider how supervision differs, 'and should differ', when practised in any new context (p.4).

Definitions of supervision can be found which describe a continuum of supervision from an evaluative activity linked to organizational purpose (and student development) to supervision as a reflective space where transformative learning develops and enriches practice. In some contexts, supervision is exclusively the domain of the novice or student apprentice, while in other contexts, it is a lifelong process of professional critique and learning. In our writing, we have chosen to use the term professional supervision, not because we necessarily see this term as the 'best' term for what is a complex set of specific relationships and tasks, but rather it is our attempt to distinguish the practice of supervision from a plethora of other terms which describe similar activities but which do not exactly capture our meaning of supervision. Ferguson (2005), in a multidisciplinary text on clinical mentoring and supervision in the allied health professions, provides a broad definition of supervision that works across disciplines and neatly manages to include the practice learning aspect of supervision and to encompass professional development:

> Professional supervision is a process between someone called a supervisor and another referred to as the supervisee. It is usually aimed at enhancing

the helping effectiveness of the person supervised. It may include acquisition of practical skills, mastery of theoretical or technical knowledge, personal development at the client/therapist interface and professional development. (Ferguson 2005, p.294)

In 2010, we commented on the unprecedented number of publications on the topic of supervision in the helping and health professions over the previous 15 years and, as detailed earlier, we see that this interest and activity have continued in the subsequent ten years. Research on supervision, although possibly still not keeping pace with conceptual material on supervision (Hawkins and Shohet 2006), has nevertheless also grown in the past ten years. While, as Hawkins and Shohet (2012) note, much of the research is situated in North American-based counselling psychology and psychotherapy and focuses on the supervision of trainees, we have also noted an upsurge in social work research from United Kingdom (UK), Canada, New Zealand and Australia which is focused on the experiences of practitioners who engage in career-long supervision.

The published research has a wide focus which has included: evaluation of supervision, supervisory harmfulness, interprofessional supervision, multicultural competence, anti-oppressive supervision, collaboration, supervision as a reflective space, emotion in supervision, stress and resilience. Studies have followed and observed supervisees and supervisors and reported their interaction with each other and with their clients; different models and approaches to supervision have been considered for their applicability to different groups of supervisees and for their compatibility with each other. Ethical practice and ethical supervision have been explored and the power structures and role of the supervisor and supervisee have been critiqued. A critical lens has been applied to supervision to challenge the blind assumptions of power and tradition and, importantly, supervision has been challenged to move to a collaborative model of relating.

Despite this progress, evaluating the effectiveness of supervision remains problematic (Davys *et al.* 2017). Watkins (2019, p.1), in a systematic review of the clinical supervision research reviews published between 1995 and 2019, concludes that 'proof' for supervision appears to be more 'proof by association' than otherwise, being primarily a product of ex post facto, cross-sectional, correlational study. Many schedules of criteria for evaluation include some form of subjective individual or parallel assessment by the supervisor and/ or supervisee, or rates of staff satisfaction, and/or service user complaint. With regard to the two latter criteria, however, it may not be the effectiveness of supervision per se, but rather the organizational culture that ultimately wields the greatest influence over these factors. This is a topic we will discuss further in Chapter 4. Two questions have typically been asked when evaluating supervision: what has been the effect of supervision on the supervisees and how does supervision benefit clients or service users (Watkins 2011)?

In response to the first question, effective supervision has been considered to have a positive impact on staff retention (DePanfilis and Zlotnik 2008; Yankeelov *et al.* 2009) while low supervisory support has been significantly related to the intention to leave (Nissly, Mor Barak and Levin 2005). Mor Barak *et al.* (2009) reported in a meta-analysis that the supervisory functions are positively and statistically significantly related to better outcomes for workers. Considering the supervision of child welfare workers, Carpenter, Webb and Bostock (2013) reviewed the research literature over a period of 12 years from 2000 to 2012 and found 'evidence of associations between the provision of supervision and a variety of outcomes for workers, including job satisfaction, self-efficacy and stress and for organizations, including workload management, case analysis and retention' (Carpenter *et al.* 2013, p.1843). Through a longer (30 years) but similar systematic review of the research on psychotherapy supervision, supervisees were found to gain 'enhanced self-awareness, enhanced treatment knowledge, skill acquisition and utilization, enhanced self-efficacy, and strengthening of the supervisee-patient relationship' through supervision (Watkins 2011 p.236). Watkins (2019), in his most recent review, somewhat revises this finding, stating that 'evidence supporting supervision impact of any type is weak at best, especially so for worker and client outcomes' (p.13).

This question of whether clients or service users benefit from supervision has been considered by others and progress to develop appropriate measures for this has been reported as slow (Falender and Shafranske 2014; Tsong and Goodyear 2014), lacking in methodological rigour (Watkins 2011) and focused on trainees as opposed to experienced qualified practitioners (Wheeler and Barkham 2014). Exploring the clinical supervision of psychotherapy trainees, Rast and colleagues (2017, p.1) suggest that efficacy of the supervision in this regard is more a matter of belief than fact: 'both supervisors and supervisees perceive supervision as beneficial and important for impacting client outcome'. Watkins (2019), while noting the enduring calls in the supervision literature for empirical research, concludes that 'If supervision is to ever be evidence based, then there is sore need for more, better and broader evidence' (p.16).

A brief history of supervision

Historically, professional supervision has been associated with the early development of social work during the latter part of the 19th century (Tsui

1997) and indeed it has been identified as 'the most original and characteristic process that the field of social casework has developed' (Robinson 1949, p. viii). As O'Donoghue astutely observes, however, it is unlikely that such an activity should 'suddenly emerge from nowhere in the nineteenth century' and it is probable that the antecedents of supervision lie in much earlier social, spiritual and cultural arrangements of family and community (O'Donoghue 2003, p.43). In illustration of this, Grauel (2002) identifies links between current supervisory practice and the 17th- and 18th-century relationships between physicians and apothecaries.

Whatever the antecedents, the end of the 19th century saw the first application of supervision as it relates to current practice. As previously mentioned, this first stage of supervision development was introduced by social workers. At this time, groups of volunteer social workers gathered around experienced leaders and, through a process that has been likened to an apprenticeship, learned through observation and instruction. Here the emphasis was on adherence to agency policy and concerned the 'appropriate' distribution of resources to those deemed to be in need and deserving of assistance (Munson 1993). Thus at the turn of the 19th century, when social work practice had begun to move away from the determination of who was deserving among the poor and become more interested in assessing the effect of poverty, so too did supervision cast a more critical eye on the broader aspects of practice. A shift of focus for supervision was recorded by Mary Richmond in 1917 who stated:

> Good supervision must include this consideration of wider aspects... Every caseworker has noticed how a certain juxtaposition of facts often reappears in record after record, and...this recurring juxtaposition indicates a hidden relation of cause and effect. (cited by Munson 1993, p.50)

The relationship between models of practice and models of supervision has continued to be noted throughout the development of supervision practice (Gardiner 1989; Scaife 2001). The development of solutions-focused practice, for example, has led to the construction of a style of supervision held to be congruent with work with service users (Juhnke 1996; Santa Rita 1998). This supervision approach will be discussed in more detail in Chapter 2.

The influence of Freud and psychoanalysis in the early part of the 20th century brought a new group of participants to supervision and also a shift of focus. Supervision was now concerned with client work. By the 1920s, it had become a requirement of psychoanalytic training (Carroll 2007). The influence of new Freudian and psychoanalytic theories on existing social work practice and supervision was also evident (Pettes 1967). Within the supervision relationship, the psychoanalytic approach emphasized the authority and expertise of the supervisor and any difficulties experienced by the supervisee were identified as personal pathology and required remedy. The boundaries between the impact of personal factors on the practitioner's work and personal issues were blurred and supervision was, at times, hard to distinguish from counselling or therapy.

At this stage of supervision practice, where difficulties were deemed to reflect the failings, psychological or otherwise, of the supervisee, supervision was considered perhaps not surprisingly as the province of the new and uninitiated worker. Trained and experienced practitioners resisted the idea of supervision, considering it an insult and a suggestion of incompetence (Kane 2001). This is a theme that follows supervision on its journey in other professions as well and will be seen later.

In the mid- to late 20th century when psychotherapists and counsellors joined social workers and psychoanalysts in adopting supervision as an integral component of practice, Carroll notes the continued blurring between clinical practice with clients and supervision (Carroll 2007, p.34). Carroll describes a new phase of supervision appearing in the 1970s. Now a clear distinction was made between counselling/therapy and supervision. Supervision became firmly focused on the 'work' of the practitioner and whatever affected or influenced that practice (Carroll 2007, p.34). In the field of practice, the development of task-centred models reflected an increased concern for accountability.

For some professions and practitioners, this focus on accountability heralded the major ideological and political changes which affected social service provision during the 1980s and 1990s. The last decades of the 20th century saw private sector management practices applied to the public sector, with considerable impact on schools, health care and social services, where formerly professional status had determined decision-making power (Healy and Meagher 2004). We are all familiar with the requirements for measurable outputs, performance management and quality assurance systems.

One significant impact of the new preoccupation with accountability practices on supervision was the strengthening of the administrative function and an associated move away from in-depth review and critique of practice. For many, particularly those in social work, this period represented a time of challenge to the integrity of professional work as management demands took precedence in supervision (Payne 1994).

The socioeconomic influences of this time, however, did not have the same constraining effect on all professions. It was during the 1970s that counselling psychology in the United States established itself as a key developer and researcher of supervision theory and practice (Carroll 2007). It was here, according to Carroll, that 'the emphasis from within counselling psychology on the "reflective-practitioner" model as the best way to define a counselling psychologist gave supervision its credibility' (Carroll 2007, p.34). This period also saw the development of other approaches to supervision which drew from theories of adult learning and development (Butler 1996; Loganbill, Hardy and Delworth 1982).

Supervision continues to change. Interest in career-long supervision has been shown from professions which traditionally only involved themselves in supervision as pre-service education (Watkins 2014b). This revitalization of supervision has also been led by changes in the nature of public services which have demanded increased scrutiny of direct practice and resulted in reduced professional autonomy for professionals (Beddoe et al. 2016; Karvinen-Niinikoski et al. 2019). Two major factors have influenced this change. The first factor is the neoliberal preoccupation with systems of accountability mentioned earlier. The second factor is the impact of 'the risk society' and the concomitant public critique of professional practice (Beddoe 2010). These features come together in a social trend described as a 'crisis of trust' in professionals (O'Neill 2002). Fear of failure, concern for public safety and a deep fear of public criticism (Stanley and Manthorpe 2004) on the part of government have led to more emphasis on compliance in oversight of professional practice and mandatory and continuous professional development.

Supervision and the health professions in the regulatory climate

The introduction of supervision into health care professions has been an interesting journey, separate though at times parallel to that of social work, counselling and psychology. Traditionally, health care professions have utilized supervision as a method of training students and as oversight for new practitioners. An example of the latter is the nursing profession's use of preceptors for new graduates or nurses commencing practice in a new role and function. Many health professions, however, have not traditionally required supervision for fully qualified practitioners, and supervision in these contexts has thus traditionally been regarded as something for those who are less expert or for those needing oversight. Leggat et al. (2016) suggest that within the allied health professions such association has resulted in continued confusion between clinical supervision, professional supervision, performance review and line management. Research from these professions thus often reflects a supervision relationship which is characterized by student/expert dynamics and open to the anxiety and pressures of assessment.

In the nursing profession, the early advocates of clinical supervision faced considerable resistance in the implementation of supervision programmes (Gilbert 2001; Johns 2001). Northcott reports that:

> Clinical supervision entered the professional language of nursing...with a flurry of interest, uncertainty and suspicion, in part I believe a result of nurses' experience of appraisal. Was clinical supervision yet another attempt to control nurses, as one of my respondents had suggested? (Northcott 2000, p.16)

As with allied health professionals, nurses made links between clinical supervision activity and those measures associated with increased accountability: individual performance review, personal therapy, management and preceptorship (White et al. 1998, p.187). While Bond and Holland (2010) note a subsequent growth in' the momentum towards clinical supervision' (p. 51), they also record their concern at the ongoing resistance from the nursing profession to major change in this area of practice.

Allied to this tension between the functions in supervision, a significant issue identified in a review of the literature on supervision in the health professions is the nature of the relationship(s) between supervisor and supervisee. In 1998, White and colleagues' research found that in nursing, supervisors were often supervisees' managers, and this was a source of tension. 'Indeed, in one setting there was an intention to develop an organizational culture using such an arrangement, while in another setting it was argued that clinical supervision actually "needed to be hierarchical"' (White et al. 1998, p.188). This is a recurring theme in supervision literature as demonstrated in a study by Williams and Irvine (2009), which 'highlighted the precarious situation of the manager as clinical supervisor arrangement' (Williams and Irvine 2009, p.481). While the ideal type of professional supervision presents supervision as 'facilitative and supportive, interpretations of government directives rather promote supervision as directed towards consumer protection and safety' and this raises the spectre of surveillance (Beddoe 2010).

The contemporary practice of supervision

The last three decades have seen this emphasis on managerial supervision in the public sector. Requirements for measurable outputs, rationalized service, efficiency, effectiveness, performance management and quality assurance created new priorities and tensions for managers and these features filtered into the supervision process. The climate of accountability also brought increased public critique of professional practice, particularly focused on those operating at a threshold of risk such as child protection and mental health and the oversight of criminal offenders (Morrison 1997, 2001). Supervision thus became a locus for output and performance measurement and risk management, rather than a place for reflection and development.

Proving yet again its adaptability, supervision entered a further period of revitalization. In the United Kingdom, supervision was significantly mandated by such public comments as the following:

> If we are to deliver the very best services across adults' and children's services we need the very best workforces who are well trained, highly skilled and passionate about their role. We know from our research that the key to building this workforce is the support, guidance and opportunities we provide to our colleagues. High quality supervision is one of the most important drivers in ensuring positive outcomes for people who use social care and children's services. It also has a crucial role to play in the development, retention and motivation of the workforce. (Skills for Care 2007, p.2)

In response to such calls, resources for supervisors have been developed and are available on public websites such as Scotland's The Institute for Research and Innovation in Social Services (2019) and England's Research in Practice online resources (2019).

Changes in the organization of professional practice have led to different emphases on the functions of supervision. In many instances, particularly in the health sector, these changes have followed increased stringency in requirements for professional registration and standards of competence of professional practice. This has resulted in a demand for increased accountability and risk-management structures within organizations. For many services and in many different professional settings, this emphasis on accountability has been played out through supervision, with the result that the managerial function of supervision has been accorded priority over the other two functions – education and support. A by-product of this drive for accountability, however, has been that the new focus on supervision, and on best practice, has created a renewed opportunity for debate and conversation and reflection about professional practice. In this postmodern era, the conditions of practice have significantly altered (Cooper 2001). Previous certainty and cohesiveness of professional practice have been dismantled and universal theories and practice have been replaced by pluralism of theory, practice and context.

Professional supervision, though buffeted in this period of major change, has retained its core functions of accountability, education and support (Bradley and Hojer 2009), and has emerged with increased diversity of styles and approaches to supervision (Cooper 2001). It seems likely that we may now experience a renewed focus on educative and supportive functions which may reflect long-standing concerns about retention of professionals (Healy, Meagher and Cullin 2009; Roch, Todd and O'Connor 2007).

In order to meet the supervisory needs of changing practice, a variety of forms of supervision have emerged. These can be independent of each other or may be conceptually linked. A growing trend towards the development of additional professional relationships (Beddoe and Davys 2016; O'Donoghue 2015), described by Garrett and Barretta-Herman (1995) as a 'mosaic of strategies accessed in different configurations over time in response to educational, administrative and support needs' (p.97), has introduced a range of options. These strategies include external supervision, internal supervision, peer supervision, line supervision, interprofessional supervision, individual supervision, team supervision, group supervision and cultural supervision. This list is not exhaustive but rather an indication of the responses of practitioners to the diversity of practice contexts and the consequent range of choices and decisions to be made around the practice of supervision. Supervision has also faced critical scrutiny from those proposing to make matters of culture, world view and social justice centre stage in supervision practice. Hair and O'Donoghue argue that the 'leading social work supervision texts offer little to inform or encourage supervisors to integrate cultural knowledge with social justice... This absence is actually an example of how dominant discourse can influence knowledge production' (Hair and O'Donoghue 2009, p.74). In countries with indigenous populations, such as Aotearoa New Zealand, the imperative for culturally safe supervision, incorporating indigenous values and world view, has seen the development of indigenous approaches and models of supervision, including what is termed cultural supervision. Cultural supervision:

> creates a mode of supervision in which practitioners of a certain ethnicity are supported to practice within a supervision process that is grounded in spiritual, traditional, and coherent theoretical understandings congruent with a unique worldview. Culture becomes the overarching environment of supervision. (Beddoe and Egan 2009, p.414)

There is also a strong emphasis on social and cultural development in these cultural models (Beddoe and Egan 2009). Davys notes that such cultural models, however, often struggle to develop in organizations dominated by western values, traditions and theory (Davys 2005a). In 2015, Beddoe asked 'Is there one supervision or many?', echoing a participant in her recent research, arguing:

> Aspects of power, cultural and geographical locations, possession of different forms of capital – economic, social, cultural and symbolic; education and

managerial barriers all impact on relations in supervision. This requires some exploration of the concepts that dominate supervision discourse. We assume that we know what it is to each of us in the room (even at the international level), and yet we know that it can have many meanings. (Beddoe 2015a, p.153)

Both Beddoe (2015a) and O'Donoghue (2015) called for new theoretical perspectives to be applied to the future development of supervision, with a diversity of models and contexts emerging. Given the certainty of change, the uncertainty of resource and the complexity of practice issues, these last decades have required models of supervision to be sufficiently adaptable to adjust to a diverse range of practice contexts, to have the professional integrity to hold the unpredictability of practice content and the structure to respond to the tensions of change. In response to these challenges, supervision models based on learning and reflexivity have been promoted (Carroll 2014).

The view of supervision as a reflective learning process, rather than a process for direction and audit, represents a 'significant difference between teaching techniques as opposed to teaching a way of thinking' (McCann 2000, p.43). It is within this framework that we propose the Reflective Learning Model of Supervision as the central model for this book (Davys 2001). We regard a reflective approach as essential to affirm practitioners' development, bringing together theory, tacit knowledge and transformative personal experience. This approach develops a more holistic understanding of the complexity of experience that practitioners encounter in their day-to-day work (Fook and Askeland 2007).

Supervision by any other name: defining supervision

Professional supervision is both context dependent and context specific. With no universally accepted definition, many professions use the term 'supervision' interchangeably with activities which range across the scale of management tools and training requirements. Any text, article or research will therefore need to be considered within the terms defined by the authors and with reference to the professional and organizational context.

A useful model developed by Northcott (2000) identifies six performance management strategies, all of which are 'designed to optimise results, increase productivity and help ensure high quality service and activity of the organization and individuals' (Northcott 2000, p.12). The determining factor in Northcott's model is 'who sets the agenda'. Thus, disciplinary action, which sits at one end of the scale, has an agenda almost entirely determined by management. At the other end, Northcott positions clinical supervision in which the agenda is created by the practitioner. The beauty of Northcott's model is that it teases out those 'other' activities often lumped together with 'supervision'. Thus, supervision is separated out from disciplinary action, management supervision, preceptorship, appraisal and mentorship.

Clinical supervision as defined by Northcott is clearly not remedial oversight for professionals whose practice has been assessed as impaired. Nor, we would argue, is supervision an activity confined to students and new professionals. Supervision in our context demonstrates an ongoing professional commitment to reflection, analysis and critique by professional practitioners who take individual responsibility to use supervision to renew and refresh their practice and ensure that they continue to work within the mandate for their work with other people. A commitment to supervision demonstrates a commitment to lifelong learning.

However, we cannot say that supervision is entirely voluntary and here is the rub. Within many professions, codes of practice and registration requirements prescribe a schedule of supervision which may vary with experience and qualification. Similarly, there may be conditions on the form of supervision and the qualifications of the supervisor. For example, many professional and regulatory social work bodies require social workers to only be supervised by someone who is a registered or qualified social worker (Beddoe 2015b).

Organizations, too, may prescribe the type, duration and frequency of supervision and, indeed, in an increasingly regulated environment where professionals practice under a statute, supervision may be considered as mandated compliance of regulatory codes. Here supervision struggles to avoid becoming a risk-management tool, an indicator of practitioner competence and a process primarily designed to ensure consumer protection. Northcott's insistence that 'clinical supervision can only operate as a voluntary activity' is therefore an interesting challenge (2000, p.16). The reality is that for many practitioners, supervision is not voluntary. While a diversity of understanding about supervision continues, there is increasing focus in the literature on supervision as a process of in-depth reflection by practitioners on their work in order that they continue to learn from their experiences and develop their skills.

We hope that this book will provide some guidance and inspiration to supervisors and supervisees alike so that supervision, regardless of whether it is compulsory or voluntary, will be a valued and welcome activity. This is captured well by Bernard:

> But at the end of the day, supervision was, is, and will be defined by the realisation of our supervisees that they understand the therapeutic process and themselves a tad better than when they entered supervision, and our

own realisation that we have been players in the professional development of another. It is as simple and profound as this. (Bernard 2005, p.18)

Our stance in this book

In 1990, we were asked to present a workshop on supervision to a group of probation officers. At the time, we were both experienced social work practitioners and supervisors who had considerable experience in providing workshops and training. We accepted this brief with enthusiasm and began to research the recent literature. This was the beginning of almost three decades of interest and excitement about supervision. The literature available to support education about supervision in 1990 was sparse and somewhat outdated. The early 1990s was possibly a time when supervision was most profoundly at risk of management capture and in 1994 (Beddoe and Davys 1994) we echoed Payne's concern that supervision in social work was under threat (Payne 1994). Since that time, we have seen an excitement and resurgence of energy for supervision within those professions where supervision has been a traditional aspect of practice, and a growth of new ideas in professions where it has been introduced more recently.

Our own position on supervision has been influenced by the contexts of practice and teaching within which we have been engaged over the past 30 years. At the beginning, as providers of tertiary education, we delivered graduate supervision programmes to classes of social workers. We were, however, increasingly asked to provide 'workshops' to mixed groups of professionals, particularly from health. Initially cautious about the boundaries of other professions, we soon discovered the generic core of supervision and also the strength of interprofessional learning (Davys and Beddoe 2008). For many years now we have delivered both graduate and post-graduate programmes to groups of professionals from a wide range of professions.

Also, as we engaged in our own practice over the last 30 years, and as we accompanied other professionals on their practice journeys, we have recognized that at the heart of all practice is the ability to assess, reflect, adapt and respond. As discussed earlier in this chapter, certainty of practice no longer exists and practitioners today need to be able to critically examine all aspects of practice and adjust their responses and understanding accordingly. Professional supervision therefore is not about complying to ensure that the rules are followed; rather it is the application of professional skills, knowledge and principles to the variations of professional practice. As such, supervision provides the forum wherein practitioners can critically engage with their practice, reflect on their actions, review their decisions and learn. There are few 'right' answers but rather a choice of 'best'.

Supervision therefore for us is a forum for reflection and learning. It is, we believe, an interactive dialogue between at least two people, one of whom is a supervisor. This dialogue shapes a process of review, reflection, critique and replenishment for professional practitioners. Supervision is a professional activity in which practitioners are engaged throughout the duration of their careers, regardless of experience or qualification. It is accountable to professional standards and defined competencies and to organizational policy and procedures.

Overview of chapters

Chapter 2, Approaches to Professional Supervision, explores supervision as an expanding professional practice. It describes and differentiates between the functions and tasks of supervision and discusses four supervision models or approaches. These include developmental models, reflective models and postmodern approaches, and finally we present the growing practice of cultural supervision.

Chapter 3, The Supervision Relationship, examines how to negotiate the conditions of supervision and establish an effective supervision relationship taking particular cognizance of issues of power, authority and managing difference. Our approach to the supervision relationship promotes supervisee ownership and participation in supervision through developing trust and an orientation towards learning, and continuing professional development.

Chapter 4, The Organizational Context and Culture of Supervision, examines how supervision acts as a significant process within professional settings and within individual careers and explores professional learning in the organizational context.

Chapters 5, 6 and 7 focus on the 'doing' of supervision and the essential skills for supervisors. Chapter 5 introduces A Reflective Learning Model of Supervision, which draws from adult learning theory and understanding of reflective practice. This approach provides a detailed process for the conduct of supervision. It positions the supervisee as the director and the supervisor as facilitator of the supervision process. Chapter 6, Developing Expertise: Becoming a Critically Reflective Supervisor, explores the relationship between reflective practice, critical reflection, social justice and the core values of the helping professions, and links these to ongoing reflective supervision, throughout professional careers. Chapter 7, Skills for Supervision, provides a framework for identifying and developing essential skills for effective supervision within a reflective learning process approach.

The next two chapters explore aspects of the emotional content of supervision and those elements of supervision that engage the functions of support and personal professional development. Chapter 8, Communication and Emotion in Supervision, explores difficult interactions in supervision processes and suggests interventions. This chapter will explore the place of strong emotion in professional practice and supervision and the relevance of this in understanding and responding to challenging moments in practice. Chapter 9, Promoting Practitioner Wellbeing, examines the development professional resilience in practitioners in health and social care. We review the role of supervision in assisting professionals to manage stress in demanding and complex health and social care environments.

Chapter 10, Supervising Students in Clinical Placements, considers the particular issues and elements of supervising students in pre-service training and education for the social and health professions. The centrality of teaching and learning concepts is identified for this supervision practice. A variation of the Reflective Learning Model of Supervision for students on clinical placements is outlined.

Chapter 11, Supervision in Child Welfare, will explore the contribution supervision can make to enhancing accountability, professional development and support of social workers in child welfare. In particular, we will explore collaborative approaches to supervision that promote critical reasoning strategies. The potential for the creation of communities of practice within and between health and social care organizations that have a common concern for child wellbeing will be considered.

We have used a number of vignettes to illustrate the many challenges faced by practitioners in health and social care and how such situations may be drawn into the supervision encounter. We wish to declare that no one situation is real but rather, all scenarios reflect a composite of the many events that have challenged us, as practitioners, supervisors and educators, and which we believe may resonate with readers.

CHAPTER 2

Approaches to Supervision

Throughout its evolution, supervision practice has responded to different contexts and different purposes, and a corresponding range of terms have been employed to describe this activity. As highlighted by Vec, Rupnik Vec and Žorga (2014) it is thus often difficult to talk 'about supervision as something uniform' (p.103). Vec *et al.* further conclude that supervision 'is poorly conceptualized with implicit theories, unrelated to empirical research, and inconsistent in the use of its own concepts' (p.104).

Commenting on the range of terms used to describe supervision, and the evolution of supervision practice as it has responded to different contexts and different purposes, Vec *et al.* conclude that supervision 'is poorly conceptualized with implicit theories, unrelated to empirical research, and inconsistent in the use of its own concepts' (p.104). Notwithstanding this seemingly haphazard development, different models and approaches to supervision are important and provide a useful to guide supervision practice. Supervisors frequently employ 'more than one supervision method' (Milne *et al.* 2008, p.183) and it is our experience that, by accessing a range of models and approaches, supervisors have the flexibility to appropriately respond to the different needs of individual supervisees.

Bernard (2005), in a review of supervision over the previous 25 years, reported that during that time the development of models had been limited and that what occurred had been a refinement, exploration and testing of existing models (Bernard 2005, p.16). In some instances, Bernard noted, the introduction of an 'ideology' such as feminist supervision had transformed existing models while the introduction of new theory, rather than creating new models, had introduced new approaches – an example of this being the influence of postmodern constructivist theory on the development of the 'strengths' and 'solutions-focused' approaches to supervision. Twelve years later, Watkins (2017) identifies more activity and development, reporting that 'supervision has continued its bold march forward, with continuing empirical work on a host of topics being conducted, new theoretical models being advanced, and the professionalization of the specialty area occurring in unprecedented ways' (p.140). Possibly more critically, in an earlier publication, Watkins and Milne (2014) identified a cluster of features which they saw as characteristic of all current supervision models. In summary, these features described supervision as more negotiated, collaborative, cognisant and sharing of the power in the supervision relationship, and valuing of the mutuality of the supervision process and outcomes (p.676).

Models of supervision are frequently considered as belonging to one of two categories (Beinhart and Clohessy 2017; Howard 2018). First, those which are based around a set of practice principles or theory and as such are an extension of a therapeutic or therapy model, and second, those which are built from the process of supervision itself and so provide a blueprint for supervision practice. This latter category has also been considered by others, for example Watkins and Milne (2014, p.675), as comprising developmental and social role approaches. Supervision-based models of supervision, it has been argued, have many similarities. Watkins (2017), in reviewing models of psychotherapy supervision, notes that where therapy (psychotherapy) is driven from many theoretical positions, psychotherapy supervision is 'fundamentally powered by a theory of learning and a learning process' and so there is a basis for commonality between these different supervision models. Using three 'common, broad-band conceptual organizers: the supervisor's (and supervisee's) way of being, the supervisor–supervisee relationship, and supervision skills and techniques', Watkins (2017, p.142) identified 50 commonalities. Such argument lends support to the proposition that supervision is a profession in its own right (Carroll 2007).

Accepting the higher-order similarities in supervision practice, we nevertheless believe that supervision is usefully and pragmatically organized around different models. In this chapter, we begin with a discussion of the functional models of supervision as we believe that it is here, within these basic parameters of supervision, that the supervision territory and framework are defined. Later in the chapter we will briefly consider four other models and approaches of supervision: the developmental, reflective, postmodern and cultural models. Our choice of models presented reflects those which have, in some part, been useful to or developed through our practice and teaching. This is not to say that any omitted models are of less value or importance. Rather, we refer readers to the original source where the authors are better able to do justice to their own ideas and work. One model which we refer to but do not address in any detail is Hawkins and Shohet's model which, after four iterations (1989; 2000; 2006; 2012), has become known as the Seven-Eyed Model of Supervision. This model has had particular value in our teaching and practice and we mention it here to note our appreciation of this very useful framework.

Functional models of supervision

Traditionally, models of supervision have identified three key functions or tasks. Although differently labelled, these functions have remained fairly constant over the years. Pettes (1967) employed the terms administration, teaching and helping, Kadushin (1976) described the functions as administrative, educative and supportive, and Hawkins and Smith (2006) have named qualitative, developmental and resourcing functions. The administrative or qualitative function describes the practitioner's and supervisor's accountability to the policies, protocols, ethics and standards which are prescribed by organizations, legislation, and regulatory and professional bodies. The educative or developmental function addresses the ongoing professional skills and knowledge development of the practitioner. The supportive or resourcing function attends to the more personal relationship between the practitioner and the work context.

Inskipp and Proctor (1993, p.6) name the tasks of supervision under 'three main functional headings' which align with those functions identified earlier. Specifically, these tasks are the normative task, the formative task and the restorative task. This model, the Supervision Alliance Model (Proctor 2001, p.25), originates from counselling supervision, and is commonly described in the nursing and health services literature on supervision. What is notable in this functional model is the emphasis on the mutuality of the supervision relationship and of the associated responsibilities of supervision. The normative task of supervision is described as the 'shared responsibility of the supervisor and (counsellor) for monitoring the standards and ethical practice of the counsellor'; the formative task of supervision is the 'shared responsibility for the counsellor's development in skill, knowledge and understanding' and the restorative task is the 'provision of space, or the chance to explore opportunities elsewhere, for discharging held emotions and recharging energies, ideals and creativity' (Inskipp and Proctor 1993, p.6).

Morrison (2001, p.9) names four functions of supervision: 'competent, accountable performance/practice' (administrative/qualitative/normative), 'continuing professional development' (educative/developmental/formative), 'personal support' (supportive/resourcing/restorative) and finally 'engaging the individual with the organization' (mediation function). The inclusion of the mediation function is an important and interesting addition. For Morrison (2001, p.29), the mediation function is the negotiation of the different, and sometimes competing, aspects of the supervision encounter.

Achieving and maintaining a balance between the functions of supervision can be a challenge for supervisors and supervisees alike. Different professions accord different priority to the accepted tasks or functions of supervision and this varied emphasis has been identified as a factor which can result in one function dominating the supervision process. Bond and Holland (2010) consider that this reflects the manner in which different professional cultures explicitly value 'management monitoring' on the one hand and 'therapeutic use of self' on the other hand (p.36). Other factors such as organizational imperatives, developmental level and experience of the supervisee and the nature of the supervisee-client environment and exchange are also relevant. When one supervision function dominates, the other functions are either ignored or cursorily addressed. When this happens, both the nature of the supervision relationship and process of supervision can be compromised.

In the social work profession, particularly in English-speaking countries, there is a traditional link between supervision and line management. Supervision here has been described as a 'process whereby line managers oversee and support their staff' (Antczak et al. 2019, p.2) and there is a real risk in these situations that the administrative/quality/normative function will dominate. The supervision conversation becomes focused on oversight and audit of cases and caseload. As will be discussed later in Chapter 8, outcomes and targets will be monitored and practice will be considered from a risk-management rather than a professional perspective. The supervision relationship becomes hierarchical and managerial and there is little time for consideration of learning and development or space for support and restoration. Figure 2.1 depicts this situation.

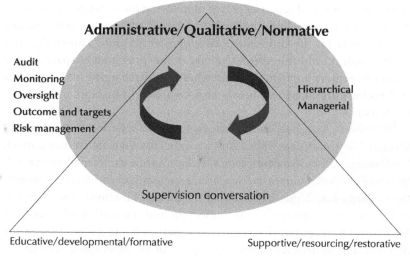

Figure 2.1: When the administrative/quality/normative function dominates

Similarly, the practice experience and level of professional development of the supervisee can tip the balance of focus within supervision. The supervision of students, new graduates and those new to areas of practice, in particular, may gravitate towards the educative/developmental/formative functions as the supervisees seek answers to new situations encountered in practice and supervisors provide them with those answers. In these supervision sessions, the supervisor is the expert and the supervisee is the novice. Conversational exchange becomes didactic, answers are provided and information is given. Supervision is dominated by teaching and education, rather than reflection and learning. These supervision conversations are one-sided. Supervisees are given little encouragement to consider the impact of the new situations on them and their work nor is there opportunity to consider the organizational and professional context of the work. When students are involved there may be additional focus on evaluation, assessment and signing off competencies (Figure 2.2).

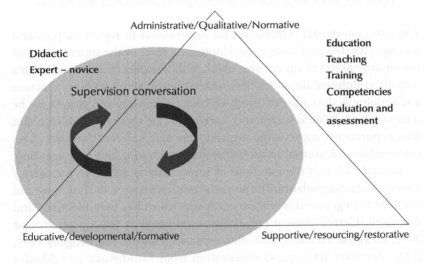

Figure 2.2: When the educative/developmental/formative function dominates

Finally, over-attention to the interface between the practitioner, the practice environment and the often stressful and complex client situations has the potential for supervision conversations to focus primarily on the impact of the work on the supervisee. Once again, without the balance of the other functions, such focus risks supervision becoming solely focused on support at the expense of broader perspectives of quality and knowledge. Supervision becomes indistinguishable from counselling and the supervisee is positioned as the client or the patient.

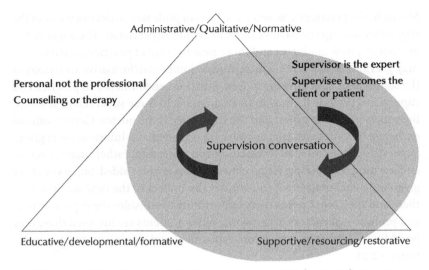

Administrative/Qualitative/Normative

Supervisor is the expert
Supervisee becomes the client or patient

Personal not the professional
Counselling or therapy

Supervision conversation

Educative/developmental/formative   Supportive/resourcing/restorative

Figure 2.3: When the supportive/resourcing/restorative function dominates

Thus, organizational imperatives for supervision to report outputs and manage risk, the professional developmental level of the supervisees and the emotional toll of supervisees' work with complex families and clients may all, at different times, tip the balance towards one particular function and in doing so the nature of the supervision relationship and process can be compromised. What is important, therefore, is for supervision to maintain its core purpose of supervision, to manage the parameters of the supervision conversation and to avoid a slide into management, education or counselling.

Consideration of the functions of supervision is, however, not merely about maintaining balance. The potential tension between the functions and the need to negotiate this tension is a theme which has been identified and discussed (Carroll 2009, p.218; Hughes and Pengelly 1997, p.24; Proctor 2001, p.23). An excellent, and often repeated (Hughes and Pengelly 1997, p.24; Morrison 2001, p.29) observation from Middleman and Rhodes (1980) captures both this tension and the choices facing a supervisor. 'The supervisor–worker relationship is the key encounter where the influence of organizational authority and professional identity collide, collude or connect' (Middleman and Rhodes 1980, p.52).

Hughes and Pengelly (1997) identify a variation of the three functions of supervision and propose a triangulated model which graphically captures the competing tensions of the supervision process. Linking the three functions of supervision to the participants of supervision (the supervisee, the supervisor and the service user or client), Hughes and Pengelly (1997) describe the functions as managing service delivery, facilitating practitioners' professional development and focusing on practitioners' work (Hughes and Pengelly 1997, p.42).

In this model, the functions are represented as corners of a triangle. 'Managing service-delivery' addresses the requirement of supervision to ensure that policies, procedures and protocols as defined by the agency (or by statute or regulation) are followed. It is also through this function that the 'quality and quantity of work' and the professional standards and ethics of practice are addressed. The ongoing professional development of the supervisee takes place within the function of 'facilitating practitioner's professional development' while the third corner of the triangle, 'focusing on the practitioner's work' allows supervisor and supervisee to reflect on and explore the practitioner's work with clients (Hughes and Pengelly 1997, p.42).

The depiction of each of the functions as a corner of a triangle neatly captures the tensions and decisions present in any supervision session. From this model, Hughes and Pengelly identify three key issues: first, that it is difficult to address all three functions of supervision in any one session; second, that the interrelationship between the three functions means that they cannot be regarded separately; and finally (and as also suggested in Figures 2.1, 2.2, 2.3), that supervision 'becomes unsafe if one corner is ignored or avoided for any length of time' (Hughes and Pengelly 1997, p.43).

Failure to address issues at any one of the corners of the triangle is therefore not an option. The challenge or dilemma they believe 'lies in having the time, skill and experience to manage the difficult tensions' (Hughes and Pengelly 1997, p.46). They also warn of the 'deadly equal triangle' where rigid adherence to each corner can stifle the effectiveness of supervision work and not allow sufficient depth. There is, they suggest, no 'right' balance but supervisors are encouraged to view the model as a map by which they can review and check where time is spent in supervision and which corners are being avoided or neglected. In this way, any imbalance can be challenged and addressed.

Representation of the functions of supervision as a triangle is most effective. It graphically locates the intersection of each of the functions of supervision at each apex of the triangle and thus heightens the sense of tension inherent in supervision arrangements. The integrity of a triangle lies in the tension at every point. The importance of holding these tensions in balance is therefore apparent, as otherwise the structure would distort or collapse.

Returning to Middleton and Rhodes' (1980) comment on how the profession and the organization come together in supervision, we note from our own experience that some supervisors fall into a quandary of how to respond in supervision when faced with the tensions of these competing functions. The choices, as Middleton and Rhodes (1980) remind us, are between collision, collusion or connection.

■ VIGNETTE: JASON

Jason was angry with the new requirement from the agency to limit the number of visits to patients in the community. In supervision, with a supervisor who was external to the agency, he expressed his anger and dismissal of the new process. The supervisor knew that Jason was a conscientious practitioner who liked to give his clients the best service.

Option 1 – Collide

The supervisor was clear and uncompromising. She reminded Jason that as this was a requirement then he had to comply. Yes, she understood that this might not be best practice, but he had no options. This was a sign of the times and a reality of current practice. Possibly he could review his time management – learn to work smarter. They could consider that in their supervision together. Jason left the session feeling angry and determined to avoid complying with the new process.

Option 2 – Collude

The supervisor heard Jason out and sympathized with his view of the situation. She shared her own practice experience in a similar situation and agreed that this policy was not in the best interest of patient care. When she asked Jason how he was going to adjust to this new policy, he replied that he had no intention of doing so and would still make the visits but not record his time. The supervisor warned Jason not to get found out. Jason left the session feeling justified in his decision to avoid complying with the new process.

Option 3- Connect

The supervisor heard Jason out and sympathized with his situation. She shared her own experience and frustration with a similar situation. She asked Jason why he thought the new system was being introduced in his agency. What gains were being envisaged? Were there any benefits he could see in the long run? What support was being offered to assist staff and patients to accommodate the new system? She asked Jason to reflect on any similar past experiences he had had – what had he learned from them? What were his professional objections to the changes and were there other ways to address those? Jason left the session feeling heard and with a plan to approach his manager to discuss his concerns and to present a proposal that would give patients and practitioners some other options.

Middleton and Rhodes locate the tensions of supervision between the expectations of the organization and the profession. Using Hughes and Pengelly's model, we believe that the tensions are between all three functions and that the role of the supervisor is to manage the tension, and build relationships and an environment where connections can be made. Carroll (2009) describes this as holding the three tasks of supervision 'in creative tension, building and creating environments that sustain learning while still monitoring the professionalism of the work' (Carroll 2009, p.219).

One of the key differences between Hughes and Pengelly's model and other functional models is the explicit exclusion of support as a function of supervision. Support, Hughes and Pengelly (1997) argue, is a means not an end. When support is identified as a function of supervision 'there is a danger of a collusive focus on the worker's needs for their own sake, rather than a focus on the worker in order to promote a better service' (Hughes and Pengelly 1997, p.48). This scenario is depicted in Figure 2.3.

Support in supervision, we agree, is a core condition of supervision but not a function. Support is a central and necessary element in supervision for it is through an awareness of, and a confidence in, the 'supportive relationship' that the challenges of practice can be tolerated and accepted. Support in supervision has been 'conceptualised as the supervisor's provision of comfort, recognition, encouragement and approval' (Lizzio, Wilson and Que 2009, p.128). This provision of support is necessary whatever 'function' is being addressed. Supervisees' need for support in supervision, however, will vary. As supervisees develop in experience, competence and confidence, the level of support they need changes (Lizzio et al. 2009). Too little support can create uncertainty and anxiety while too much support may be 'too permissive' and mean that issues of 'competence and performance' are not addressed (Lizzio et al. 2009, p.129).

The positioning of support as a *condition* rather than a function of supervision has a subtle but significant effect on the role of the supervisee in the supervision relationship. The supervisee is liberated 'from being the passive recipient of support' and instead is positioned as 'an active participant in a *supportive* supervision process which in turn is keenly focused on the provision of a better service to clients' (Davys 2005a p.5). Supportive supervision encourages supervisees to express and explore their feelings and their work, not only so they will 'feel' better but also in order that they may 'know' their practice. We will discuss the place of emotions more fully in Chapter 8.

The relationship between supervision and counselling is often confused at this interface of supervision and support, and as depicted earlier, when the supportive function dominates it can be difficult to distinguish between supervision and counselling. The understanding of support to be a condition rather than a 'function' of supervision in our view helps to differentiate between these two activities. But this will not be sufficient unless all parties are clear about the boundaries between the two allied, but different, activities of counselling (therapy) and supervision. Yegdich (1999) demonstrates this confusion when she describes the boundary between supervision and therapy in nursing:

> It may be inadequate simply to proclaim that supervision is not therapy, as ultimately, it is the techniques utilized, not the stated goals that determine the form of supervision, or therapy. (Yegdich 1999, p.1266)

We argue that it is indeed the goals that distinguish supervision from therapy and counselling. The techniques of supervision do utilize the skills and interventions of practice but the goals of each are distinct and so shape how these techniques are employed. Fox (1989) provides a guide when he usefully describes the supervision relationship as therapeutic rather than therapy. He identifies two significant differences between therapy and supervision. The first is personal change which, he states, is the primary goal of therapy but occurs only as 'a by-product of the supervisory process' (Fox 1989, p.51). That is to say that the very process of exploration, reflection and learning which occurs in supervision (which we discuss in detail in Chapter 5) can lead to transformational change and inevitably to personal growth. The intent of supervision is, however, to develop a practitioner's professional not personal persona. The second difference arises out of the dictates of the professional and organizational standards, ethics and expectations which define the boundaries and accountabilities of supervision. 'The supervisor, unlike the clinician, does not suspend critical judgement' (Fox 1989, p.52) and therefore whatever is brought to supervision must be considered within these accountability frameworks.

It is well reported in the literature that supervision is the appropriate place for practitioners to express and explore the wide range of emotional responses they experience in relation to their work (Carroll 2014; Lombardo, Milne and Proctor 2009; Winter *et al.* 2019). This is both necessary and professionally responsible. It is also important that neither supervisors nor supervisees confuse 'personal problems' with the 'appropriate emotional reactions to highly painful work or unsatisfactory work conditions' (Hughes and Pengelly 1997, p.49).

Incorporating the above, we propose our representation of the functions of supervision in Figure 2.4. Based on Hughes and Pengelly's (1997) model, we have included on each side of the triangle, as a supervision task, the management of the tensions. This task involves making connections between the sometimes conflicting functions and accountabilities of supervision. Support, the core condition of supervision, sits in the centre of the triangle and includes validation, respect, the creation of a safe environment, conflict management and anti-discriminatory practice.

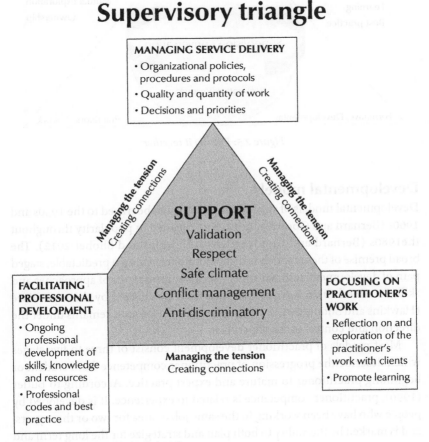

Supervisory triangle

MANAGING SERVICE DELIVERY
- Organizational policies, procedures and protocols
- Quality and quantity of work
- Decisions and priorities

Managing the tension
Creating connections

Managing the tension
Creating connections

SUPPORT
Validation
Respect
Safe climate
Conflict management
Anti-discriminatory

FACILITATING PROFESSIONAL DEVELOPMENT
- Ongoing professional development of skills, knowledge and resources
- Professional codes and best practice

Managing the tension
Creating connections

FOCUSING ON PRACTITIONER'S WORK
- Reflection on and exploration of the practitioner's work with clients
- Promote learning

Adapted from Hughes and Pengelly (1997).

Figure 2.4: Functions and tasks of supervision

Finally then, when attention to the functions of supervision is balanced and when support is a central tenet, the supervision relationship and process are subtly but importantly changed. Supervision can be considered as a professional conversation which takes place within clear boundaries of accountability, learning and reflection. The relationship is collaborative and allows for mutual exploration and ownership of the process (see Figure 2.5).

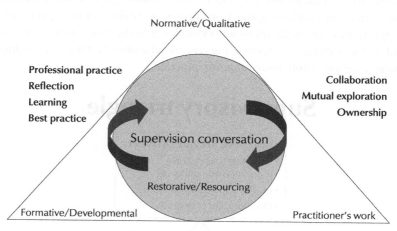

Figure 2.5: Putting it together

Developmental models

Developmental models of supervision, which can be traced to the 1950s and 1960s (Bernard and Goodyear 2014, p.33), gained in popularity throughout the1980s (Bernard and Goodyear 2014; Hawkins and Shohet 2012). The broad premise of these models is that practitioners follow a predictable, staged path of development and that supervisors require a range of approaches and skills to attend to each sequential stage as it is achieved by the supervisee (Hawkins and Shohet 2012). It is implied that the process remains under the direction and control of the supervisor.

Most models of practitioner development consist of three to five stages which describe the progression of practitioner competence from student or beginning practitioner to mature and expert practice. According to Butler (1996), practitioner competence is related to experience. It is developed by people who have been working in the same job or area for two or three years, and is marked by the ability to both plan and strategize for the long term and to analyse complex problems (Butler 1996, p.278). Competence is, however, not the ultimate goal of his model but rather he charts the journey from externally prescribed professional development to self-directed development.

Butler (1996) describes five stages of performance development. The first, *novice* (rule governed), leads to *advanced beginner* (seeking the external answer) to *competent* (personal analysis of each situation) to *proficient* (having the big picture in focus) and finally to *expert* (tacit understanding). The supervision of a competent practitioner will be different from the supervision of a novice/student. A novice practitioner will need 'rules and procedures to follow so that the performance can be done without experience' (Butler 1996, p.277), whereas the competent practitioner centres their actions 'on a plan which is based on considerable conscious, thoughtful, analytic reflection' (Butler 1996, p.278). Expert practitioners, according to Butler 'have an accurate grasp of each situation' and do not waste time on 'a large range of unfruitful, alternative diagnoses and solutions' (p.279). They are expert because 'personal knowledge is continually renewed by the uniqueness of some encountered events. Beliefs and assumptions are evaluated against the changing context' (Butler 1996, p.279).

Developmental models have been subject to a variety of critique, but as Bernard and Goodyear (2014, p.51) note, 'probably the safest conclusion at this point is that there is limited evidence to support some aspects of stage development models' and the models require more research. More general commentary has been offered by others over time. Alert to the prescriptive nature of developmental models, Gardiner (1989) warns that there is a risk of equating compliance to a norm with success and pathologizing those who 'differ from... expectations of normal progress' (p.11). Hawkins and Shohet (2012) also present their developmental model with a warning that too rigid an application of the stages may blind the supervisor to the uniqueness of the supervisee, the supervision context and the supervision relationship. Cultural bias and the associated assumptions implicit in developmental models must also be considered for 'the information they leave out, such as a person's experience due to race, class, gender or sexual orientation' (Moffatt 1996, p.49). To this list we would add religious beliefs and spirituality. Stoltenberg et al. (2014), noting the influence which age and gender can have on the balance of power within the supervision relationship, urge for this to be considered when supervision partners are determined. Considering these factors and the uniqueness of individual supervision partnerships, Stoltenberg et al. (2014) citing Richards (2000), warn that supervision 'should not be taken out of the cultural context in which it was developed and simply implemented in another context' (p.583). Finally supervisors, it is acknowledged, will also be on a journey of development and the influence on the supervision process of the supervisor's own developmental stage cannot be overlooked (Hawkins and Shohet 2012; Scaife 2009).

A general and challenging critique of traditional models of development is offered by Nye (2007). Western models of development, she argues, typically describe a linear progression from novice to expert, from dependence to autonomy. Value is placed on the 'autonomous' 'expert' practitioner. Nye (2007) suggests that such models limit learning to the realm of 'actual development' as opposed to the 'potential development' of which a practitioner is capable 'or has access to in collaboration' (Nye 2007, p.90). Competence in these models is equated with 'knowing' while 'unknowing', associated with failure and shame, is often hidden or denied. Pack (2009a, p.660) argues that the 'potential for shame' 'which leads to withdrawal from contact', can result in supervisees acting on their own without consulting their clinical supervisor. This inappropriate and unsafe 'independence' can result in clinical errors with dire consequences.

Vygotsky's developmental learning theory, Nye (2007) suggests, is a helpful framework by which to re-value and recognize 'dependence' on an*other* as 'essential to learning and development across the life course. For Vygotsky, this is not a process with an end point…something to be outgrown…[but] inevitable if learning and development are to occur' (Nye 2007, p.84).

Despite these limitations, developmental approaches can usefully provide supervisors with a framework for thinking about how practitioners develop skills and competence over time, and can offer strategies for working with a range of practitioner experience and knowledge. More particularly, developmental models support supervisors to consider their supervisees against key professional competencies or dispositions. Through the application of interventions, relevant to the supervisees' stage of development, supervisors can then facilitate the professional growth of those supervisees. Davys (2002) has suggested that if the developmental framework is considered as a dynamic, as opposed to a mechanistic structure it can provide a useful conceptual framework from which to understand the difference of both relationship and dialogue which occurs between supervisors and students on the one hand and, more particularly, supervisors and competent practitioners on the other (Davys 2002, p.65).

Loganbill *et al.* (1982), in a classic formulation, 'one of the 25 most-cited articles *The Counseling Psychologist* has published' (Bernard and Goodyear 2009, p.89), provided a framework for utilizing a developmental theory in supervision. This 'Conceptual Model' (Loganbill *et al.* 1982), in development for the subsequent 30 or more years, has become known as the Integrative Developmental Model of supervision (IDM) (Stoltenberg *et al.* 2014). The IDM describes domains of professional practice against which practitioners' competency is considered alongside 'changes over time in three overarching structures (motivation, autonomy, self-, and other awareness)' (Stoltenberg *et al.* 2014, p.576). Three levels map practitioners' movement until the final achievement of level 3i, which indicates integration across all domains at level 3. Change or movement may occur as a natural progression of experience and awareness or it may be facilitated through appropriate planned intervention on the part of the supervisor (Stoltenberg *et al.* 2014). Three transition points are identified where particular interventions can be applied. An important characteristic of the IDM model is that a practitioner, in response to personal and professional events, may cycle or recycle through 'similar developmental processes for various domains of clinical practice' (p.548). Learning and development are therefore ongoing and a supervisee may be functioning at different levels for different domains.

When considering this particular developmental model, it is important to recognize its North American origin and that as such it has at its core the supervision of trainees. Career-long supervision for post-graduate practitioners may be available but is not assured. Stoltenberg *et al.* (2014) conclude:

> Independent reflective practice now becomes more of a reality, and less aspirational. Supervision, if available, is still useful in providing additional breadth of perspective, but has become increasingly collegial and less hierarchical. (p.593).

Developmental models are thus frequently paired with the supervision of trainees and as Hawkins and Shohet (2012) recommend, acquaintance with such models allows supervisors to 'plan what supervision is most appropriate for trainees in different stages the course' (p.82). Notwithstanding these perspectives, we have found that an understanding of developmental stages and issues has been beneficial in the supervision of all practitioners from the very new to the very experienced. In the earliest iteration of the IDM, Loganbill *et al.* (1982) included a category of experienced supervisee who was, at level 1, in a state of 'stuckness or stagnation. The supervisee may be experiencing a blind spot with regard to their functioning surrounding one of the supervisory issues' (p.17). Such understanding of 'stuckness' can provide useful insight and guidance for the supervisor of those experienced practitioners who have become less reflective in their practice or who experience burnout and the associated cynicism and protective blindness in their approach to practice. In a similar fashion, we have seen experienced practitioners who have displayed all of the confusion and ambivalence characteristic of stage 2 (Loganbil *et al.* 1982) or level 2 (Stoltenberg *et al.* 2014). Following a change of work context, change of role or through promotion, these practitioners find themselves moved from a state of calm competence and assurance to one of heightened energy. Self-doubt and anxiety in the face of new challenges may lead them to seek reassurance and support, hitherto unneeded, from their supervisor. Or in an equally unsettling manner, they may be overloaded with excitement and possibility and seek structure and order from supervision conversations. An understanding of a developmental framework in these situations has proven very useful for both the supervisor and supervisee.

Reflective approaches to supervision

Watkins and Milne (2014) in their review of the development of supervision models, as mentioned earlier in this chapter, identified as a consistent theme, that supervision was increasingly 'more egalitarian, collaborative, co-participative, and co-constructed' (p.676). This shift, along with the recognition and sharing of the power within the supervision relationship, was, they proposed, aligned to the principles of adult learning development. This finding supported an earlier review by Milne *et al.* (2008) which found that 82 per cent of the supervision studies reviewed 'described outcomes consistent with the experiential learning cycle of Kolb (1984)' (p.183). This, as Milne *et al.* suggested, indicated the centrality of experiential learning to the practice of supervision. Reflection, one of the four phases of experiential learning, is embedded as a process in many supervision approaches and has been considered an approach in its own right. Exploring the elements of reflective supervision, Williams *et al.* (2019) report a focus 'on being "present" for others, the quality of relationships formed with supervisees, and a collaborative approach to supervision' (p.12).

Fook and Gardner (2007) consider a reflective approach as affirming other ways of knowing, such as personal experience and its interpretation, by supporting a holistic understanding of the complexity of experience that practitioners encounter in their day-to-day work. 'A reflective approach tends to focus on the whole experience and the many dimensions involved: cognitive elements; feeling elements; meanings and interpretations from different perspectives' (Fook and Gardener 2007, p.25). Such an approach facilitates the discovery of the kinds of knowledge relevant to the unpredictability of contemporary practice. According to Fook and Askeland (2007), reflective learning is a process that seeks to unsettle assumptions in order to change practice and helps us to understand the connections between our public and private worlds (pp.522–523), while Scaife (2010, p.4) highlights the criticality of reflection which she says 'involves making discriminations, evaluating, judging, assessing, and weighing up options… which can result in more elegant, integrated and useful know how'.

Butler's (1996) Model of Human Action (pp.270–271) explains these connections well. Two contexts, the *social* (which comprises public knowledge and professional practice) and the *self* (comprised of personal knowledge and world view) are connected by reflection. In this model 'public knowledge' is 'all that abounds outside the self in the form of theories, formal knowledge, policy directives, research results, quality assurance processes, hints and folk lore, community expectations' while professional practice is 'informed by beliefs, undertaken to achieve important goals in particular contexts'. World view which 'influences all thoughts and actions' is formed largely through an individual's 'culture and traditions'. And personal knowledge is 'knowledge and understanding attained through lived experience'. Reflection, positioned at the centre of these contexts 'is the open, active communication channel between the outside social context and the inner self' (pp.270–271).

World view, Butler notes, seeks to remain stable but 'to be effective it must be continually revised' (p.271) and it is through the process of reflection that an individual's world view is challenged and this revision occurs. We will return to consider how reflection is crucial in effective supervision in Chapter 5 where we discuss the Reflective Learning Model (Davys 2001) and in Chapter 6 where we examine the role of the critically reflective supervisor.

Postmodern approaches to supervision

Postmodernism, described by Ungar as a 'collection of interpretations made about the world that are constantly changing' (2006, p.60), has influenced approaches to supervision, just as it has influenced practice in many professions. Postmodernists try to avoid imposing organizing ideas about how the world (and practice) should be but rather focus on interpretations made by participants in social processes, through the language and narratives and the search for meaning. Postmodernism influences the helping professions in its advocacy of in-depth consideration of the language of the encounters between workers and clients (Edwards and Chen 1999). In postmodern thinking, there is a fundamental shift from the 'grand narrative' of science and positivist approaches to an emphasis on the social construction of meaning in professional life. 'Post-modernist approaches focus on strengths rather than deficits, potential rather than constraints. In social constructivist practice it is held that there are multiple perspectives instead of universal truths' (Edwards and Chen 1999, p.351). Strengths-based and solution-focused approaches have been applied to the supervision process over the last two decades (for a detailed discussion see Beddoe and Davys 2016). All share the movement away from assessment of deficits and problems, characteristic of the medical model, to reflect a postmodern view of human-systems interaction.

Postmodern supervision brings to the forefront issues of identity, stories and the language of supervision encounters. Ungar (2006) asserts that supervisors bring into supervision relationships their identities as individuals, professionals and supervisors, along with the expression of different culture, gender, ability and so forth. Thus, 'starting with such a plurality of possible selves, when we encounter supervisees we have much to draw on and much to account for', (Ungar 2006, p.60). For Ungar, a postmodern supervisor 'accentuates aspects of their identity in order to participate with supervisees in a co-construction of the supervisees as competent in their practice' (p.60).

Collaborative relationships in supervision are also emphasized by Edwards and Chen (1999) who discuss two meta-frameworks for strengths-based supervision: a postmodern view of human systems interaction, and an understanding of the isomorphic nature of the supervisor/worker/client relationships. Ungar identifies six roles in supervision, each imbued with meaning by the participants: supporter (to the supervisee), supervisor, case consultant, trainer/teacher, colleague and advocate (for both the client and/or the supervisee) (p.61). In summary, postmodern approaches imbue supervision with social constructionist ideas and:

- advocate careful consideration of the language of the encounters between workers and service users and workers and supervisors

- posit an approach to supervision which emphasizes the way the participants in professional encounters construct meaning

- focus on strengths rather than deficits, and on the potential for change rather than constraints and barriers

- acknowledge that there are numerous perspectives instead of universal truths

- are less hierarchical and focus on establishing collaborative approaches and co-constructing solutions

- avoid labelling people in ways that emphasize their differences as deficits or pathological in some way.

Social work and counselling in particular have strong links to 'social constructionist' approaches in which the social circumstances and power relations are examined and where social justice ideals are central. Applied to supervision, a social constructionist perspective 'invites supervisors to shape a supervisory relationship that encourages transparency, collaboration, and an exchange of ideas' (Hair and O'Donoghue 2009, p.76). Noble and Irwin (2009) argue that applying a constructionist lens requires supervisors to 'explore and reflect on the way the supervisors, the supervisees and the agencies work with the service users/clients' thus ensuring that 'practitioners' actions and those of the organization are more explicit and conscious' (Noble and Irwin 2009, p.354). Noble and Irwin cite O'Donoghue (2003) whose earlier work explicitly explored the relationships and the process of supervision from a social justice perspective. They point to O'Donoghue's movement away from the 'more traditional atheoretical notions of the separate functions of supervision towards a social constructionist approach' (Noble and Irwin 2009, p.354).

The differences between social constructionist and traditionalist approaches to supervision have been explored by Hair and O'Donoghue (2009). These differences include: the recognition of plurality and diversity of knowledge; an emphasis on collaboration; the acknowledgment that supervisees have agency in a co-constructive process; the engagement in various relational forms such as dyadic, group, and in-session supervision; increased sensitivity to power and the politics of empowerment and disempowerment in supervision; and the explicit recognition of the influence of the social and cultural context within which supervision is immersed (Hair and O'Donoghue 2009, p.77). Hair and O'Donoghue's social constructionist perspective suggests supervisors include the following processes:

- 'Ask "curious" questions about idiosyncratic descriptions of local community knowledge of the supervisees and clients, including the influence of dominant socio-political and economic contexts such as national laws, tribal expectations, and spiritual understandings' (p.78).

- Develop supervisory conversations which 'consider structural barriers such as poverty, legislative policies, and suitable housing alongside clients' relational conflicts and distresses' (p.78).

- Acknowledge barriers to enable 'supervisors and supervisees to weave multiple strands into a comprehensive, time-bound snapshot of culture' (p.78).

- Ensure that dialogue between supervisors and supervisees includes 'the exploration of their own cultural narratives over time' (p.78).

- Note that those educated in the dominant western practices supervision require 'continual critical self-reflection about the use of taken-for-granted authority and privilege, so that domination over others is not silently reinforced' (pp.78–79).

Reflective questions encourage collaborative practice and, Hair and O'Donoghue argue, perspectives that have been marginalized may surface and 'ideas and values can be prevented from forming rigid "truth" that inevitably means ascendancy for a select few persons and tyranny and oppression over others' (2009, p.79).

Strengths-based supervision

Strengths-based supervision has its roots in strengths-based practice, postmodern counselling and family therapy practice and is underpinned by the same principles and ideas. Isomorphism, which implies a similarity of process from one system to another, can be used to influence change. In strengths-based work, supervision centres on the development of supervisee-focused and directed supervision. Essentially this approach is a 'way of being' with supervisees, where attention is given to power 'with' rather than power 'over', and the environment is such that both supervisor and supervisee contribute their expertise to the relationship. Strengths-based supervision seeks to address the hierarchical nature of supervision by favouring the co-construction of ideas with those supervised (Edwards and Chen 1999, p.351). Recent research has found that strengths-based supervision is an approach that in child welfare practice can integrate 'many worthwhile supervisory activities into a coherent program'. That 'five of the six scales measuring varied components of strengths based supervision were associated with higher levels of satisfaction suggests that training supervisors in this model may provide one strategy for improving supervision satisfaction, thereby impacting worker retention' (Lietz and Julien-Chinn 2017, p.151).

The key principles of strengths-based supervision are as follows:

1. All practitioners possess strengths that can be activated – supervision is future focused and assumes success, 'rather than problem-saturated talk' and the potential for further competence of the supervisee to build further competencies (Presbury, Echterling and McKee 1999, p.150).

2. Supervisees are experts about their own practice, in the same way that service users in strengths-based practice are viewed as the experts of their own lives. A supervisor encourages comfort with uncertainty and rather than assuming expertise, is open to the many ways people construct experience with a focus on utility (what works) (Edwards and Chen 1999, p.352).

3. Supervisors need to suspend their beliefs and assumptions (Thomas and Davis 2005, p.192) in order to be open to hearing the supervisee's story.

4. Supervisors support their supervisees' goals (Santa Rita 1998) and enable their strengths to be present in the work. This approach also incorporates and encourages talk about challenging issues in a safe process which is initially negotiated at the outset of the supervision contract.

5. Supervisors need to be respectful and hopeful and the language used needs to avoid pathologizing explanations (Edwards and Chen 1999, p.354).

The supervisor does not assume a normative approach and attempt to 'correct' or dominate the supervisee's aims or views but will work to create a strengths-based supervision with a future focus on potentials, possibilities and multiple perspectives. In doing so, the supervisor models an ideal of practice that is service user driven and empowering.

Edwards and Chen (1999), in their framework for strengths-based supervision, see supervision moving to what they call 'co-vision' and 'co-created' vision (p.353) where the 'co-visee' is expected to be the expert in what is happening in their work. Their experience in the supervision context will be carried over to the counselling context (p.353). Edwards and Chen identify six supervision contexts for use in training counsellors.

1. 'Symmetrical voices – rather than provide a directive monologue where one narrative dominates, the supervisor supports the supervisee to explore options for working with client problems and emphasizes the supervisee's competence' (p.353).

2. 'Competence focus – a supervisor must model the values they want the supervisee to demonstrate with their clients. By focusing on strengths and successful interventions, supervisees will feel more competent. This is also reflected in the non-pathologizing language used when talking about clients' (pp. 353–354).

3. 'Client-participated supervision – by including clients into the supervision or imaging they are present in the room, the tone of the supervision changes from one in which their deficits are analysed, to one of respect, curiosity and hopefulness' (p.354).

4. 'Unassuming transparency – supervisors will share their own professional struggles with their supervisees which enable them to more readily take on a "not-knowing position"' (p.354).

5. The 'Reflecting team' – live supervision in therapy contexts where group input offers a resource for the generation of new ideas (p.355).

6. 'Tag-team group supervision format' – a supervisee describes then role-plays a service user they are working with, assigning roles to other members of their training class – one from the rest of the class will take the role of counsellor until 'tagged' by another observer who takes over from where the previous one left off. This allows for different perspectives to inform discussion and reflection (p.355).

The solution-focused model of practice developed by de Shazer (1985) also applies the principle of isomorphism to the context of supervision (Santa Rita 1998, p.129). Solution-focused supervision has some distinctive features and is underpinned by four basic assumptions (Santa Rita 1998, pp.129–133). First, supervisees inevitably cooperate with their supervisors, and have a range of cooperative responses (p.129). Second, supervisors identify and *amplify* exceptional behaviour of supervisees in order to highlight positive, productive experience and the challenges present in the work (p.130). A third assumption is that supervisors will use interventions that have been effective previously and will only actively try new approaches when supervision gets stuck (p.131). Finally, solution-focused supervision assumes that the supervisee will define the learning goals in the supervision process, with the supervisor acting as guide. Solution-focused supervision aims to encourage the supervisee to set small achievable goals for each session (p.132) and noticing and highlighting achievements builds morale (Presbury *et al.* 1999, p.150).

A variety of interventions from solution-focused therapy are utilized in solution-focused supervision. While these essentially philosophical principles underpin the strengths-based/solution-focused approach to supervision, a range of tools and techniques, especially questions, have been developed to assist the supervisor in their facilitation. Supervisors familiar with strengths-based practice will recognize these as similar to techniques in client work, re-focused on the thinking of the practitioner and their experience. Supervisors use 'pre-suppositional' language (Presbury *et al.* 1999, p.152) to promote confidence and self-efficacy now. Presbury *et al.* (1999) argue that there is a vast difference between using subjunctive language (supposing a possibility) and using pre-suppositional language (assuming an actuality). Pre-suppositional questions avoid yes/no answers and reflect positive expectations of change:

'What has worked well since we last met?'

'Tell me the best thing you've done this week.'

'As you get better at dealing with (this situation), how will you know you have become good enough?'

'If you are feeling more confident, what will you be doing differently?'

'What would I notice if I was watching you working better with these service users?

'How will you have changed?'

The beliefs underpinning these questions are that: there are always exceptions; there will be circumstances that hold promise of the alleviating problem and it is important to provide the opportunity and encouragement to recall a time of greater confidence (Presbury *et al.* 1999, p.148). Scaling questions (de Shazer 1985) can be used to help supervisees determine their progression toward pre-identified time specific goals:

'At the onset of our supervision relationship you indicated a goal of being able to appropriately use authority and power when working with high-risk situations. On a scale of 1 to 10, with 1 indicating little progress toward this goals and 10 indicating completion of this goal, what score would you give yourself?'

Presbury *et al.* (1999) suggest the use of scaling questions to help to establish small realistic goals and engender expectations of success; for example, 'On a scale of 1 to 10, with 1 being that the problem is at its worst, and 10 being that the problem is completely solved, where would you say you are today?' After the worker offers their estimate, 2, the supervisor says, 'When you are on your way to 3, how will you know?' (Presbury *et al.* 1999, p.151).

'What will have changed?'

'What will be different about how you handle the situation?'

'What will have changed as a practitioner?'

Using these techniques, the changes identified become the supervision goals. To identify a time-specific goal, a supervisor might ask, a 'miracle question' (de Shazer 1985), for example, 'If a miracle happened just before your next family meeting, and you became the fantastic nurse you wanted to be, what would be the first thing you would notice suggesting your increased confidence and skills?'

Developing strengths-based approaches: reflections for supervisors

- How do I notice and celebrate success with my supervisees?

- How do we talk about service users in supervision? What am I modelling about expectations of success and change?

- Does our supervision model match the way we approach our professional practice?

- How often do we highlight what is working well and the times of exception to problems?

- What different kinds of power do I utilize in this relationship and what is the impact of this? How important is it for me to be expert? How do I invite feedback from supervisees and respond to it?

- How do we talk about challenging issues?

- How do I reflect on my own supervision process? What goals do I set for myself?

(Adapted from Thomas and Davis 2005, p.195)

A note of caution

In our second book (Beddoe and Davys 2016), we explore solution-focused and strengths-based approaches in greater detail. We noted the need to avoid uncritical adoption of some of the underlying 'tenets of these models. Like all supervisory and practice approaches they are not innocent of their context' (p.174). Gray (2011, p.10) suggested that those advocating for strengths-based approaches consider applying a critical lens, arguing that, 'while stemming from sound philosophical foundations, [the strengths perspective] is in danger of running too close to contemporary neoliberal notions of self-help and self-responsibility and glossing over the structural inequalities that hamper personal and social development'. In supervision too, there is the potential for solution-focused and strengths-based approaches to apply expectations of practitioners that focus on individual resilience and adaptation to work stresses, and reflect neoliberal ideological assumptions uncritically. Edwards (2012, p.97) describes three categories of supervisees. 'Customers' come to supervision ready to go and knowing what they want. They make their own use of what is shared. 'Complainants' bemoan their workplace, clients and workload and should be helped to see their own locus of control. 'Visitors' come to supervision because it is scheduled but may not bring anything to work with. Edwards regards this framing as informing him as to 'how I might use language to engage what some call resistance' (p.98). With all we know about the impact of corrosive environments and the workload impacts of austerity politics in many countries (Baines *et al.* 2014) there is a real danger here that supervisors could unwittingly be contributing to an individualizing, ultimately blaming culture where one's inability to become the perfect self-regulating model practitioner is evidence of failure and 'resistance'. Participants in supervision are not neutral actors, but carry their cultural and spiritual beliefs and political perspectives into the supervision space. Taking a critical social constructionist approach means understanding that the narratives we create and the meanings we make may be incomplete without an understanding of the material conditions that shape our conversations (Beddoe and Davys 2016).

Supervision and culture

According to Watkins and Milne (2014, p. 674, '[We] are fast becoming a world committed to supervision and its enhancement. In our view, all indications point to further embrace and strengthening of supervision's stature as educational *sine qua non* across countries and continents.' Furthermore, they argue, an exploration of culture within supervision, via 'deliberate and studious consideration is vital for supervision's future' (2014, p.681). We argue that, if supervision is to be inclusive, then culture must be an inherent focus in supervision (Beddoe 2015a).

Both supervisor and supervisee take into the supervision process their own attributes and aspects of their personal identity: their gender, sexuality, age, educational background, ethnicity, religious beliefs and values. Tsui and Ho (1998) have emphasized that within the context of supervision are ideas and practices determined by cultural considerations, the context of supervision and the prevailing culture informing it. Tsui and Ho have challenged the traditional approach to supervision as being influenced most by the organizational context and drivers. Rather, they argue that any model of supervision is shaped by the cultural system in which it occurs. Beddoe and Egan (2009) note that the influence of culture is relevant to consideration of agency purpose and goals, the supervisor's roles, style and skills, the supervisee's working experience, training, and the emotional needs, including those of service users (Beddoe and Egan 2009, p.414). Active recognition of the practitioner's culture is best considered as an essential condition and function of effective supervision, as this 'legitimises and anticipates the tensions which will arise from different value bases and perspectives within the work context' (Davys 2005a, p.7). In Aotearoa New Zealand, the practice of 'cultural supervision' has developed in recent decades (Eruera 2007; Mafile'o and Su'a-Hawkins 2005; Wallace 2019) but this is not the same as the recognition of culture within the supervision process and relationship. Rather, it represents a new and 'independent contribution to supervision' (Davys 2005a, p.7). In Aotearoa New Zealand, where development of cultural supervision is being pioneered (Hair and O'Donoghue 2009), Eruera's work (2007) articulates the uniqueness of some of these developments in differentiating *kaupapa* supervision (representing a Māori world view) from cultural supervision. *Kaupapa* supervision can be defined as:

> …an agreed supervision relationship by Māori for Māori with a purpose of enabling the supervisee to achieve safe and accountable practice, cultural development and self-care according to the philosophy, principles and practices derived from a Māori worldview. (Eruera 2007, p.144)

The development of explicitly cultural approaches to supervision, is as Hair and O'Donoghue (2009) have stated, closely tied to broader aspirations of indigenous and minority cultures. Developing local models, such as the creation of cultural supervision, reflects community responses to the oppression and inequalities experienced by colonised peoples. In Aotearoa New Zealand, this development critically encompasses 'active engagement of Māori and *Pasifika* [Pacific Island nations] social workers in the elevation of their own indigenous ways of knowing. These configurations demonstrate how dominant discourse and emerging local narratives intersect to shape culturally relevant practice' (Hair and O'Donoghue 2009, p.82). Cultural supervision practice such as described by Eruera (2007) supports practitioners with supervision 'grounded in spiritual, traditional and theoretical understandings that are congruent with their worldview. Culture becomes the overarching environment of supervision' (Beddoe and Egan 2009, p.414). Cultural supervision is thus linked to 'personal, family, community, cultural and professional domains. ... Cultural supervision is also about supporting Pasifika social workers to operate in predominantly non-Pasifika contexts' (Mafile'o and Su'a-Hawkins 2005, p.120).

Where multicultural competencies are in focus Arkin (1999) argues for training of supervisors based on four dimensions:

- The awareness dimension – 'the supervisor must be aware of his/her own cultural and personal values, stereotypes, prejudices and biases, as well as the differences between the supervisor and supervisee in terms of values, styles of communication, cognitive orientations and emotional reactions' (p.12).

- The knowledge dimensions – 'facts and information about the... political, social and economic history...research, world views, cultural codes, (differences in) verbal and non-verbal language and emotional expression' (p.12).

- The relationship dimension – 'this requires examination of supervision in cultural terms...cultural identification, expectations, criticism, initiative, passivity, roles' (p.12).

- The skills dimension – important to develop 'the ability to intervene in a culturally sensitive way without detracting from the quality of the professional training...the culture must be legitimized by showing a keen interest in it and by respecting the practitioner's own cultural identity and group membership' (p.12).

There are limitations in multicultural approaches to supervision. First, multicultural approaches don't always address power and authority issues nor the structural inequalities, roles and status of minority cultures within mainstream institutions. There is often an assumption that the supervisor's knowledge of practice is superior and the biases of western thinking may be under-emphasized (Beddoe 2015a). There is a danger that the minority students'/supervisees' differences are still pathologized – to be worked around and accommodated. There are often assumptions that the minority person is always the student or supervisee – what if they are the supervisor? How does this impact on power in the relationship if there are hidden agendas or racist assumptions? What strategies could be used to reduce these oppressive elements of the multicultural approach? Table 2.1 outlines some key requirements for the development of positive cross-cultural and multicultural supervision relationships.

Table 2.1: Requirements for non-oppressive supervision practice

Awareness	of the holistic and dynamic nature of culture in human life and how this influences our thinking as service users, supervisees and supervisors
Conceptual frameworks	applied to understanding the cultural and social construction of knowledge for practice
Understanding	of the way the dominant culture is maintained through policies and practices
Removal of barriers	that limit the utilization of knowledge from other cultures in decision making and critical reflection
Insight	into one's own self and how one perceives and values alternative views
Ability	to culturally deconstruct dominant 'group think' in the practice context and in supervision
Respect	for rituals of encounter and engagement that may be essential for safety within practice
Capacity	to honour, respect and develop perspectives derived from other world views and knowledge bases

Putting it together

As identified earlier by Milne *et al.* (2008), models or approaches to supervision are not mutually exclusive and many supervisors employ more than one model. Watkins (2019, p.15) also ponders the place of supervision models and suggests that 'perhaps such models provide supervisors with the bits and pieces from which they construct those unique integrationist perspectives, with some of those larger bits and pieces'. We agree with this perspective and Figure 2.6 represents how, in our experience, different models and approaches can be used together in a complementary way.

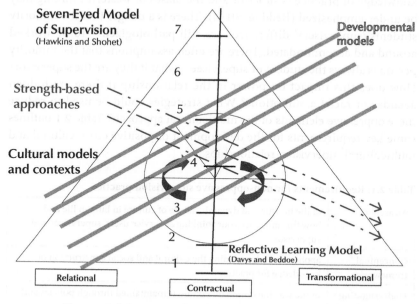

Figure 2.6: Bringing together different models and approaches

Criteria for evaluating approaches to supervision

Given the importance of considering the social and cultural contexts and practices of supervision that we have explored in the preceding sections of this chapter, it is useful to consider the development of criteria for evaluation. Whatever approach to supervision is chosen it will be influenced by professional and personal preference, cultural considerations and the context within which supervision takes place, whether this be large governmental agencies, smaller non-governmental organizations or private practice. The following structure may provide a useful beginning guide:

- structure

- attention to relationship

- attention to process

- attention to context

- underlying theoretical orientation

- technical or clinical detail
- evidence for success
- applicability and utility across professions
- focus on the supervisee's development
- attention to issues of power and influence
- cultural aspects and values
- issues of difference
- time.

In Table 2.2 we have used these criteria to summarize the four of the models presented here.

Table 2.2: Comparison of key features of four supervision approaches

Evaluation criteria	Developmental	Reflective Learning	Strengths-based	Cultural
Structure	Developmental stages Transition points for interventions	Action-reflection cycle	Not prescribed	Follows cultural rituals of engagement and encounter
Purpose	Assists supervisees to move from novice to expert Recognizes key points of transition between stages	Facilitates supervisees to find solutions within themselves through reflection on their experience and actions	Facilitates supervisees to find solutions within themselves based on their existing strengths and prior positive experiences	Supports supervisees through a process that is grounded in spiritual, traditional and theoretical understandings that are congruent with their world view
Attention to relationship	Reflects progression through developmental stages (supervisee and supervisor)	Trust and safety Collaborative	Trust and safety Collaborative	Negotiates and affirms cultural roles and responsibilities

Evaluation criteria	Developmental	Reflective Learning	Strengths-based	Cultural
Attention to process	Uses a range of interventions suited to supervisee developmental stages and transitions between stages	Follows the steps of the action reflection cycle	Language critical to address strengths Isomorphism requires supervisor to model strengths-based interventions	Close adherence to processes which are culturally explicit i.e.: beginning with a prayer/ reflection, acknowledgement of kin and community connections
Attention to context	Based on supervisee's level of experience	Based on supervisee's actual experiences and responses – past, present and future	Based on supervisee's 'reality'	Personal, family, community, cultural and professional domains
Underlying theoretical orientation	Developmental theory	Adult learning theory, reflective practice and experiential learning	Postmodernist ideas about language and meaning Social constructionism Isomorphism	Holistic orientation Spiritual and traditional knowledge
Technical or clinical detail	Supervisor led with input from supervisee Five interventions: Prescriptive, confrontative, conceptual, catalytic and facilitative	Mainly supervisee's agenda Cyclic process of reflection, exploration, analysis, experimentation and review	Supervisee's agenda Construction of narratives based on exploration of strengths and reframing old 'stories'	Reflects cultural practices and understandings of participants who share a similar world view
Utility across professions	Can be applied to any profession	Can be applied to any profession	Can be applied to any profession	Can be applied to any profession

Attention to power	Supervisor's authority assumed. Supervisee's authority develops with expertise	Collaborative to develop supervisee's self-awareness and learning	Collaborative: reframing to empower supervisee and raise self-efficacy	Consideration of the power of the dominant culture and the position of cultural minorities. May include explicit hierarchy related to cultural roles and responsibilities
Cultural aspects	Assumption of homeogenity. Traditional western determination of stages of development	Exploration of context and content	Understanding of social constructionism of ideas, values and beliefs that underpin practice	Validation and support for cultural identity. Explicit links to cultural and social development
Issues of difference	A developmental issue	Recognizes and values individual perceptions and differences	Recognizes and values individual differences and strengths	Homogeneity is important and deliberate. Status is recognized. Recognizes impact of dominant culture. Isomorphic
Time	Stages are recycled over time at deeper levels as practitioners develop in their experience and competence	Uses past and present to measure change and access experience and to bring to the fore for future action and understanding	Pre-supposes the actuality of success	Time is imbued with cultural meaning and often linked to traditional knowledge and ways of 'knowing'

Supervision: an overview

The following is a list of the characteristics of supervision which have been shared by the participants of our supervision training courses. It is not definitive nor exhaustive but rather a reflection of the complexity of this very personal professional practice.

- It is an interpersonal, negotiated relationship in which both parties have rights and responsibilities.

- It is accountable – to the organization, the profession and to the service user.

- It is ethical.

- It is confidential.

- It is ongoing and regular (a process rather than an event).

- It has boundaries.

- It has power dynamics.

- It is a forum for reflection, learning and professional growth.

- It is educative (but not education).

- It is managerial in that it relates to organizational standards and policies but it is not management or appraisal.

- It is professional in that it references professional standards, ethics and codes of practice.

- It is supportive but it is not counselling.

- It is a safe place to express and explore emotion.

Supervision is the chance to stand apart from our work and to reflect on what we do, the context of what we do and the impact that this has on ourselves as people (in particular, as professional people). This reflection brings a greater objectivity and personal understanding to our work. It is an opportunity to evaluate our work in terms of both progress and challenge and it allows us to develop and learn from our experiences. The development of a safe environment encourages mistakes and vulnerabilities to be examined as learning opportunities and not disciplinary occasions. Supervision recognizes the stress and vicarious trauma of those in the helping professions and aims to support practitioners so that they remain healthy in their job.

In summary, supervision is primarily to develop an improved service to clients. It is a practice which is accountable to organizational policy and associated legislation. It is underpinned by the knowledge, skills, competencies and codes of practice and ethics of relevant professions. These three elements provide the framework for supervision. Within this framework sits the supervision relationship which is the medium through which all else is accomplished.

CHAPTER 3

The Supervision Relationship

Within the diversity of ideas about supervision, the one least contested is the significance of the supervision relationship. As Beinart and Clohessy (2017) conclude following their examination of recent research and practice, 'the overwhelming finding from the emerging international evidence base within dyadic supervision literature is that the SR [supervision relationship] is pivotal' (p.4). While the quality of this relationship between supervisor and practitioner has been identified as the most powerful determinant of the success or quality of the supervision experience, the relationship has also been noted for its complexity. Lizzio et al. (2009) comment that it is 'perhaps one of the most conceptually ambiguous and challenging topics in the supervision and professional development literatures' (p.128).

While in some situations supervisors and supervisees share early information via electronic media, it is generally considered that the first face-to-face meeting between the supervisor and supervisee marks the beginning of the supervision relationship. For an increasing number of supervisors and supervisees, this meeting is the time when the 'fit' between the supervision partners is explored and confirmed. As such it precedes the identification of the concrete details of time and place, and other negotiations, which accompany the formal establishing of a contract for supervision (sometimes referred to as the supervision agreement). The supervision contract thus in turn grounds and sets the foundations of the relationship and the subsequent supervision structure and process. It is here, in the contracting discussions, that expectations can be laid out, boundaries mapped, differences identified and negotiated, and goals established.

The supervision relationship has long been considered to influence clinical practice. One early study, which found a significant connection between the supervisee's perception of the supervision relationship and the client's perception of the therapeutic relationship, concluded that the supervisees 'are taking the knowledge they are gaining in supervision about building and maintaining relationships and applying it to the relationship with their client' (Patton and Kivlighan 1997, p.113). Such assertions about the connection between good supervision and effective practice, however, have not gone unchallenged. 'What do we really know about the supervisory alliance? What do we need to know about it?' (Watkins 2014b, p.19). Watkin's critique of 50 years of theory and research concluded that the supervision alliance, while widely accepted as an important component of supervisor practice, is not well supported by empirical evidence. It is this question which Beinhart and Clohessy (2017) address through their examination of supervision research and practice. While acknowledging the limitations and challenges which accompany research on the supervision relationship and the work still to be done, they nevertheless conclude that 'there is now substantive research on the qualities of effective SRs and on the multiple influences on the supervisory dyad' (p.164).

The establishment and maintenance of the supervision relationship, traditionally seen as the responsibility of the supervisor, has become viewed as the responsibility of both the supervisor and the supervisee as supervision has increasingly been considered and practised as a collaborative exchange where learning is the central tenet (Beinhart and Clohessy 2017; Hair 2014; Watkins *et al.* 2018). Honesty, disclosure, respect, and thus the effectiveness of supervision will all be affected by the quality of this relationship. When understanding the tasks and responsibilities of the supervision relationship it can be helpful to view these as components of the four stages of a supervision partnership, as outlined in Table 3.1.

Table 3.1 Stages of a supervision relationship

Stages of a supervision relationship	
Preparation – personal and professional audit	What does each participant bring to the supervision relationship? What does each person want?
Beginning – 'fit' and the process of contracting	Is there is an appropriate 'fit' of expectations, knowledge, skills, values and personality? How are the different needs, expectations and requirements of supervision articulated and agreed?
Middle – developing and maintaining the relationship	Doing the work of supervision and maintaining the relationship through review and feedback
End – finishing the relationship	Conclusions: summary and tying up the ends

Preparation: personal and professional audit

A number of inventories have been complied which list the qualities and attributes that supervisors need to possess in order to be a 'good' supervisor. Our favourite is that compiled by Loganbill *et al.* (1982), possibly because of the richness of the language and the strong sense of personal engagement and commitment to the supervision process. The list includes: genuineness, potency, optimism, courage, sense of time as a gift, sense of humour, capacity for intimacy, openness to fantasy and imagery, respect and consideration (Loganbill et al., pp.28–29).

Subsequent inventories of supervisory competence have located supervision more firmly as a collaborative practice of the 21st century where tensions around power, discrimination, diversity and multicultural competence are recognized. Supervision frequently operates in practice settings which are buffeted by change and uncertainty and often involve some aspect of interprofessionality. Importantly, supervisees are regarded as active contributors, as opposed to passive recipients of their 'expert' supervisor's wisdom, in the supervision process.

Common to more recent lists of supervision skills and attributes is the need for humility, defined by Watkins *et al.* (2018) as: '(a) openness; (b) willingness and ability to accurately assess one's own personal characteristics and achievements; (c) ability to recognize one's own imperfections, mistakes, and limitations; and (d) other-orientation' (2018, p.3). Humility, Watkins *et al.* maintain, not only lessens the potential for supervisors to do harm but also builds and develops the supervision relationship. In a study of interprofessional supervision, one of the authors (Davys 2019) found that 'willingness to learn' was valued in both supervisors and supervisees, as was the ability to sit with and tolerate the uncertainty of 'not knowing'. The ability to recognize and respect the plurality of knowledge, culture and perspectives brought to supervision by both parties, to acknowledge the power dimensions of supervision and to collaborate through critical reflection and decision making, also require humility and are seen as important contributors to effective supervision relationships (Hair 2014; Hawkins and Shohet 2012).

In an early study which explored 'good' supervision as experienced by a group of supervisees (Davys 2005b, p.16), the following list of supervisor characteristics were identified which we believe remain apt:

- competence and knowledge as practitioners

- competence and training as supervisors

- an ability to challenge in a supportive manner

- an openness to feedback and an ability to be self-monitoring

- an ability to provide support and containment for a range of situations and emotions

- an ability to manage power and authority

- an ability to receive and value their own supervision.

In the same study (Davys 2005b, p.16), the supervisee characteristics included:

- clarity about what is wanted from both the supervision process and the supervisor

- openness and willingness to participate actively in the supervision process

- honesty to share practice dilemmas and personal responses to practice

- skills to prepare and plan for supervision

- ability for self-reflection

- willingness to give feedback

- confidence to challenge the supervisor

- training in supervision.

We think that it is significant that training for supervision is included in both these lists and take heart that Watkins (2014a), in a review of clinical supervision in the 21st century, notes the increased availability of supervision training opportunities internationally. In our first edition of this book we noted the number of practitioners we met who were assigned supervisor roles by managers who were seeking to comply with changing codes of practice and legislative requirements. These, often reluctant, supervisors may have never experienced supervision themselves and were catapulted into supervising 'colleagues' who were understandably suspicious of a new process which had been thrust on them. Ten years later we meet fewer of these supervisors and hear less about such situations. In a hopeful trend, we are meeting more practitioners for whom supervision is not a requirement, but who understand its potential and wish to learn the skills in order to add benefit to their professions.

An understanding that training is important for supervision is, however, not universally accepted. We also continue to see, and hear reports of, progression to a supervisory role as an item included on professional or career development plans as rite of passage. Providing supervision is considered here to be an activity for which practitioners are deemed to be equipped by dint of having been a supervisee, and of having years of experience and breadth of practice (Hair 2013; Maidment and Beddoe 2012). For supervisors, as will be further discussed in Chapter 7, skills, attributes and experience are important but are not a substitute for specific training in supervision.

Preparatory training in supervision, for those who are engaging in supervision as supervisees is also important and, though again in no way universal, is in our experience becoming more common. Here it is useful to distinguish between those practitioners and professionals who receive supervision in their training years, and those for whom supervision is a career-long activity and a professional expectation. For the former group, particularly in the North American context where supervision is predominantly focused on the trainee or student, Watkins (2014a) in the review cited earlier, believes that 'career-long supervision will continue to slowly rise on the agendas of a growing number of professional associations and eventually become more established practice' (p.254).

Supervision with students and trainees, discussed in Chapter 10, is the beginning of the supervision journey for those professionals, and introductory supervision orientation or training is generally offered in some form by educational institutions. Student supervision, however, is also a journey tempered by the anxieties of new learning, the development of professional identity and of assessment. These preoccupations, we believe, introduce different tensions and challenges into the supervision relationship, and can unduly shape and influence subsequent expectations of supervision. Hence, we believe that supervision for post-qualified practitioners is based on different premises. Preparation and training are important here to shift the focus from student to qualified practitioner. Freed from an evaluative agenda it is valuable for post-qualification supervisees to have a clear base from which they can truly enter into the supervision partnership as a collaborator who understands their role, their responsibilities and their rights as a supervisee. It is frequently said by students and workshop participants who attend our supervisor training courses that 'I am not sure how well I am doing as a supervisor but I am a much, much better supervisee!'

With or without training, however, there are other ways in which supervisors and supervisees can prepare for supervision roles. One useful activity is a personal and professional audit which can assist the supervision participants to know who they are, what they bring and what they may need or expect from supervision.

Such an audit involves a review of the supervisor's or supervisee's professional history, supervision history, strengths, weaknesses and interests, which will all influence who that person is in the supervision relationship and what they offer or need. While we are very clear about the importance of separating the personal from the professional, in these situations it can be helpful to also reflect on where the supervision participants are in their personal life stages – and how that may influence how they view their work, and how they view supervision in particular. Before entering into any supervision relationship, it is important therefore to have this clarity about who you are, where you are in your professional career, what theories, ideas, experiences and values shape your practice, and to be able to articulate your view of the profession and how you understand the role of supervision in your work and the work of others. Carroll (2014) extends this examination and adjures supervisors to 'review [their] interior condition and mine out [their] reasons for supervising others' (p.64).

Supervision is a two-way relationship. It is important for supervisors and supervisees alike to ask themselves the question, 'How open and prepared am I to engage in my side of this relationship?' The following questions in Tables 3.2 and 3.3 may be useful to help supervisors and supervisees to shape this audit.

Table 3.2: Supervisor audit

History
What do you bring to practice from your personal experiences?
What do your bring to supervision from your practice experience and training?

• What are the key events, milestones and achievements of your life to date? • How have these shaped your professional career? • What are your current interests, achievements and challenges? • What comes next in your life journey? • How do you take care of yourself and ensure your wellbeing? What are the implications of the above for your current and future practice? 	• What training, qualification(s) and work experience underpin your professional practice? • What theories, methods, models and/or people have influenced (or continue to influence) your current practice? • What have been the highlights of your professional practice? • What have been the greatest learning situations? • How have these experiences shaped how you currently work? • What areas of practice do you not enjoy? • What is your current area of interest or learning edge? How will the above impact on your supervision of other practitioners?

Supervision What is your experience of supervision? How do you use your own supervision?	
Supervisor as a supervisee	**Engaging in supervision**
• In your own current supervision how do you contribute to the supervision relationship? • Are you receiving the sort of supervision you need at this point of your career? • What are your current questions or dilemmas about the practice of supervision? • How much of your own supervision time is spent on your role as a supervisor (as opposed to other roles such as clinician or manager?) 	• What are your experiences of providing and receiving supervision? • Who, or what, has had the most influence on your supervision to date? • What training have you had to prepare you for the role of supervisor? • What is your definition of supervision and what models and theories underpin your supervision practice? • What are your expectations of supervisees? • How good are you at giving and receiving feedback?

Table 3.3: Supervisee audit

History What do you bring to practice from your personal history? What do your bring to supervision from your professional experiences?	
• What are the key events, milestones and achievements of your life to date? • How have these shaped your professional career? • What are your current interests, achievements and challenges? • What comes next in your life journey? • How do you take care of yourself and ensure your wellbeing? What are the implications of the above for your current and future practice? 	• What training, qualification(s) and work experience underpin your professional practice? • What theories, methods, models or people have influenced (or continue to influence) your current practice? • What have been the highlights of your professional practice? • What have been the greatest learning situations? • How have these experiences shaped how you currently work? • What are your areas of strength and competence in practice? • What areas of practice would you like to develop? • What areas of practice do you avoid?

Supervision What is your experience of supervision? What do you want from supervision?	
A new supervision relationship	**Engaging in supervision**
• What qualities and experience are you looking for in a supervisor?	• What experiences of supervision have you had in the past?
• What approach or model of supervision best suits your needs?	• What stands out as effective and good supervision? Why?
• What do you want from supervision?	• What have been obstacles to effective or good supervision?
• How will you collaborate in the supervision process?	• How have you contributed to supervision in the past?
• What areas of practice do you want to celebrate, address, explore and/or develop?	• How have you addressed supervision issues in the past?
• What are your career aspirations, short term and long term?	• What have you learnt from your past supervision experiences?
• What are your immediate goals for supervision?	

Supervision partners

A range of suggestions have been made about ways to optimize the supervision process: matching of gender, culture, sexual orientation, age and physical ability (Brown and Bourne 1996; Howard 1997), consideration of learning styles (Scaife 2009), while Clare (2001) proposes supervision matches across the continua of specialist/generalist, learning/teaching styles, local/cosmopolitan dimension and professional/anti- or non-professional dimension. Others, however, have described a more eclectic 'fit', a 'match of such things as skills, philosophy, needs, expertise and personality' (Davys 2019, p.124), as being the factor which determines the quality of the supervision process. 'Supervisee–supervisor fit strengthens the supervisory relationship [and] that has been shown in empirical studies to be the single most important factor that influences the quality of supervision' (Ducat et al. 2016, p.33). Bernard and Goodyear (2014), in an examination of competent multicultural supervision which included difference of race, gender, sexual orientation and culture, again found that it was the strength of the relationship, not the similarities, which bridged the differences and provided 'the necessary sense of safety and support to permit what often are difficult and challenging dialogues' (2014, p.130). Similarly, in a study of interprofessional supervision, Davys (2019) found that competence as a supervisor and a good relationship transcended the differences of profession.

Choice

The relationship between choice, trust and effective ('good') supervision has been well documented (O'Donoghue and Tsui 2012; Sloan and Grant 2012). Choice, or lack of choice, of supervisor (or supervisee) shapes the supervision negotiations and the subsequent quality of the supervisory relationship. For many supervisees, 'having a real choice of who to see as a clinical supervisor is essential to building a working alliance' (Bond and Holland 2010, p.254).

The desirability, and the feasibility, of supervisees making a choice of supervisor are discussed in the literature (Bond and Holland 2010; Davys *et al.* 2017). Here the benefit to supervisees of choosing their supervisor is supported by such statements as 'the greater the opportunity to choose, the more likely the supervisee will positively anticipate engaging in the supervisory process' (Scaife 2009, p.19). Cooper and Anglem (2003) report supervisees' dissatisfaction with the lack of choice of supervisor and their supervisor's availability and, Sloan (2006) found that supervisees placed less value on internal supervision because they were not able to choose the supervisor. In a study by Davys (2005b), the ability of supervisees to choose their supervisors was highlighted as an attribute of good supervision. In this study, supervisors and supervisees alike saw the benefits of choice as including the ability to both enter and to leave the relationship. These acts of choice, which also included deciding to continue in the relationship, were considered by the participants as reinforcing the ultimate commitment to the relationship.

Caution, however has to be exercised as it has also been suggested that 'an agreeable supervisor and a pleasant SR are not sufficient for effective supervision' (Beinhart and Clohessy 2017, p.164). The question arises as to 'whether supervisees choose that which is good for them or that which makes them feel good' (Davys 2005b, p.17). This question was posed by participants themselves in the research cited above. One respondent wondered if her choice of supervisor reflected an easy, less challenging relationship (Davys 2005b, p.17), while a supervisor pondered the possibility that she was chosen because she provided 'a cosy support system' (Davys 2005b, p.17). These reflections we believe highlight the importance of an awareness of the processes of supervision rather than a need for greater or less choice.

In all supervision arrangements where the focus is on learning and the professional development of supervisees, there will be an element of challenge. This challenge, which can provoke anxiety, discomfort or defensive self-protection (Lizzio *et al.* 2009, p.129), will occur whether or not there has been a choice of supervisor. It will need to be acknowledged and managed as part of the supervision process. 'The struggle inherent in learning may not always be experienced as the most satisfying' (Ladany, Ellis and Friedlander 1999, p.453). Supervision which is deemed 'good' by the supervisee, may in fact be attending to the supervisee's comfort and reinforcing the 'known' rather than encouraging development and change by challenging the practitioner's growing edge. Such comfort in supervision can affect the outcomes of practice. Rieck, Callahan and Watkins (2015) report from their study that supervisor agreeableness had 'a significant inverse association with [and was] inversely predictive of client change scores' (p.192). Good supervision, Reick *et al.* believe, requires an 'appropriate balance of support *and* challenge' (2015, p.192).

It is our contention that at times the issue of whether or not a supervisee, or supervisor for that matter, can choose their supervisor (or supervisee) assumes an importance which distracts from the issue at hand. The key issue is how to develop a supervision relationship which will enable both parties to attend professionally to the consideration and development of the work of one of them (the supervisee). Supervision does not occur in a professional vacuum and all good supervision contracts include, or should include, a process for feedback and review. Further, the majority of supervision relationships occur between 'professionals' who know about relationships as their work includes, or depends on, a relationship with others. Is it possible that preoccupation about choice becomes an end in itself and detracts from the core ability of competent practitioners (and supervisors) to get on with it and develop the best relationship possible for the given period of the supervision arrangement? It is certain that many of us have experienced supervision where there has been no choice of supervisor and which we would not have chosen. We have developed skills to extract the best we can from the supervision experience, or we have used the processes available to challenge and hopefully constructively move on. What is important is for there to be a clear process for review which does allow supervisees to remove themselves from unproductive and destructive relationships. The supervisee who embraces supervision and takes an active role in making supervision work opens an opportunity for learning and professional growth. A wise mentor to one of the authors once said, 'The best therapist is the one who pushes your buttons – because all your issues will be to the fore'. Is there possibly a parallel truth here for supervision? Do we always choose the right supervisor?

It is worthy of note that many practitioners are employed in public organizations within health, social service or justice systems. The clients of these practitioners, unlike fee-paying consumers of private practitioners, have no choice of their practitioner. Isomorphism, the 'matching between the form of supervision and the form of practice' (Edwards and Chen 1999, p.352 citing Kerlinger 1986), would suggest that there is an appropriate parallel between the limited choices in the supervisor/supervisee relationship and the practitioner/client relationship. Be that as it may, it is a useful and important exercise to clarify what, ideally, we want from a supervisor at any given time regardless of whether or not we have a choice in the matter. If we know what we want from supervision we are better equipped to ask for it and to discuss with the supervisor how we can be facilitated to get the most out of supervision. We are in a good position to consider with our supervisor whether they are able to meet all of our needs and to identify how any gaps can be filled in other ways outside the relationship. Carroll and Gilbert (2011) remind us that, whether or not you have chosen a supervisor or had one chosen for you, 'you are the consumer and it is essential that your learning needs be adequately met in supervision' (p.27). In this manner, a supervisee can take active responsibility for their role. While we may not all be able to choose our supervisor, we do have choices about how we conduct ourselves in supervision.

Traditionally supervision has been between a supervisor and a supervisee who share the same professional identity and has been conducted within the boundaries and parameters of their particular profession. As supervision has developed as a profession, or as a professional activity, in its own right (Inman *et al.* 2014; Lizzio *et al.* 2009; Sewell 2018), however, it has stretched to include supervision relationships which bridge a range of professions in a range of organizational and private settings. This break from tradition has seen the emergence of interprofessional supervision, 'professional supervision which occurs between a supervisor and a supervisee who do not share the same professional training or practice' (Davys 2017, p.79) sometimes referred to as 'cross disciplinary' (Hair 2013; Hutchings, Cooper and O'Donoghue 2014), 'multi-disciplinary' (Gillig and Barr 1999) and 'multi professional' (Mullarkey, Keeley and Playle 2001). Many professional and regulatory bodies address this issue directly and prescribe the qualifications and experience necessary for supervisors and the occasions when same-profession supervision is required and interprofessional supervision is acceptable. It is generally recognized that students, new graduates and those new to areas of practice are best supervised by a supervisor who shares their profession or discipline (Davys and Beddoe 2016). Bernard and Goodyear (2014) note that one of limitations of interprofessional supervision is the absence of the 'socialisation function' of supervision to assist, particularly new, practitioners to create a sense of professional identity (Bernard and

Goodyear 2014, p.12). They also warn of the 'cuckoo' effect where, like the cuckoo laying her egg in another nest, a novice practitioner is socialized into the practice 'mores' of another profession, thus losing some of the uniqueness of their own (Bernard and Goodyear 2014, p.12).

Research conducted by the authors (Beddoe and Howard 2012; Davys and Beddoe 2008) into interprofessional supervision and interprofessional learning contexts for supervision also contributes to this debate and adds other perspectives. Difference of profession between the supervisor and supervisee, rather than being considered as a limitation of supervision has been viewed by many as 'a source of stimulation, excitement and growth' (Davys 2019, p.142). When the supervisor does not share the same work context it allows the practitioner to have the benefit of an outside perspective which is free from some of the unspoken assumptions within professions. The supervisor is indeed a true naive enquirer whose need to understand requires an explanation from the supervisee, which in turn prompts consideration of those often 'taken-for-granted' practices so often accepted without critique when practitioners and supervisors share a knowledge base. This exploration can bring forward new ideas and challenge practice which has previously been accepted without question. Similarly, in order to communicate clearly across professions, supervisees take more time to clarify their thoughts and avoid the short cuts offered by jargon. A supervisor from another profession may introduce a new and extending range of skills and perspectives.

When the development of professional insights, reflection, learning and responsive practice is considered to be a primary function of supervision, then supervisors require higher order skills which transcend the day-to-day task focus of profession-specific practice. '[Interprofessional] Supervision is driven through a knowledge of *supervision* practice as opposed to *profession-specific* practice' (Davys 2019, p.177) and could be said to represent 'best practice' supervision. Once again, supervisor knowledge and expertise in supervision is recognized, echoing other assertions that competence as a supervisor is more important than a shared professional base (Bogo *et al.* 2011). Lynch and colleagues (2008) bring this neatly into perspective by suggesting that identification of what a practitioner wishes to achieve from supervision is more productive than a debate about whether the supervisor should share the same profession as the supervisee.

We believe that there are many benefits to interprofessional supervision; however, care does need to be taken to ensure that profession-specific skills and protocols are not compromised. This may lead to a distinction between professional supervision and clinical mentoring or oversight. It is recognized that all supervision sits within a network of professional relationships which support the professional practitioner. Interprofessional supervision in many instances is supported by particular adjunctive relationships which ensure safety and accountability to professional and clinical requirements (Beddoe and Howard 2012; Davys 2019). If the supervisor does not share the same professional base as the practitioner, we stress that it is important that there is some other form of 'professional critique' of clinical practice in order to ensure safe practice. This idea, that all supervision needs may not be addressed in one relationship is not new, particularly in the social work supervision literature (Beddoe and Davys 2016; Davys 2002; 2017; Garrett and Barretta Herman 1995; Hirst 2001; O'Donoghue 2015).

Beginning

Supervision is 'strongly influenced by infrastructure and relationship variables. In other words, the performance will be as good as the attention that has been paid to these seemingly extraneous variables' (Bernard 2005, p.9). The beginning stage of a supervision relationship is characterized by two activities: establishing 'fit' and negotiating the supervision contract.

The supervision contract, it is generally agreed, underpins and defines the parameters of any supervision arrangement and provides a structure for the relationship (Beinart and Clohessy 2017; Scaife 2009), but before this occurs many supervisees and supervisors meet to make a preliminary assessment as to whether they think this relationship will work (Carroll 2014; Davys 2017). Is there an appropriate 'fit'? For those who have chosen the relationship it can confirm the choice; for those who have not chosen, it is an early opportunity to make connections and to find reassurance or to identify mismatch and consider other options. In a study on interprofessional supervision (Davys 2019), supervisors and supervisees alike described the benefits of this first meeting. The conversation, which many of those supervisors who were in private practice provided free of charge, occurred prior to any contract negotiation, was intentional and aimed to confirm 'fit' for both parties. Participants asked themselves: does this supervision relationship have the potential to meet the supervisee's needs and do both parties believe that there is an appropriate 'fit' of expectations, skills, values and personality (Davys 2019, p.176)? When a preliminary connection has been established, and when the 'fit' has been confirmed, supervisors and supervisees are in a good place to begin a more focused conversation about the formal aspects of the supervision arrangement, variously called the supervision contract, supervision agreement.

Morrison (1993, p.29) has defined the supervision contracting process as 'a means of making explicit the aims of the parties to work towards agreed goals in agreed ways'. Preparation is useful. When a practitioner knows what they want, or don't want, from supervision then they are in the best position to negotiate a supervision contract which delivers what is needed. In subsequent work, Morrison makes the proviso that a contract will not guarantee a successful supervision relationship, but it will provide the best beginning place from which a 'good' relationship can grow (Morrison 2001, p.114).

The contract document is the record of those conditions of supervision which are prescribed by organizational and professional policy and, equally importantly, contains the agreements and goals which have been independently negotiated between the supervisor and supervisee. It is the process of negotiating this contract, however, that is as, if not more, important than the content (Bond and Holland 2010; Hawkins and Shohet 2012).

By declaring and discussing their expectations of supervision, both the supervisor and the practitioner are able to acknowledge the constraints, the opportunities and the possible areas of difficulty of their working alliance. 'The process, of discussing and establishing both general principles and the nitty gritty of the alliance, is the vehicle through which an intentional and unique relationship is initiated between this particular practitioner and this particular supervisor in this particular context' (Proctor 2001, p.31). It is, however, not always the experience of practitioners that the supervision process begins with discussion, either to consider 'fit' as described earlier, or to discuss how they will work together. Many of the supervisees we meet report that they are simply presented with a formatted contract to sign as a fait accompli. While it is readily accepted that a prepared 'contract' is expedient in terms of time and ensures that basic organizational and professional requirements are explicit and equivalent for all practitioners, it is important that the piece of paper does not become a substitute for the beginning relationship building conversations which take place between supervisor and practitioner.

In general, the conditions which need to be specified in a supervision contract include:

- the aims of supervision
- frequency
- duration
- venue
- cost (if appropriate)
- confidentiality (and its limitations)

- accountability to professional or registration bodies and organizational policy

- issues of safety: how they will be recognized and the process for addressing them

- limits to clinical accountability: if the supervisor is external to the organization or not from the same profession, who the person(s) is to whom the supervisee is professionally accountable or whom can they access for support an information

- additional supervision arrangements (cultural, managerial, clinical etc.)

- record keeping: what records will be kept, where will they be kept and who will have access to them

- preparation: what preparation for each session is agreed between the parties

- agenda setting: how the agenda will be set, and whose agenda it is

- feedback and review: when this will occur, how it will occur and who will have access to the review

- processes for dealing with conflict and complaint

- the relationship of supervision to performance management, appraisal and counselling

- degree of access the supervisee has to the supervisor outside supervision sessions

- missed supervision appointments

- interruptions: what the rules/exceptions are.

Negotiate a supervision contract or working alliance

The negotiation of the supervision contract, as we continue to stress, is a process as much as it is a task. Proctor (2001, p.29) identifies two levels of engagement when negotiating what she terms the 'working agreement'. First, there is the level of practical clarification and negotiation. This is the clarification that will occur through discussion of items such as those identified on the checklist above. It is, however, our contention that the second of Proctor's levels, that of shared information, is the more significant and potent. Information is shared verbally and intuitively and it is during the process of sharing of this information that the core conditions of trust, openness and respect begin to develop. Others are no doubt referring to this level of negotiation when they refer to the psychological contract (Carroll and Gilbert 2011; Scaife 2009):

> The psychological contract refers to the agreement (on a more implicit level) that the supervisor is committed to co-creating with the supervisee a safe and facilitative environment in which work can be discussed and evaluated. (Carroll and Gilbert 2011, p.41)

Carroll and Gilbert (2011) reinforce the importance of making explicit any assumptions and expectations because, they warn, unless these expectations and assumptions are explicit the potential for 'misunderstandings and disappointments' is high. The acknowledgement of power in the supervision relationship and a clear definition of the boundaries around power is one such necessary conversation in order to avoid misunderstanding.

Traditionally hierarchical in nature, the supervision relationship confers considerable authority on the supervisor (Hair 2014). From this authority are derived various types of power which are exercised through the filter of organizational, professional, cultural and personal values, beliefs and norms (Bond and Holland 2010). Supervisors are frequently uncomfortable with this power and at times their failure to exercise their authority can amount to collusion with the supervisee and result in poor and unsafe practice (Bond and Holland 2010; Morrison 2001). A focus during supervision negotiations, on mutuality and the 'shared' two-way relationship can, on occasion, lead to a mistaken belief that the supervision relationship is an equal relationship. It is important that supervisor and supervisee alike are clear about power in the relationship and have a candid discussion which acknowledges that, while this is a collaborative relationship, there are defined boundaries. Supervisors' professional, organizational and ethical accountabilities may require them in certain situations to exercise their authority. This is not to be confused with threats or disguised control. On the contrary, open discussion is aimed to avoid misunderstanding and to ensure that the parameters of the relationship are explicit. In a study of 636 post-qualified social workers Hair (2014) found that:

> Social workers have a need for supervisors who are transparent about their positional power and who are willing to create a quiet space for a mutual exchange of knowledge and critically reflective decision making. The power relations identified by research participants can help transform supervision from being a binary relationship of the dominator and the dominated, to becoming a dynamic interrelationship that is a positive, energizing aspect of peoples' lives. (p.111)

Typically, a conversation about power in supervision will cover legitimate power. This includes the responsibilities of the supervisor as defined in the policies and protocols of the organization and in the codes of practice and codes of ethics of the professional or regulatory body. It is useful of course to note here that the supervisee will similarly be accountable to such policies and codes. Where a supervisor has power to reward or withhold reward, which often occurs when the supervisor also holds a line management responsibility or, in the situation with a student, where the supervisor has an assessment role, these conversations need to include a discussion about the effect that this power will have on trust and disclosure.

Equally important, but sometimes more difficult, are conversations about personal power. Hawkins and Shohet (2012) describe this as the power an individual has which is outside their role(s) and task, '...it derives from both the authority of their expertise, as well as from the presence and impact of their personality' (p.122). These conversations require more disclosure on the part of both supervisor and supervisee and are thus more likely to be overlooked. Finally, there is charismatic power, which is possibly the most complex form of power and harder to define. Charismatic personalities can be associated with relationships which are characterized by acceptance and or rejection – the in-crowd and the out-crowd. Charismatic power from community or cultural status, however, can at times create genuine difficulties of divided loyalty for supervisees, while Eurocentric models of practice can play out the assumptions of dominant cultures and can render supervisees voiceless (Hair and O'Donoghue 2009). How will a supervisee give critical feedback to a supervisor who holds status as an elder in a particular cultural structure? Or in cultures where gender and age have specific status, how will that be accommodated in supervision, particularly if it is the supervisor who, in cultural terms, has less status?

In a more general sense, through the process of sharing information and negotiating the expectations of supervision, similarities will be discovered and differences uncovered. The supervisee will be making assessments as to how safe they feel in the relationship with the supervisor and the supervisor will be assessing how the supervisee is likely to respond to challenge and how much support might be needed. During this process of negotiation, respect can be demonstrated and trust begins to be established. 'Often, to make the deepest changes the relationship between supervisee and supervisor needs to be based on a high level of mutual trust and confidence' (Owen 2008, p.63).

The establishment of that trust is a complex process in supervision. Paradoxically, one of the ways to begin to establish trust is to take risks through the willingness to be open. The discussions which take place during the negotiation of the supervision contract provide a key opportunity where, at the beginning of the supervision relationship, openness can be modelled and beginnings of trust seeded. Lizzio *et al.* (2009) highlight the significance of the supervisor in this process, 'If a supervisor is perceived as not being open, the supervisee may in turn, not trust their supervisor sufficiently to be open themselves' (Lizzio *et al.* 2009, p.136). Openness for the supervisor begins through early preparation by knowing their own strengths and the limits of their abilities and knowledge and being willing and able to articulate these with the supervisee. It includes a supervisor knowing what they expect from supervisees and saying so. A supervisor's openness contributes 'to a virtuous cycle of trust building between supervisor and supervisee' (Lizzio *et al.* 2009, p.136) which will continue to grow with the supervision relationship.

The establishment of the supervision relationship begins with the first meeting and develops through the discussion of the contract. It requires both the supervisor and the supervisee to accord the time to have these conversations and to withstand the pressure to get on and 'do' supervision before these fundamentals are discussed. It requires the supervisor and the supervisee to both value and respect the 'other' so that needs and expectations can be heard, middle ground defined and creative options developed where there are differences.

Essentially, the negotiation of the supervision contract or working agreement can be considered as the process of working through three key questions: Who are we? Where do we want to go? How will we get there?

Like many documents and processes, the supervision contract is a living document which needs to be reviewed and renewed on a regular basis (Bienhart and Clohessy 2017). Many supervision arrangements agree to have an initial review process three months after the contract is first signed and annual reviews thereafter. As supervisees develop in skill and confidence, what they require from supervision changes. Supervision activities and focus will change accordingly and it may be necessary to revisit and redesign the contract. Where third parties are involved in the supervision negotiation, such as a manager or practice leader, particularly when the supervision is external to the organization, it is important that their involvement in the review is identified in the original contract (Beddoe and Davys 2016). The challenges of external supervision are explored further in Chapter 4.

Morrison (2001) in his most useful four-stage process for negotiating the supervision contract includes a stage which he calls 'acknowledging ambivalence' (Morrison 2001, p.107). This is the stage where the supervisor and the supervisee identify possible blocks which can occur during a supervision relationship, discuss how these blocks may be recognized when they occur and negotiate ways of dealing with them. Morrison (2001) identifies three possible areas of block:

- the potential effect of the 'work' on the supervisee and the personal expectations the supervisee may have around resilience and coping

- the general feelings the supervisee may have about the supervision process and its benefit

- the potential effect of 'difference' between the supervisee and supervisor.

An exploration of ambivalence and resistance during the contracting stage provides an opportunity to pre-empt difficulties, particularly those which arise as the result of difference. When a supervisee and their supervisor identify that they have different experience, around any of the difference continua of practice, culture (including ethnicity, gender, sexual orientation, spirituality, ability etc.), values or beliefs, they can anticipate possible difficulties and negotiate how best to deal with them if they do arise. It might be that they identify their own process and structure for discussion or that they agree to engage a third person to act as a mediator or advisor to assist understanding or resolution of disagreement. Situations where the supervisee may be unable to voice their discomfort, disagreement or point of view are also usefully identified. In the face of such a possibility, the supervisor and supervisee can explore how the supervisor might notice this difficulty or withdrawal on the part of the supervisee and how best to assist the supervisee to convey their concerns. Once again, these conversations require honesty and disclosure. Where supervisors have encouraged and invited supervisees 'to have a voice' it has been found that there is a reduction in 'resistant behaviours' and an increased 'willingness to receive feedback' (Lizzio *et al.* 2009, p.136). Unfortunately, these honest conversations which can be uncomfortable are often hurried, superficial or overlooked.

Middle

Thus far we have described and discussed the preparation for the supervision relationship, given some consideration to the selection of a supervisor and establishing whether there is an appropriate 'fit', and reviewed a process for negotiating the conditions for conducting this alliance. In this next section, we wish to consider the ongoing development and maintenance of the supervision relationship.

Traditionally the role of the supervisee has been portrayed as passive and indeed the very construction of the language of supervision places the supervisee in the role of a recipient. The supervisor is active – they 'supervise' while the supervisee's role is defined by passivity, they 'are supervised'.

The ultimate quality of the supervision relationship, however, as we have seen in the earlier discussion, is dependent on the development and maintenance of this arrangement as an active and collaborative exchange. The supervision contract and the process of its construction and negotiation set the scene for the manner in which this relationship will mature. One factor which will influence the manner in which the relationship evolves is the developmental progress of the practitioner.

Models of practitioner development have been discussed in Chapter 2 and we refer to those models here only to provide a framework to consider how the supervision relationship will be altered according to the level of supervisee development.

Where the new practitioner depends largely on rules and structures, the experienced practitioner organizes their work around 'more conscious, thoughtful, analytic reflection (Butler 1996, p.278). Lizzio *et al.* (2009, p.129) note that supportive behaviour in supervision may be more beneficial in the early stages of the supervision relationship when practitioners are more anxious about their professional role and the supervision relationship. As the practitioner develops in competence and experience, the level of support in supervision lessens and, consistent with a wish to reflect on and critique practice, the experienced supervisee seeks challenge through corrective rather than confirmatory feedback (Lizzio *et al.* 2009, p.129).

A developmental framework for supervision may thus depend, not so much on the adaptation of approach and skills of the supervisor, but rather on adaptation and changes within the relationship between the supervisor and the supervisee. As the relationship changes, so will our understanding of mutuality within the relationship. As the supervisee moves from novice to expert and beyond, they will, at each stage, attend to a different level of self. So will the supervisor respond from a different place within themselves. Supervisors are reminded to consider this mutuality and to ask what the supervisee has considered or done, before telling or issuing directives (Enlow *et al.* 2019), or in Hawkins and Shohet's (2012) words 'never know better, never know first' (p.93).

We believe that there are three qualities which are fundamental to a good supervision relationship: authenticity, respect and positive regard, and mutual investment in or openness to learning. When a supervisor is present, open and authentic and conveys genuine interest and regard, supervisees are encouraged to trust and share their work. There is an exchange of energy and enthusiasm which becomes a cyclical process. The supervisees' honesty and their willingness to share material reinforces the regard and respect from their supervisor. Positive regard and respect are the conditions required by the supervisees to continue to share. This process of sharing we believe defines the supervisory space and it is within this space that transformational learning can take place for both supervisor and supervisee. 'The personal connection that results from openness related strategies appears to have the strongest influence on keeping supervisees engaged in the learning process' (Lizzio *et al.* 2009, p.136).

Ruch (2009), describing the connections between curiosity, 'not knowing', critical reflection and learning, notes that in order to be curious one must also be able 'to tolerate "not knowing" both in terms of what is going on and "not knowing" in terms of how best to respond' (p.352). Such openness leads to an ability to consider multiple possibilities and realities. The mutuality of shared goals, and a commitment to a shared process of relationship, may have different outcomes for both parties and requires an authentic presence, respect and a willingness to create and explore that supervisory space into which the supervisee places their work. To move into this supervisory space requires courage and trust and a knowing that both parties may emerge with new learning and be possibly altered. Not all supervision arrangements and relationships achieve this level of learning.

Explicit in any good supervision contract should be a schedule for review. Typically, supervision is reviewed annually and this provides an opportunity for the participants to take stock and reflect on the relationship, the process and the outcomes of supervision. Is the relationship still relevant and vital and are the supervisee needs being met? (Davys *et al.* 2016).

A study of evaluation of supervision in Aotearoa New Zealand (Davys *et al.* 2017) found that a majority of the 24 participants reviewed supervision in some way, and that the most common rationale for reviewing supervision was 'to develop and maintain an effective supervision relationship' (p.254). The participant group, which comprised supervisees, supervisors and managers from the professions of counselling, mental health nursing, psychology and social work (and did not include supervision partnerships), reported that the review was mostly conducted through informal verbal feedback and discussion. The focus of these reviews, which occurred either at the end of every session, every three, six or twelve months or through a combination of all timeframes, considered:

- usefulness of the supervision provided
- whether the current supervision arrangement should continue
- quality of the both the supervision relationship and the supervision process
- supervisee practice development

- supervisor's interventions/strategies

- what was not being addressed in supervision. (Davys *et al.* 2017)

In supervision, the contract can become the focus for this review and the following questions itemized in Tables 3.4 and 3.5 can discussed between the supervisor and supervisee.

Table 3.4: Reviewing supervision – a supervisee's perspective

For the supervisee
Is the supervision meeting the stated goals?
Is the supervision meeting your needs?
What needs to be added or removed from the original contract?
At the end of this period of supervision, what have you learned?
How has supervision made a difference to the way you work?
How has the process of supervision affected your learning?
What do you like about this present supervision arrangement?
What would you like to change?
What feedback would you like to give your supervisor?
What areas of feedback would you like to receive from your supervisor?
What are your current goals for practice and are they reflected in your supervision plans?
Are your culture and values recognised in supervision?

Table 3.5 Reviewing supervision – a supervisor's perspective

For the supervisor
Does the supervisee feel heard?
Is supervision supportive?
How do you assist the supervisee to reflect and learn?
If you hold a dual role (supervisor and line manager), is there a clear boundary?
Is the contract still relevant?
Do you do things the supervisee wants to change?
Does the supervisee feel safe?
Are you approachable?
How do you recognize the supervisee's culture and values?
Do you impose your culture or values on the supervisee?

How do you facilitate a learning environment?
Does the supervisee feel that on leaving the supervision session their goals have been met?
What areas need to be improved or developed?
Does this relationship work?
What feedback do you want to give the supervisee?
What areas of feedback would you like to receive from the supervisee?
How has supervision influenced the way in which this supervisee practises?
What has changed in the supervisee's practice?

Endings

Given the amount of attention paid to the establishment of the supervisory relationship in the literature, it is interesting that so little attention is paid to its end. In this section, we will consider how to conclude a supervision relationship.

The supervision relationship may end for a number of reasons:

- The contracted period for supervision has finished.

- The supervisor or supervisee is leaving the organization or the role.

- There has been a break down in relationship and the contract is terminated.

- It is time for a change.

Whatever the reason, it is useful to consider how we finish this relationship. In a parallel with practice, where the client or patient together with the practitioner reviews the achievements and details the work still to be done, we recognize the place and opportunity for review and consolidation at the conclusion of a supervision partnership.

At the end of a supervision relationship, it is important to take the time to reflect on, to review and to honour the time spent together. If this has been a relationship where significant moments of practice have been shared then the relationship may hold deep, celebratory and sometimes painful moments of the practitioner's professional history. If the supervision arrangement has been more problematic, the prospect of ending may be viewed with some relief by one or both participants. Regardless, tying up the ends and closure are important.

The ending of supervision relationships, as we have suggested above, occurs for a number of reasons. Sometimes these are mutually timed and agreeable to all concerned. In other circumstances, the timing may not suit one or both parties and the very ending may create discomfort and ambivalence. What is important is that time is allowed for either party, but particularly the supervisee, to express their response to the change and to come to terms with the consequences. Marris (1974) cited in Ford and Jones (1987, p.149) identifies three tasks in response to change. When confronted with change, people need to have an opportunity to react, to articulate their ambivalence and to work out their own defence of it.

In supervision, time needs to be allocated to allow these processes to occur, and particularly where change has not been the choice of the supervisee it is important that the supervisee is given time to accommodate the implications of, and responses to, the impending change. Time must be allowed for the supervisee and supervisor to review and reflect on the relationship and note and celebrate any significant development and learning which has occurred. Where relationships have been more problematic, it is even more important for opportunity to be given for any unfinished business to be aired and if possible put to rest before the relationship finishes. Either together or separately, the supervisor and supervisee can consider the following questions:

- What do I, as the supervisee or the supervisor, take away as learning and development from this relationship?

- How does this fit into my professional development plan?

- What have been the challenges of this relationship?

- What professional development remains to be addressed?

- How will this reflection and learning be brought in to my next supervision relationship(s)?

The supervision relationship is possibly the most basic and yet the most complex feature of supervision. It is the medium through which the work of supervision is achieved. To accomplish this work, the relationship needs to be founded on integrity, honesty, courage and faithfulness. This chapter has considered ways to develop and maintain such a supervision relationship while at the same time acknowledging the challenges and hurdles which may need to be overcome.

CHAPTER 4

The Organizational Context and Culture of Supervision

Supervision is a significant element in the complex system of professional and organizational processes designed to ensure competent practice in health and social care. In the 21st century, most helping professionals work in highly bureaucratic organizational contexts and increasingly fewer can truly claim to be fully able to control their own work, or even their own knowledge (Karvinen-Niinikoski *et al.* 2019). This is particularly so where their profession exists under the control of central government or local authority-controlled services (Bierema and Eraut 2004). The nature of the climate in any given workplace has a major impact on the effectiveness of supervision and learning in that workplace. This chapter examines the way organizational culture in workplaces supports or hinders supervision and the professional development of staff. The nature of workplace cultures will also be examined with consideration of external societal influences. The increasing focus on the psychosocial aspects of workplace health and safety will be critically examined.

So what is organizational culture? The study of organizational culture began in the 1970s and grew from critical examination of what sort of culture (which was made up of beliefs, norms, and values) organizations create and perpetuate, and thereby what effect that culture has on individual and organizational effectiveness (Glisson 2000). Schein (1996) defines 'culture' as:

> A set of basic tacit assumptions about how the world is and ought to be that a group of people share and that determines their perceptions, thoughts, feelings, and, to some degree, their overt behaviour. (Schein 1996, p.11)

Most descriptions of organizational culture define it as the whole of the traditions, values, attitudes, work practices and policies that constitute an all-encompassing context in which the work of the organization is carried out (Hawkins and Shohet 2012). A commonplace definition is 'it's the way things work around here', and at its simplest it is grounded in the everyday life of a workplace: it may be about greetings, breaks, meetings, celebrations, welcomes and farewells. In its more complex dimensions, it concerns the way workers relate to each other, the interpersonal dynamics and histories and the hierarchies, visible and invisible, that determine informal roles in the agency. Significant elements are found in the manner in which 'workplace relationships are developed and maintained and how boundaries between work and private life are constructed. At a deeper level culture will include the taken for granted and shared meanings attributed to actions in the agency, and the values and beliefs which underpin those actions' (Beddoe and Maidment 2009, p.82), with much literature emphasizing that many aspects of the 'culture' will be unspoken rather than spelled out to newcomers.

The oft-cited typology provided by Hawkins and Shohet (2012) delineates the impact of dysfunctional workplace cultures on the supervisory climate. It is clear that the best and worst features of the organization often accompany the participants into supervision. Hawkins and Shohet (2012) described five common 'cultural dynamics' and their impact on supervision (pp.229–234). The optimal culture from their stance is the learning development culture in which there is a high degree of congruence between organizational polices, staff development goals and the actual day-to-day work practices which impact on staff (Hawkins and Shohet 2012, pp.235–237).

As we have seen in earlier chapters, contemporary authors have presented models and approaches to supervision in health and social services which strongly ground supervision within learning and development policy and practice. These approaches to supervision have been influenced significantly by ideas about how professionals learn in practice (Butler 1996; Eraut 1994; Schön 1987). Professionals are not empty vessels to be filled. From their own lives they bring to the practice context their beliefs, culture, values and relevant prior experience. Competence in professional practice requires practitioners to form 'judgements through a process of negotiating shared meanings' (Jones and Joss 1995, p.29). Individuals are constantly adding to their store of knowledge, where their formal knowledge, skills, experience and intuitive wisdom are augmented and refined through contact with colleagues, other professionals and of course patients and service users. In addition to ideas derived from knowledge about individual learning, another set of ideas has been employed from the study of organizational learning (Hawkins and Shohet 2012; Senge 1990). The site of learning is of increasing importance and distinct accounts of learning for professional practice are identified in the workplace (Eraut 1994; Wenger 1998). Health and social care service organizations don't exist in a vacuum; they are shaped by history, government policy, evidence, professional cultures, requirements of regulatory bodies and broad social trends. As we have noted in Chapter 1, the 'risk society' and conceptualizations of danger and vulnerability of service users and communities we work with occupy our thoughts as we interact with each other and make decisions in cut-back health and social services (Fawcett 2009; Mänttäri-van der Kuip 2014; Warner 2014).

Bradley and Hojer argue that 'the worker/supervisor relationship may be constructed and viewed as an integral and interdependent part of a broader dialogue within the organization and beyond, one that actively seeks feedback, interaction and improvement that is less reliant on the more usual form of hierarchical communication' (Bradley and Hojer 2009, p.82). To achieve its aims, supervision must be held as a central component of a culture that nurtures learning. In an ideal workplace, in which the prevailing approach is the fostering of a 'learning and development culture', one would expect to see the following practices in place:

- greater engagement of frontline staff in determining local and personal professional development goals (Beddoe 2009)

- recognition of the emotional impact of constant exposure to illness, distress and trauma with effective processes to mitigate any deleterious effects (Hughes and Pengelly 1997; Knight 2018; Koivu, Saarinen and Hyrkas 2012)

- professional learning as continuous throughout careers and including learning within practice activity, especially for newly qualified practitioners (Moorhead, Manthorpe and Baginsky 2019)

- facilitative, learning-focused supervision which is valued, supported and well resourced (Hawkins and Shohet 2012)

- all staff members, including the most senior, participating in supervision and professional development (Hawkins and Shohet 2012)

- review of mistakes and problems to provide opportunities for learning with a focus on practices and potential improvements not on finding scapegoats (Green 2007; Stanley and Manthorpe 2004)

- good practice based on a cycle of learning – action, reflection, planning and evaluation (which includes evaluation of process, structure and relationship) (Davys 2001)

- individuals and teams making time to review their effectiveness (Hawkins and Shohet 2012)

- provision of ongoing feedback including 'immediate comment on aspects of a task or a role given on-the-spot or soon after the event by a co-participant or observer' (Eraut 2006, p.114)

- informal conversations away from the frontline of service delivery via supervision or formal mentoring, and formal appraisal is a more formal and less frequent process (Eraut 2006)

- opportunities for feedback between the levels of the organization (Hawkins and Shohet 2012)

- room for professional autonomy and discretion and practice which is not dominated by rule-bound proceduralism (Cooper 2001; Franks 2004; Karvinen-Niinikoski *et al.* 2019).

Frequently, health and social care organizations promote policy statements exhorting that they are 'learning organizations'. The rhetoric, however, is sometimes not matched by evidence of what really happens. Genuine commitment to cultural change in organizations creates 'spaces for generative conversations and concerted action. In them, language functions as a device for connection, invention, and coordination. People can talk from their hearts and connect with one another in the spirit of dialogue' (Kofman and Senge 1993, p.16). Similarly, supervision policies can be acceptable on the surface but not meet their promises in reality. Gardner (2009) found that participants in a critical reflection process felt that there were problems with their supervision. Among the problems were: 'supervision that's confusing, not clarifying', poor quality of supervision that does not help develop skills, a lack of direction, inconsistency, and 'rules of supervision – that do not meet needs of team' (Gardner 2009, p.184). Benton, Dill and Williams (2017), discussing the organizational context in a study conducted in Northern Ireland, found that insights came from identifying what was missing in the workplaces of their participants. They saw that shifts in perceptions of supervision were linked to a shift in the workplace towards greater emphasis on compliance and very procedural practice. It became clear in their study that supervision wasn't consistently occurring and was often irregular. This lack of regular supervision led to feeling that the process was not valued. As a participant stated, 'For me I would think the ideal supervision would be a very, I almost want to use the word sacred at times, that's very honored and held' (Benton *et al.* 2017, p.296).

Peach and Horner comment that low levels of public and political tolerance of mistakes in contemporary human services and health organizations mean that the main purpose of 'supervision is in danger of becoming the elimination of risk through the micro-management and surveillance of practitioners and their outcomes' (Peach and Horner 2007, p.229). This is far from the idealized nurturing restorative process in which supervision is the 'quiet profession' (Alonso 1985) focused on the provision of reflective, supportive, yet challenging facilitation of the supervisee's professional development. As Jones asserts, 'the nursing literature concerning clinical supervision is consequently anything other than quiet. There is a burgeoning discussion concerning many complexities of clinical supervision' (Jones 2006, p.579). An impression is formed in much supervision literature that the impact of organizational culture is such that supervision is not happening in practice, or is under pressure (Stanley and Goddard 2002; Stevenson 2005). It is also the experience of many that supervision time or focus is inadequate or that it does not occur (Benton *et al.* 2017; Hunter 2009).

Health and social care agencies have faced many decades now of escalating demands, an adverse climate of scrutiny and public criticism. Such a climate is corrosive of core values of helping professions and undermines public confidence. The significance of these concerns is discussed in further detail in Chapter 11, where we explore supervision in child welfare and protection practice.

Learning and workplace cultures

Workplace cultures can exert positive and negative influence on the attitudes of staff and their motivation to fully participate in learning activities, including supervision. Unhappy workplaces in health and social care organizations can be unduly bureaucratic and stifle innovation, or become crisis driven, without time for reflection. They can be risk averse, with high levels of anxiety, or highly competitive environments which lead to severe overworking (Hawkins and Shohet 2012). In the case of 'workaholic' dynamics, managers may collude with unsafe working conditions rather than challenge the leadership. Often dysfunctional workplaces have faced significant or continuous change that has placed many key processes beyond the control of professional leaders; for example, where the external decisions of funders and policy makers create a highly competitive environment that imposes targets (and sanctions) on individuals, teams or sites. Restructuring and downsizing have contributed to crisis conditions and demanding workloads with concomitant stress (McFadden, Campbell and Taylor 2014).

Austerity and downsizing

Economic rationalism, managerialism and the growth of management as a new and distinct profession, the emphasis of outcome and output-led service delivery, contracting, and consumer advocacy all have had an influence on the organizational contexts in which supervision occurs. Casey (2003) describes how decades of change, manifest in such features as continuous or repeated organizational restructuring, downsizing, the introduction of flexible employment practices such as temporary jobs and changes to working hours have impacted on the nature of working life. She notes that 'many of these developments occur in conflict with other social and cultural aspirations, such as for secure employment, social inclusion, community development and quality of working life' (Casey 2003, p.622). In a study of workers in the non-governmental sector in Canada and Australia, Baines (2010, p.940) found cuts and restructuring led participants to feel their mission was badly impacted: 'unless the sector gets back to where it was before the cuts and managerialism, it will be difficult to generate solutions that are good for the community, rather than good for governments or "the bottom line"'. Baines reported that few resources were available and little time was allotted for developing creative responses to community problems.

Awareness of the impact of organizational culture on learning, reflection and supervision practices has been informed by consideration of research and development happening in the broad fields of organizational development and lifelong learning. Koivu, Saarinen and Hyrkas (2012) found that the reasons for attending clinical supervision for nurses working in medical and surgical units of an acute hospital could be quite different depending on the basic tasks and organizational culture of the hospital. The past two decades have seen a movement towards greater recognition of the importance of work cultures with regard to both pragmatic concerns about productivity and competence and to more altruistic efforts to ensure worker happiness and empowerment (Koppes 2008). Using Proctor's terms Koivu et al. (2012) found that different work cultures, in different services within the hospital, created differences in the emphasis on a *restorative* goal of promoting nurses' health and wellbeing and the *normative* goal of improving the quality of patient care.

Table 4.1 sets out features of dysfunctional workplace cultures and their impact on learning and development and contrasts this with features of resilient organizations. Where resilience is a feature, developments in positive psychology (Collins 2008; Luthans 2002; Wright and Quick 2009) are encouraging workplace leaders to reassess and affirm values (Gardner 2009) and foster learning in order to promote resilience and retain committed professional staff. In addition, many western governments have placed commitment to post-school learning as a significant feature of economic and social development in the past few decades. There is sustained political support for whole societies to be engaged in continual learning and development. Policy-driven terminology such as 'lifelong learning', 'the learning society' and 'the learning organization' has entered everyday language in health and social services. In particular, the ideal of the 'learning organization' has taken firm hold.

Table 4.1: Contrasting the features of organizational cultures

Organizational type	Common themes	Impact on learning and development	Robust organizations
Blame and shame culture dominates (Hawkins and Shohet 2006)	Defensive practice Risk averse Scapegoating Focus on identifying individual deficits Staff cover up any difficulties	Fearfulness about admitting mistakes. Surveillance dominates supervision (Peach and Horner 2007) Failure to reflect and change practice Supervision resisted and undermined Supervision focus on surveillance Low support for reflection	Collective responsibility for problems and mistakes Supervision and group consultation processes embed culture of collaboration (Jones 2008; Lietz 2009)
Efficiency model dominates	Rigid hierarchies High on task orientation and low on personal relatedness (Hawkins and Shohet 2006)	Efficiency valued over communication (Cooper 2000) Audit processes create additional overload and limit learning activities Stifles innovation – seeks standardization and routine Supervision focus on targets and output	Recognition that professionals in health and social care use their own personal emotional resources in the work and these resources need care, oversight and 're-stocking'
Perpetual crisis dominates (Hawkins and Shohet 2006)	Constant state of stress and vigilance Low social connectedness Little planning Problem-solving focus	Little space for understanding, stories, reflection and exploration Supervision focus on debriefing and 'survival'	Hardy organizations (Collins 2008) foster hope and optimism (Koenig and Spano 2007) Strengths-based, positive approach (Luthans 2002)

Organizational type	Common themes	Impact on learning and development	Robust organizations
'Workaholic' culture (Burke 2001; Hawkins and Shohet 2006)	Enthusiasm and commitment warps into 'missionary' zeal Denial, collusion or reward for overwork (Burke 2001)	Climate is overtly politicized or highly competitive Supervision and support for the 'needy' and less heroic Professional development support may be a reward not a right	Work-life balance and empowerment (Koppes 2008) Collaborative decision making and space for reflection

The learning organization

The concept of 'the learning organization', developed in the 1980s, is often cited in supervision literature. The rise in prominence of this concept has been attributed to Peter Senge whose influential text, *The Fifth Discipline: The Art and Practice of the Learning Organization* (Senge 1990) has gained a place on the bookshelves of many managers in health and social care. The origins of the learning organization are found in the work on organizational development undertaken by Argyris and Schön in which organizational learning was viewed from a systems perspective (Argyris and Schön 1974, 1978). Senge's prescription for a learning organization requires the mastery of five core disciplines: self-mastery, shared vision, team learning, mental models and systems thinking (Senge 1990). Common features include a systemic view of organizational learning and development, a cycle of continuous critical reflection on the business of the organization, empowerment of individuals within the work world, emphasis on communication and the harnessing of knowledge and energy through commitment to teamwork. The learning organization's influence beyond the business sector is indicated by articles that refer to it in professional contexts such as health, social services and education (see, for example, Eraut 2004; Gould and Baldwin 2004).

'Lifelong learning' and 'learning organizations' are interesting aspects of contemporary professional life as, on superficial examination at least, it seems that government policy and organizational practices are rather well aligned with the professional values of the helping professions, 'on the surface what could possibly not be "good" about "lifelong learning"?' (Beddoe 2009, p.724). Is there a dark side? Beddoe (2009) found that practitioners in social services were highly conscious of these learning 'discourses' and their impact on the workplace, but that they were rather cynical. First, learning discourses are acknowledged as influential but practitioners recognize personal costs and may experience this as yet further encroachment of work on their time (p.728). Second, learning organizations aspire to foster learning from mistakes; however, practitioner perspectives suggested that feedback loops were unlikely in low trust environments (Beddoe 2009, pp.728–729). Last, participants felt that health and human services organizations were far too unstable to manage continuous improvement (Beddoe 2009, p.731).

A critical examination of the learning organization suggests that it is vital to retain a sense of the value of learning for its own sake, where it is self-directed and free from manipulation by short-term political agendas (Beddoe 2009). Other kinds of knowledge – cultural, transformative and personal – are valuable and contribute to the professional knowledge base. Knowledge is enriched by critical reflection, the practice wisdom uncovered by examining practice over time. Overly technical and proceduralized 'training' approaches risk objectifying service users and minimizing the complexity of professional practice by assuming that assessment tools and limited 'system' responses create sufficient skill to keep disasters from occurring. The Laming inquiry report (2009) clearly identified the importance of embedding regular time for reflection, supervision and peer learning, recognizing the impact of target-driven management:

> There is concern that the tradition of deliberate, reflective social work practice is being put in danger because of an overemphasis on process and targets, resulting in a loss of confidence among social workers. It is vitally important that social work is carried out in a supportive learning environment that actively encourages the continuous development of professional judgement and skills. (Laming 2009, p.30)

At the time of writing the first edition of this book, announcements were being made about the development of extensive training for social work supervision in Britain, to ensure that the recommendations of the Laming report could be met. In examining various accounts of 'managed' implementation of supervision strategies, there are often problems with top-down approaches, see for example Froggett (2000). One enterprise, reported in Davies *et al.* 2004, described how a 'computerised auditing system is being used to track the occurrence of supervision and the nature of any events which prevent supervision from taking place' (Davies *et al.*, p.41), perhaps indicating a concern that compliance might be patchy. What seems to have happened was a system, in England at least, where case management systems led to supervision being dominated by case management rather than reflection and support (Turner-Daly and Jack 2014). A study conducted in 2017 found that while supervisors believed that supervision should be reflective, supportive and analytical, audio recording showed that sessions were primarily aimed at managerial oversight (p.89). While they asked supervisees about their wellbeing, feelings were rarely sought and 'there was only limited consideration of why the social worker felt a particular way or how their feelings might be impacting on their behaviour and decision-making' (Wilkins, Forrester and Grant 2017, p.946).

It is also important to consider the significance of the mediating capacity of supervision and its potential to contribute to multiple levels, and direction, of feedback within health and social care (Morrison 1993). Failure to communicate, anxiety and lack of trust within organizations can lead to poor or unsafe practice. Austin and Hopkins (2004) cited in Kaiser and Kuechler (2008) have described this mediative function as having three parts: 'managing down' (transforming the vision of the administration into action); 'managing up' (advocating for the needs of clients and staff); and 'managing out' both in the agency (dealing with tensions between diverse professionals in an agency) and in the community (addressing the interests of and pressures from multiple agencies who might be involved in client services) (Kaiser and Kuechler 2008, p.78). Baines *et al.* (2014) found that strong supervision, supporting an agency social justice mission, when higher level managers seem to have lost sight of the vision of change, can 'buffer the demoralizing aspects of lean care work and may contribute to staff remaining' (p.448). Strong supervisors provided support and improved 'the quality of work life' (p.444).

Table 4.2 suggests some questions which may assist supervisors to consider the context of their particular organization.

Table 4.2: Organizational context

Considering organizational context
• Power: who decides the learning goals in this organization?
• Collaboration: what processes are used to elicit employee ideas about learning needs?
• Do managerial interests dominate decisions about supervision?
• Are there opportunities to learn in groups?
• Is group supervision or consultation used to tap collective learning power?
• Is there a continuous improvement strategy and, if so, does it focus only at the micro level, ignoring macro problems that frontline health and social care workers can't control?
• Is there room for honest reflection and evaluation of supervision and professional development to guide the organization in its decision making about development and improvement?

Workplace learning

It is part of a professional's personal obligation to remain competent. Increasingly this shifts workers' study time to their non-work hours and into their home life. As we saw in Chapter 1, many professional bodies have now embedded these expectations within requirements for annual practising certificates. One of the problems is that there is still a great deal of work to be done to understand how professionals do continue to learn during their careers and how to motivate practitioners who struggle to participate because of time constraints, costs and personal responsibilities. In reality, most practitioners are learning all the time whether this is conscious or not! For most practitioners in the health and social services professions, their professional work is carried out within group and agency settings. Informal learning is constant, 'everyday' and sometimes accidental.

Much of this development of everyday knowledge occurs informally through trial and error, observation, discussion and sharing stories as well as more formal guidance and mentoring. Supervision is most effective when it is led by the supervisee's agenda and is learning focused. This makes practitioner narratives significant and locates learning centrally in the work context and not remote from practice. This does not mean that professional development via external training, study towards higher qualifications and practitioner research do not contribute to learning, but all these are likely to be more successful and lead to change and improvement if supervision provides a conduit for their support. A consequence of learning activities being located in the world external to the practitioner's employing agency is that distance is created between the educational institution and the site of practice. This distance is unhelpful and limiting and does not align with practitioners' accounts of their learning. Dirkx, Gilley and Gilley (2004, p.36) argue that in these situations 'learning and change are conceptualized largely as cognitive, decontextualized, individualistic, and solitary processes.' Furthermore, Dirkz et al. note:

> Practitioner stories suggest that lifelong learning and change in continuing professional development reflect an ongoing struggle to keep the rational deeply connected with the richly felt experience of practice... From this perspective, the knowledge we use to inform our practices evolves in an ongoing way from dialectical relationships that involve the relevant technical or scientific knowledge, the sociocultural context of practice, and the practitioner's self. (Dirkx et al. 2004, p.38)

Table 4.3 suggests some questions which may assist supervisors to consider how the culture of their particular organization affects learning.

Table 4.3: Organizational learning

Organizational learning exercise
• What are the particular strengths in your workplace? • What particular expertise do team members have? • How do the learning activities in the workplace facilitate sharing of expertise? • What supports or hinders innovation in your workplace? • What would you like to strengthen about learning in your setting? • What would you like to discard? • What would you like to develop or create which is currently missing?

Supervision, given its location close to the workplace, often in peer and professional relationships, offers considerable potential for promotion of a more practice-grounded learning. In considering the links between supervision and career-long learning, it is important to note there is common agreement that professionals learn in the job through a combination of work experience, clinical practice, clinical or professional supervision and ongoing post-qualifying learning. However, good facilitation is needed to ensure that reflection and critical review assist professionals to turn this collected information into enhanced practice. In an ideal health and social care organization, supervision is valued and training and ongoing support encourage and maintain excellent communication among supervisees, supervisors and managers alike.

Managerialism, 'the risk society' and supervision

In our first edition, we noted the links between the revitalization of supervision and the impact of 'the risk society'. The term 'the risk society' is used to describe a society that is organized in response to risk (Beck 1992) and preoccupied with safety (Giddens 1999, p.3). We live in a world in which there is a belief that we must keep and be kept safe (Fawcett 2009). One of the consequences of this heightened awareness of risk is that professionals are expected to take particular responsibility for identifying, managing and reducing risks to which patients and service users are exposed. Risk features at all levels. Individual practitioners are recommended to develop a personal safety plan, while in health and social care organizations, risk assessment of intake procedures and fiscal accountability require organizations to identify the potential for costly risk. As we will examine further in Chapter 9, this concern extends to the role of supervisors in identifying the potential for supervisees to be harmed by their work and in assisting in prevention.

The raised awareness of public accountability and the desire of governments and other health and social care organizations to avoid exposure to reputational and other risks has, in a rather paradoxical manner, led to a revitalization of supervision. In 1994, Beddoe and Davys asked, 'What is the future for social work supervision in crisis-driven bureaucratic agencies?' (1994, p.21). At that time, involvement in providing supervision training for probation officers had suggested to us that supervision had become captured by the gathering of information about case management and there was little room for practitioners to focus on their practice issues and even less to think about their professional development. Supervision had become a 'checklist' exercise that was essentially a managerial tool.

Payne, around the same time, suggested that supervision was a practice in danger of becoming captured by 'unthinking adherence to politically and bureaucratically defined roles' (Payne 1994, p.55). Payne's hopeful view was that there might be a reconciliation of managerial and professional supervision models through the increased focus on quality (pp.54–55), and indeed the extension of professional supervision as a practice which developed in social work, counselling and psychotherapy is very much underpinned by the risk-averse cultures within contemporary health and social care. Beddoe (2010) argued that this revitalization of supervision emerged during a period in which risk comes to occupy central stage in health and social care. Supervision, however, has not always been welcomed as a consequence of this association with risk culture and the preoccupation with audit that has characterized much of the change in health and social services over recent decades (Gilbert 2001; Johns 2001).

The current preoccupation with 'quality' and the numerous mechanisms to interrogate professional practice has clearly strengthened the mandate for supervision. The links between quality assurance and clinical supervision have often been used to support and protect supervision. In social work, Peach and Horner cautioned that because of low tolerance of mistakes in contemporary human services and health organizations, 'the sole goal of supervision is in danger of becoming the elimination of risk through the micro-management and surveillance of practitioners and their outcomes' (Peach and Horner 2007, p.229). Statutory social work in particular has a high public profile and is especially vulnerable to political scrutiny and public criticism. Supervisors in statutory child protection work face major challenges in the face of an overwhelming focus on avoiding mistakes. They need to manage the expectations of multiple stakeholders in a high-stress environment and yet find the time, skill and emotional energy to provide supervision to frontline workers. Bogo and Dill (2008), in a study of child welfare supervisors, reported that 'walking the tightrope' was the metaphor for a significant theme of struggle in their supervision practice:

One side of the tightrope relates to their relationship to the workers they supervise and indirectly to the workers' clients. They struggle to achieve enough trust about their workers' competence and practice so that they can share power with these workers. The other side of the tightrope refers to their relationship with those senior to them, their managers, the agency director, and the government ministry that decrees new legislation and policy. (Bogo and Dill 2008, p.151)

Chapter 11 examines more closely the importance of supervision in child protection services.

Clouder and Sellars (2004) provided an interesting counter to the problematizing of supervision as a spectre of increased surveillance. Their article offered a pragmatic response to Gilbert's important critique of supervision in which he argues that clinical supervision can be shown to operate as a 'mode of surveillance disciplining the activity of professionals' (Gilbert 2001, p.199). Clouder and Sellars argue that rather than a consequence of new work practices, 'surveillance is ubiquitous and an inevitable concomitant of the social practices in which professionals engage', citing the numerous public encounters health professionals have with colleagues, managers, patients and others and which means that 'professionals are constantly in the spotlight under which competence is being evaluated' (Clouder and Sellars 2004, p.264). Indeed, at work we 'are under constant surveillance, whether or not we are consciously aware of it or its effects on us, because we are social beings operating within a system of social practices' (p.265).

As outlined in Chapter 3, the quality of the supervision relationship is a significant factor in determining the effectiveness of supervision. A review of the literature identifies the range of managerial elements in the relationship between supervisor and supervisee. The linking of supervision and managerial concerns has been a significant issue for nurses (Bond and Holland 2010; Butterworth *et al.* 2008; Johns 2001) but it is contested in other professions as well. Carroll (2014), from a background in counselling psychology, warns that 'where managerial and clinical supervision merge, supervision can be seen as a form of control, creating docile and conforming practitioners' (p.11). Social work has a longer tradition of supervision and in practice has always included some managerial or administrative functions.

Supervision and wellbeing

This chapter has explored the dimensions of effective organizational arrangements for supervision and ongoing professional development.

Supervision is also held up as an important mechanism to promote staff wellbeing, to contribute to resilience and to reduce attrition (Beddoe, Davys and Adamson 2014; Chiller and Crisp 2012). However, as Adamson (2011) pointed out, supervision is not a 'politically or organizationally neutral practice but one that must be constantly aware of its context, purpose, and application' (p.186).

Organizations sometimes offer toxic environments that work against developing healthier working cultures. Oates (2019) found many examples of barriers to staff accessing support services. Among these was 'the fear of being seen as incompetent' and fear of bullying, intimidation and retribution (p.5). In such a climate, supervision may go beyond being inadequate and cause harm.

Ellis *et al.* (2014) considered what factors were essential to the provision of adequate supervision and, correspondingly, how it might be distorted so it is actually harmful. They noted that for supervision to be minimally adequate, the supervisor would need to hold the correct credentials and have had training to ensure that they had the necessary knowledge and skills. It was also suggested that the supervisor 'provides a minimum of one hour of face-to-face individual supervision per week' [and] 'observes, reviews or monitors supervisee's therapy/counseling sessions' (p.439), reflecting the supervision needs of students and interns rather than fully qualified practitioners. Supervisors should also provide helpful, constructive and reflective feedback, being aware of their supervisee's professional growth and development. Supervision should be consented, and confidentiality and its limits clarified. Finally, supervisors should be 'attentive to multicultural and diversity issues in supervision and in therapy/counseling' (Ellis *et al.* 2014 p.439).

While there has been much consideration of situations where supervision has failed to deliver its promises, over the last few years *harmful supervision* has emerged as a focus of scholarship and research. In 2017, *The Clinical Supervisor* published a special issue on harmful supervision. Harmful supervision is defined by Ellis *et al.* (2014) as:

> supervisory practices that result in psychological, emotional, and/or physical harm or trauma to the supervisee... The two essential components of harmful supervision are (a) that the supervisee was genuinely harmed in some way by the supervisor's actions or inactions, or (b) the supervisor's behavior is known to cause harm, even though the supervisee may not identify the action as harmful. (p.440)

It has been our experience as supervision educators that most supervisees have variable supervision experiences across their careers. In a mixed methods study, Ladany, Mori and Mehr (2013) found that *good* supervisors work towards establishing a strong supervisory alliance and mutually agreed goals and are capable of critical or challenging feedback via a positive respectful relationship. As we explored in Chapter 3, the core supervision skills of listening, reflection and empathy are crucial in building the supervision relationship. For participants in Ladany *et al.*'s study, the absence of these skills led to unsatisfactory experiences for interns, with negative experiences impacting beyond their training. Harmful supervision, usually found in distortions in the supervision relationship and poor management of authority and power, is also, by definition, inadequate supervision (Ellis *et al.* 2015).

Supervision has an accountability to the professions in which it is practised and 'must create the forum for challenge and critical feedback' if it is to achieve its aims (Beddoe 2017, p.90). In examining harmful supervision, Ellis *et al.* (2014) argue that we need to distinguish between the struggles novice and beginning practitioners have managing painful matters and challenging feedback in supervision from those situations where 'the supervisee's best interests were not primary' (p.440). Harmful supervision may include sexual, physical and emotional abuse, gendered and racialized micro-aggressions, misuse of power, along with supervisory incompetence and neglect (Beddoe 2017).

External supervision – the debates

To a large extent, this practice climate encourages the individualist response which characterizes the shift towards external supervision (Cooper 2006). External supervision is a term often used as synonymous with non-line-management supervision. Points in favour of external or privatized supervision generally focus on the importance of supervisee choice and direction and the negative influence of power differentials in the supervisory relationship when it is located within an organization or when the supervisor has a dual supervisor/manager role. Supervisee choice, especially in relation to group membership and professional identity, was reported by Davys (2005b) as a major indicator of satisfaction. Matching of supervisee and supervisor characteristics, particularly in relation to ethnicity, culture, gender, age and professional and theoretical orientation, is also often considered to be important. It is expected that with an external supervisor, where power and authority issues have less impact, supervisees will have greater freedom to express concerns and frustrations about organizational issues, and external supervisors may feel freer to assist the discovery of possible responses and solutions to workplace problems.

External supervision, however, located as it is outside the agency, should allow more intensive focus on clinical issues and personal professional development rather than becoming bogged down in the detail of organizational concerns (Beddoe 2011). In addition, this external supervision arrangement, subject to clear contracting, may improve the likelihood that supervision actually does take place. In busy agency settings, supervision can often be neglected or deferred to accommodate the latest crisis unless it is made a high priority by management.

While these arguments are valid, there remains justification for some scepticism about the efficacy of external supervision arrangements. The following questions are pertinent:

- To what extent can the external supervisor be an advocate for stressed and troubled workers when their mandate is ambiguous?

- Does the absence of organizational authority in the supervisor lead to a lack of real challenge?

- What do supervisors do to check out other perspectives?

- How do supervisors assess clinical practice and ensure safety?

- To whom is ultimate loyalty and confidentiality owed when a third party is paying for the supervision?

We are aware that these questions may represent social work models of supervision where the organizational context has favoured line management supervision. Nevertheless, it is a reasonable assumption that other approaches may be influenced by traditional assumptions about context. Counselling and psychotherapy supervisory approaches are frequently based on a private practice structure which is strongly predicated on a set of assumptions about the relative autonomy of the individual practitioner. The private or semi-private (group practice) practitioner may make choices based on reputation, therapeutic or theoretical orientation, style and, of course, more pragmatic concerns such as cost, access, professional accreditation requirements and third-party funding bodies. The private supervisor will be able to determine the length and nature of the supervision process and will largely self-monitor and evaluate their interventions. These conditions are likely to be replicated in the supervision arrangements. Knowledge and training in supervision, clear supervision contracts and three-way conversations between managers, supervisors and supervisees, however, have all been identified as important to the practice of external supervision. 'For the external supervisor, and for the practitioner, a balance needs to be achieved between the independence of supervision and professional and organizational accountability' (Beddoe and Davys 2016, p.111).

Disadvantages of external supervision

There are a number of pitfalls in the separation of supervision from clinical accountability:

- There may be an ambiguous mandate for dealing with issues of poor performance where supervisors become aware of performance matters but have no mandate or clear contract to address these.

- Unhealthy collusion can occur where there are grievances in the practitioner relationships with line managers.

- Separation may deepen the experience of the gulf between 'management' and 'practice' and thus reduce the flow of information between the layers of the organization.

- There is a tendency to rely on reported performance rather than 360-degree information collected through day-to-day interaction and observation of performance in teams and case consultations.

- There is the potential for unhealthy triangulation of practitioner, line manager and clinical supervisor if there is not sufficient attention paid to the clarity of the mandate.

- The line manager may be relieved of responsibility to ensure that anti-oppressive polices are satisfied, including cultural support for particular staff, addressing conflict between team members, and the monitoring of personal and practice safety issues in the workplace.

- Duty of care issues can remain unclear and yet be vitally significant when things go wrong.

- Dissonance between organizational goals and the focus and direction of supervision may remain unaddressed.

In spite of these problems, external supervision has become more prevalent. External supervision raises the issue of the mandate and accountability for supervision practice and what kind of relationship might be understood to operate between internal and external stakeholders with an interest in practice. O'Donoghue (2015) asserts that agencies delegate the authority to external clinical supervisors, via supervision contracts and agreements between the parties. Professionals are also likely to be accountable via registration or licensing by, or membership of, professional bodies. O'Donoghue (2015) outlines four sources of a mandate to act as a supervisor. The supervision mandate in social work, for example, comes from 'the same four sources that a social worker's mandate for work with clients comes from;

namely, from their agency, profession, by law and from people to whom the service is provided' (p.145).

A comparison of United Kingdom and Scandinavian approaches to supervision of social workers discusses the Scandinavian model where supervision provided by external consultants is 'combined with a system of internal, method-oriented supervision, from the line manager to the social workers (Bradley and Hojer 2009). This latter aspect of supervision focuses on the management of cases and may be seen to be within an administrative model (Bradley and Hojer, p.75). Bradley and Hojer cite Bernler and Johnsson (1985) when suggesting seven criteria that form the basis for supervision in social work (p.75). These are 1) that supervision should be a continuous activity, 2) it should assist the integration of all aspects of their work, 3) the process should encourage reflection on the use of self and feelings, 4) ideally it should be a non-linear organizational relationship between supervisor and group of practitioners, 5) supervisors should be responsible for the process of the supervision, not for supervisee's direct work with client, 6) all social workers should have supervision, and finally, 7) the supervisor should have expertise in social work (theoretically as well as practically), education in supervision theory and method, and cultural competence in the specific area of practice (Bradley and Hojer). Table 4.4 identifies a list of questions through which to consider external supervision from the perspective of the external supervisor, the manager and the supervisee.

Table 4.4: Reflections on external supervision

Reflections on external supervision
If you are an *external supervisor:* • What can you do to support the full professional learning of your supervisee? • Could you influence your supervisee's organization? • How can you ensure you get good information? • How do you influence in both directions and *should you*? • What arrangements are in place for you to provide feedback to your supervisee's manager?
If you are a *manager or professional leader* and your team members have external supervision: • How do you negotiate the lines of accountability and feedback on supervision issues and process? • What arrangements do you have to liaise with the supervisor if you have concerns about your practitioner's work performance? • What agreements are in place if the supervisor has concerns about the practitioner and/or the work context?
If you are a *supervisee* with external supervision: • What should you do to ensure that your supervision is accountable to your manger/workplace? • What are the boundaries of confidentiality that you consider to be important?

Conclusions

Supervision has a major role to play in safeguarding practitioners in health and social care in a process which can assist them to cope with their emotions, manage uncertainty and to continue to grow and learn professionally. The culture of the organization will shape the manner in which supervision is valued and accepted within that organization. Organizational culture will also filter the effects of public and legislative surveillance and ultimately determine how effective supervision can be in promoting learning and renewal of practice. In the organizational setting, supervision practice is 'at the intersection of the personal and professional, where "dangerousness" may be a fear and optimism may be muted' (Beddoe 2010, p.1288) and, whether supervision is internal or external, there are inevitable difficulties of balance.

To retain critically reflective practice, exploration of practitioners' emotions and their understanding of risk and uncertainty need to be given a central space in supervision (Parton 1998). Moral reasoning and a more nuanced exploration of emotional responses and concerns can strengthen supervision practice. We will explore this in more detail in Chapter 8.

Contemporary professional practice is scrutinized, audited and open to the public gaze. Most professionals do much of their work in crowded, noisy, public and stressful environments where meaningful dialogue and reflection are impossible. Supervision can at the very least allow, albeit briefly, the doors to be shut, the noise to be reduced and a quiet space for satisfying professional conversation.

CHAPTER 5

A Reflective Learning Model of Supervision

The fundamental proposition and underlying premise of the Reflective Learning Model (Davys 2001) is that supervision is first and foremost a 'learning process', regardless of whether the supervisee is a trainee or an experienced practitioner. This is a proposition which aligns with Butler's (1996) 'assumption' that practitioners are 'always in the process of "becoming" what is required by the ever changing parameters of the learning context' (Butler 1996, p.265). Within the Reflective Learning Model, the learning process is driven from the experience of the supervisee rather than from the wisdom and knowledge of the supervisor. The model was first developed by one of the authors (Davys 2001) and has been the basis of an interprofessional supervision programme taught at the University of Auckland. Over the years, it has been adapted and updated. Supervision models based on learning and reflexivity offer the flexibility needed for practitioners to adjust theory and practice to the ever-changing and messy shapes of the modern practice context. When supervision is regarded as a reflective learning process, a shift occurs which moves the supervisor from an 'expert' to a 'facilitator' in the supervision forum. As a facilitator, the supervisor's role becomes one of ensuring the space and context for learning. McCann (2000, p.43) has described this role as one of co-explorer. The supervisee defines the problem and is responsible for their own learning as generated from this co-exploration with the supervisor. The Reflective Learning Model of Supervision promotes a way of thinking rather than a blueprint for doing. Solutions which emerge from the supervision process are discovered and owned by the supervisee rather than 'taught' by the supervisor.

As discussed in Chapter 2, supervision is not practised in a vacuum, and the boundaries of accountability which accompany both the mandate and the role of supervisor require both participants to understand and respect the limits of exploration. This means that in given situations such as safety or crisis, the supervisor may, and indeed should, assert appropriate authority. These, however, are the exceptions.

Without reflection, practice becomes a routine of mindlessness (Carroll 2014). As described by Johns and Freshwater (2005, p.2), reflection is 'a fusion of sensing, perceiving, intuiting and thinking related to a specific experience in order to develop insights into self and practice. It is vision driven, concerned with taking action towards knowing and realising desirable practice.'

Beliefs and values within each individual person's world view, however, determine what is perceived and so influence not only what experience is offered for reflection, but also the outcomes of the reflective process (Butler 1996). In the nature of homeostasis, perception acts to reinforce an individual's world view. Thus, discrepancies and events which could disturb that world view will be filtered out and only those that reinforce and confirm the position of the practitioner are available for reflection (Butler 1996, p.275). For this reason, it can be difficult for any individual to 'critique' their world view, as 'reflection on its own can so easily become self-indulgent navel-gazing that leads nowhere' (Carroll 2014, p.134).

In the supervision process a practitioner's work is presented for consideration by both the practitioner and the supervisor and it is here that the practitioner's world view may be identified. Opportunities for new options and ideas are uncovered when different 'filters' are applied to a situation and so, with the assistance of an 'other', transformational learning can take place. Learning, Carroll concludes, 'is as much between people as it is within people' (Carroll 2009, p.213). Supervision thus can provide the place and the space where practitioners can reflect in the presence of another, or others, and where reflection can be encouraged which tests the boundaries of routine practice and ideas and where new learning can emerge.

The Reflective Learning Model of Supervision, which combines the closely related ideas of reflective practice and adult learning, offers a framework within which these principles can be enacted. The model is underscored by our belief that 'the key to learning and development lies in the ability to engage in, and make use of, the worker's experience' (Morrison 2001, p.57) and reflection is central to this learning. It assumes that supervision and learning are lifelong processes in which a practitioner engages from the beginning of formal training until retirement from practice.

Reflection as a learning process is not new and can be traced to Aristotle's 'distinction between technical, practical and theoretical forms of reasoning' (Kondrat 1992, p.239). In more recent times, John Dewey's 'reflective activity in learning' has been identified as influential (Boud, Keogh and Walker 1985, p.11). Dewey determined that the boundaries to 'a complete act of reflective activity' were 'a perplexed, troubled, or confused situation at the beginning and a cleared-up, unified, resolved situation at the close' (Dewey 1998, p.139). For Dewey, failure was instructive and he argued that 'the person who really thinks learns quite as much from his failures as his successes' (Dewey 1998, p.142). While Dewey led the way, it is Kolb's (1984) 'experiential learning model' which is probably the best-known model of adult learning. Kolb's definition of learning is 'the process whereby knowledge is created through transformation of experience' (Kolb 1984, p.38). According to Kolb (1984), demand for change and versatility of response in the workplace has emphasized the very challenges which Dewey's approach was designed to address.

Kolb's model has four stages, beginning with a 'concrete experience' in which the learner is 'fully' involved. In other words, something happens and the learner, or person involved, not only notices that it has happened but also places value on the moment. Without this noticing and valuing, no learning can occur. 'It is not sufficient to have an experience to learn, for the experience may be suppressed, denied or rejected as irrelevant or of no significance' (Morrison 2001, p.137). Hewson and Carroll (2016) note the importance of this in their list of the principles which underlie reflection in supervision. Noticing needs to be intentional and pausing allows that to happen – 'pause to notice and then consider what you have noticed' (p.43).

When it is noticed and valued, 'experience' can then be 'reflected' on in order to establish its impact on the 'learner' and also how the 'learner' impacts on the experience. Once the experience has been reflected on, a 'conceptual analysis' of the experience allows for the implications and meaning of this experience, in terms of theory and context, to be considered. Finally a new action plan is formulated on the basis of the assimilation of the reflection and analysis and the cycle is ready to be repeated with new experience or action. We are not the first to incorporate Kolb's experiential learning cycle into supervision and others have offered their own descriptions of the stages. Driscoll (1994) added, 'What? So what? Now what?' and Carroll and Gilbert (2011) describe the stages as 'Activity-Reflection-Learning and Application'. Figure 5.1 illustrates these interpretations.

Where Kolb's model lays the basis for experiential learning, reflective practice has been moulded by the seminal work of Donald Schön (1983, 1987). Schön's idea is that 'knowledge is directly constructed through engagements with problems encountered in the field, and built through successive stages of hypothesising, testing and reflection' (Gould and Harris 1996, p.224).

In order to learn from reflection, the practitioner must examine the effect of events, actions and interactions on themselves. Consideration must also be given to how the practitioner impacts on those same events, actions and interactions. The practitioner must locate themselves in the situation in order to fully understand what has occurred. Learning is not the application of rules and theory but rather, the uncovering and understanding of the intuitive wisdom which underpins practice (Gould and Harris 1996). Such examination also encourages practitioners to notice and to value their intuitive response. 'At the same time' Moffatt (1996, p.53) warns, 'intuition is one of those "moments of knowing" which should be open to inquiry to ensure that it is used in a responsible manner'. Hence the process of learning from reflection requires more than intuition. Intuition must be critiqued and considered alongside thoughtful analysis and concrete data. Hewson and Carroll (2016) advise: 'notice how the problem has been framed' (p.106); 'hunt down and challenge deepest assumptions' (p.113).

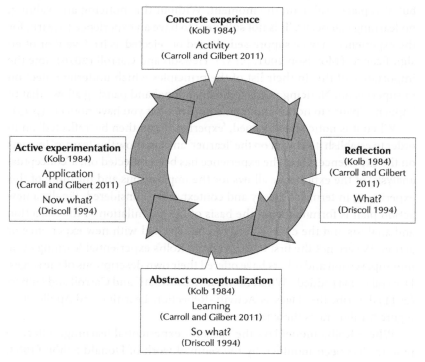

Figure 5.1: The Reflective Learning Cycle

In a similar vein, Kondrat argues that:

> Critical reflexivity involves the practitioner-knower in the process of making explicit the knowledge that is implicit in action so that it becomes available

for both critique and enquiry. The effort called for includes, but goes well beyond, the task of outcome evaluation. (Kondrat 1992, p.250)

Reflection thus does not uncover the 'ultimate' truth, but rather a subjective truth relative to time, place and person. It allows practitioners to examine dissonance between espoused theory and theory in action – that is, what they intend or say they do as opposed to what they actually do (Argyris and Schön 1974). Reflectivity requires a subjective examination of experience which includes engagement with and respect for 'the emotional world of self and others' (Papell 1996, p.14). Such views offer contradictions and inconsistencies and thus, importantly, reflectivity also offers the possibility of a number of perspectives. From this postmodernist view, the possibility of plural views equips practitioners well for the changing perspectives and the uncertainties which characterize current practice contexts. The rate of change of these confusing practice contexts far outstrips the possibility of 'right' answers and responses. The possibilities of practice are therefore more certain than the 'rules' of practice. Hewson and Carroll (2016) urge us to 'embrace uncertainty and be willing to be unsettled' (p.191).

For some practitioners, however, a desire for clean solutions wrestles with the anxiety and challenge of choice. And of them Schön observes:

> Many practitioners, locked into a view of themselves as technical experts, find nothing in the world of practice to occasion reflection. They have become too skilful at techniques of selective inattention, junk categories, and situational control, techniques which they use to preserve the constancy of their knowledge-in-practice. For them, uncertainty is a threat; its admission a sign of weakness. (Schön 1983, p.69)

These may well be the practitioners we need to challenge and monitor as they seek to impose stability onto an ever-changing and evolving landscape of practice.

Schön's work on reflective practice identified two central forms of reflection: reflection 'in action' and reflection 'on action' (Schön 1987). 'Reflection in action' relates to conscious considerations, evaluation and decision making which occur during the performance of a practitioner's daily tasks. 'Reflection on action' is the consideration, analysis and evaluation of a situation or event after it has occurred. Both forms of reflection lead to new understandings and new knowledge of practice.

The role of supervision in this creation of new understanding and learning is to focus on, and develop, the process of *reflection on action*. In this manner, supervision provides the foundation for effective *reflection in action*. By internalizing the supervision process, the practitioner is able to access the reflective process more readily when engaged in practice. The reflective process in supervision can therefore be considered as a transportable learning process which can be internalized and accessed at the worker–client interface.

Overview of the model

The Reflective Learning Model of Supervision follows the cycle of experiential learning with specific tasks at each stage for both supervisor and supervisee. As with all models, it has a beginning and an end and in between is a cyclic process of reflection, analysis, experimentation and evaluation. This cycle is repeated for each item that is placed on the supervision agenda.

The structure of the model – beginnings and endings

We have noted elsewhere the importance of acknowledging beginnings and endings of a supervision session (Davys 2001). Unless an appropriate space and context is defined, the 'work' of supervision is at risk of being undervalued or discarded. If we truly wish to invite our supervisees to reflect on and consider those hidden and sometime painful intuitions and details of practice then the supervision 'space' must reflect respect, regard and trust. Both parties need to be 'present' if the truths of practice are to be considered. Supervisors and supervisees who have completed a thorough initial contracting process will have agreed on the manner in which each session will start. The form will vary from dyad to dyad. In some situations, a ritual of prayer, song or reflection may start the session and reflect cultural responses. At other times, it may be the offer of refreshment or simply a brief hello and 'how are you?' Whatever the form, it is an important moment where both parties can tune themselves to the rhythms of the other and focus on the task and relationship at hand.

The 'end' of the session will also vary from dyad to dyad and may include individual or cultural rituals. Once again, the 'process' is important and an analogy can perhaps be made to knitting. Good beginnings cast on the stitches of the garment to be knitted and set the shape of the final product. When the knitter has finished the garment, unless they cast off, the work is at risk of unravelling. Good beginnings set the shape of the session and good endings assist the learning to be contained, valued and transported into practice.

Agenda setting

When supervisor and supervisee are sufficiently settled and present it is time to build the agenda for the session. Different models of supervision have varying expectations about the setting of the agenda. It is our contention that the agenda for supervision is primarily the responsibility of the supervisee. Supervision is the 'learning' and 'reflection' time for the supervisee and hence it is they who need to have primary responsibility for setting the agenda. That said, it is important to recognize the limitations of 'supervisee knowing' and awareness and at times supervisors will need to lead.

Developmental approaches to supervision (Loganbill *et al.* 1982) remind us that supervisees do not always know what they do not know and, within the tensions and roles of supervision, there may be agenda items which the supervisor has a responsibility to draw to the supervisee's attention. It is therefore important that the supervisor also has an opportunity to contribute to the agenda. When a supervisor does place items on the agenda, the process of supervision is subtly altered. It is therefore important for the supervisor to monitor their contributions. If the 'learning' is dominated by the supervisor, the session risks becoming hijacked as one of instruction and control rather than of reflection and discovery (see Figure 2.2).

As the agenda determines the content and focus of supervision it is important that adequate time is given to the setting of the 'agenda'.

■ SCENARIO 1A

Marsha arrived at supervision directly from a service user interview. It had been a difficult interview which had challenged her skills and patience. When she entered the supervision room she was delighted to give full vent to her recent experience. Her supervisor heard her story with interest and encouraged her to review and consider the interaction. Marsha left the supervision session feeling buoyant and good about her morning's work, but also troubled. She was aware that she had not dealt with any of the pressing issues she really wanted to discuss with the supervisor. The morning's visit had hijacked the supervision time and she was aware that while she appreciated the opportunity to reflect on that visit, it was not the priority of her caseload at present.

Priorities for discussion need to be considered regardless of the seemingly pressing items which arrive with the supervisee.

■ SCENARIO 1B

Marsha arrived at supervision directly from a service user interview. It had been a difficult interview which had challenged her skills and patience. When she entered the supervision room she was delighted to give full vent to her recent experience. Her supervisor heard her story with interest but stopped her after several minutes and asked if this was where she wanted to spend her supervision time. The supervisor was aware that Marsha was an enthusiastic practitioner who engaged strongly with her work and wanted to be sure that this issue was actually the best use of their time together. Marsha appreciated the intervention. She was able to table the 'other' supervision issues and prioritize so that when she left she knew she had covered the most pressing concerns.

A cyclic structure

The Reflective Learning Model of Supervision describes a four-stage cycle of supervision comprising *the Event, the Exploration, the Experimentation and the Evaluation stage*, illustrated in Figure 5.2.

The Model

Event – awareness of experience

The first stage of the supervision cycle considers the item on the agenda which the supervisee identified as being the most important.

The cycle begins with the identification of the goal for the issue or item which the supervisee has placed at the top of the agenda. The supervisee is invited to explain why they wish to discuss this item. What do they want to resolve about the issue? How does the supervisee want to work on the issue in supervision? In order to answer this question the supervisee may need to spend some time reviewing the 'event' or 'experience' and identify, define and locate it in context. For some, this process may lead to 'telling the story'. Through this 'telling', the supervisee may reawaken the thoughts and feelings which have been aroused by the situation and thus bring to the fore useful material for supervision.

For the supervisor, this can be a difficult stage to manage. The task is to assist the supervisee to 'describe' the situation in order to reconnect with the events but not to become so immersed that they are unable to identify why this situation is worthy of supervision time. There is a risk that the supervisee (and the supervisor) will become so involved in the 'story' that they lose focus of what it is that the supervisee wishes to resolve. Keeping a tight focus on the goal clarifies the real issues and avoids the narrative 'swamping' reflection with detail. We have noted that it is the experience of many supervisees that they 'leave a supervision session with a sense of achievement but still carrying the same issue they brought to the session. The supervision time, useful though it may have been, has not been focused on the problem at hand' (Davys 2001, p.92).

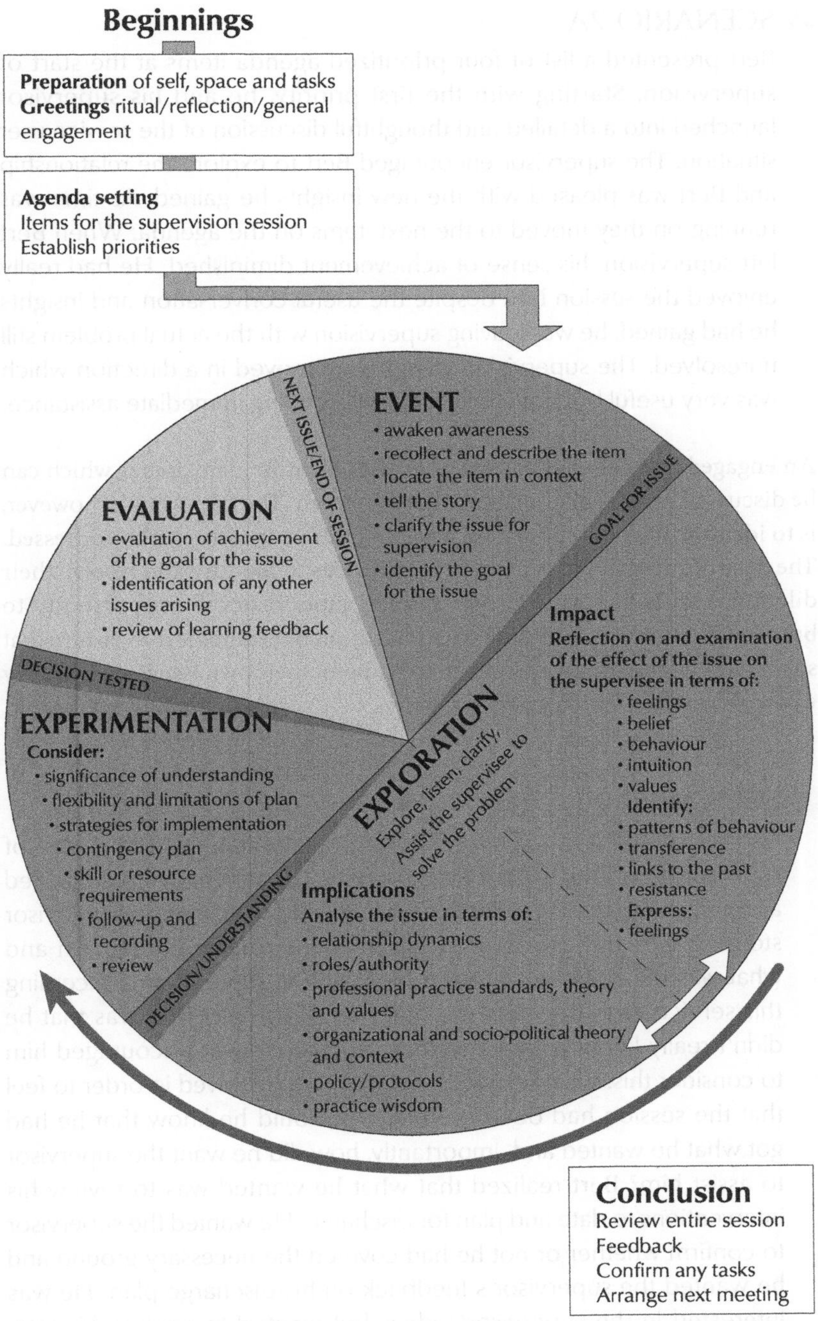

Beginnings

Preparation of self, space and tasks
Greetings ritual/reflection/general engagement

Agenda setting
Items for the supervision session
Establish priorities

NEXT ISSUE/END OF SESSION

EVENT
- awaken awareness
- recollect and describe the item
- locate the item in context
- tell the story
- clarify the issue for supervision
- identify the goal for the issue

GOAL FOR ISSUE

EVALUATION
- evaluation of achievement of the goal for the issue
- identification of any other issues arising
- review of learning feedback

DECISION TESTED

EXPERIMENTATION
Consider:
- significance of understanding
- flexibility and limitations of plan
- strategies for implementation
- contingency plan
- skill or resource requirements
- follow-up and recording
- review

EXPLORATION
Explore, listen, clarify.
Assist the supervisee to solve the problem

Impact
Reflection on and examination of the effect of the issue on the supervisee in terms of:
- feelings
- belief
- behaviour
- intuition
- values
Identify:
- patterns of behaviour
- transference
- links to the past
- resistance
Express:
- feelings

DECISION/UNDERSTANDING

Implications
Analyse the issue in terms of:
- relationship dynamics
- roles/authority
- professional practice standards, theory and values
- organizational and socio-political theory and context
- policy/protocols
- practice wisdom

Conclusion
Review entire session
Feedback
Confirm any tasks
Arrange next meeting

Figure 5.2: The Reflective Learning Model

■ SCENARIO 2A

Bert presented a list of four prioritized agenda items at the start of supervision. Starting with the first priority, he and his supervisor launched into a detailed and thoughtful discussion of the service user situation. The supervisor encouraged Bert to explore the relationship and Bert was pleased with the new insights he gained. As time was running on they moved to the next items on the agenda. When Bert left supervision, his sense of achievement diminished. He had really enjoyed the session but, despite the useful conversation and insights he had gained, he was leaving supervision with the actual problem still unresolved. The supervision session had moved in a direction which was very useful but not where Bert was seeking immediate assistance.

An engaged and competent supervisor will identify many issues which can be discussed in any situation placed before them. The importance, however, is to identify what the supervisee has identified as the issue to be addressed. The core of supervision is to assist supervisees to identify and resolve their dilemmas. This of course is not to deny supervisors the opportunity to broaden the supervisee's vision of the situation but rather it is to ensure that supervisees are encouraged to learn to pinpoint their own issues and identify where they need particular assistance.

■ SCENARIO 2B

Bert presented a list of four prioritized agenda items at the start of supervision. Starting with the first priority, he launched into a detailed account of the service user situation. After a few minutes the supervisor stopped him and asked him what he wanted from the session and what was the issue he wanted to deal with in supervision concerning this service user. Bert realized that part of the problem was that he didn't really know what he wanted. The supervisor encouraged him to consider this: what he would need to have resolved in order to feel that the session had been useful. How would he know that he had got what he wanted and, importantly, how did he want the supervisor to assist him? Bert realized that what he wanted was to review his interventions to date and plan for discharge. He wanted the supervisor to confirm whether or not he had covered the necessary ground and he wanted the supervisor's feedback on his discharge plan. He was interested in the supervisor's ideas but wanted to explore his own first – he did not want advice. When Bert left supervision, he felt a great sense of achievement. He had really enjoyed the session and was leaving feeling affirmed for his work to date and with a clear plan for the coming weeks of work with this service user. His supervisor's feedback and comments had also given him some very useful insights which he valued and wanted to take away and reflect on.

When the supervisee has clarified what they want to get from supervision in relation to the issue presented the session can move to the next stage.

The task of clarifying 'the issue' for supervision is a valuable exercise for all supervisees and is vital in positioning the supervisee as an active, rather than a passive, participant in the supervision process. When a supervisee names the issue, identifies what sort of outcome they would like and is able to articulate the 'type' of assistance from the supervisor then the supervision process becomes one of joint responsibility and collaboration. Each participant has clearly defined separate roles and functions but has an equal responsibility to achieve a 'good' outcome from supervision. In this manner, a more 'passive' supervisee is challenged to be accountable to the process and outcome of the session and joint ownership of the problem-solving discussion is promoted. As supervisees become familiar with this process of establishing a clear question for supervision, it becomes incorporated into their preparation and they arrive at supervision with clearly formulated goals. This not only saves precious supervision time but also often means that smaller supervision problems are more easily resolved leaving time for the more difficult dilemmas.

Supervisee passivity or disengagement may at times be disguised as autonomy and independence (Nye 2007). In an interesting exploration, Nye notes that these practitioners bring solutions, answers or old rehashed cases to supervision. The supervisor has therefore 'limited access to the supervisee's on-going work or the supervisee's learning process' (Nye 2007, p.82). This stance on the part of the supervisee, Nye suggests, may be in response to cultural models which promote independence and autonomy as desirable traits and dependence as shameful. Using Vygotsky's model which promotes ongoing 'dependence' as necessary for learning and development throughout one's professional career, Nye translates this into the supervision arena and recommends supervisors to find an 'appropriate balance between dependence and independence' (Nye 2007 p.96). By positioning the supervisee as co-explorer, the Reflective Learning Model encourages ownership by the supervisee of both the problem and the solution. As Scaife (2010) notes, while another person can assist and guide a practitioner to access alternative contexts and perspectives 'the responsibility for change and development lies with the person doing the reflecting' (Scaife 2010, p.21).

Before moving to the next stage of the model the supervisor may privately review the following questions:

Event

- *Do I understand the supervisee's question or issue?*

- *Am I clear about how the supervisee wants to work on this?*

- *What is the significance of this issue/question in relation to this supervisee – how does this connect with previous supervision conversations?*

Exploration

With a clear goal established for the agenda item, the supervisor and supervisee can move on to the next stage of the cycle. Here, with knowledge of the supervisee's purpose or issue, the supervisor is able to focus their listening and ensure that the supervisee's question or dilemma is addressed. Just as it was the supervisee's role to identify the problem so it is for the supervisee to solve their own problem albeit with the assistance of the supervisor. The supervisor's role is to listen, explore and clarify. While there is always a place in supervision for the supervisor to share ideas, practice wisdom and knowledge, premature sharing of this may prevent the supervisee from discovering their unique solutions. Hence, before creating new options, it is important for the supervisor and supervisee to start at the place where the supervisee stands so that they both understand and acknowledge what has already been done, what has been considered and how this has been experienced. Some supervisors approach supervision with a belief that they must 'solve' the problem for the supervisee. Such an approach not only creates stress and undue expectations on the performance of the supervisor but also diminishes the supervisee's role and responsibility for the session. Supervision is at risk of becoming a competitive sport where the supervisor attempts to resolve the supervisee's problems and the supervisee measures the success of supervision according to the supervisor's performance. In this situation, independent growth and learning are problematic for the supervisee and there is considerable potential for game playing.

The exploration stage is divided into two parts: Impact (Reflection) and Implications (Conceptualization).

The exploration stage is the place where the 'work' of supervision takes place. In order to undertake this work and to fully examine, understand and learn from a situation there needs to be balance between the emotive/personal and the cognitive. The supervisee is thus encouraged to explore and examine the issue from two perspectives. The first is from a personal perspective: 'impact'. The second is from an analytical perspective: 'implications'.

Impact

Effective exploration of any supervision issue involves the consideration of that issue in terms of its impact or effect on self. The boundaries between 'self' and 'other' are important and supervision is a forum where these boundaries can be reviewed in order to identify and prevent any blurring or breach of this separation.

The supervisee is invited by the supervisor to locate themselves in the situation. What impact have they had on the situation and how have they been affected by the situation? Feelings, beliefs, attitudes, behaviour and intuitions are considered. The supervisee's personal assumptions and expectations of their own reactions to the surprises and challenges of practice can be explored. 'Messy' feelings can be allowed to surface. Patterns from the past can be identified and transference acknowledged. From the place of 'knowing' what has occurred, the supervisee has the opportunity to consider what could be different and to uncover what is not known and what needs to be known. The supervisor's role is to create the space within which the supervisee can explore the possibilities of their own behaviour and feelings and those of the 'others'.

■ SCENARIO 3

Jackie was bothered by a situation she had encountered with the mother of a client with whom she was working. Her goal for supervision was to identify why she felt uncomfortable and to plan how to approach this woman in her next session. As the supervisor listened to her story he noticed that Jackie began to minimize the situation and to list reasons why she should just close the case. The supervisor pointed this out to Jackie and asked her what sorts of feelings she had about the situation and if this sort of situation had occurred before. Jackie was initially surprised but on reflection identified feelings of incompetence and inadequacy. These were old feelings which she associated with her very competitive and successful older sister. With her supervisor's assistance Jackie explored the transference with her sister and was readily able to recognize how those old feelings were intruding on, and undermining, her sense of competence in the present situation. She was surprised to recognize that her first response in these situations had been, and continued to be, one of withdrawal.

This stage of exploration also provides an opportunity for supervisees to express the emotional impact of their work. In a safe and trusting environment the emotions and feelings which inevitably accompany practice can be expressed, acknowledged and validated. The importance of the validation of the 'personal self' is well captured by Horney:

> A healthy integration is a result of being oneself, and can only be attained on this basis. If we are sufficiently ourselves to have spontaneous feelings, to make our own decisions, and to assume responsibility for them, then we have a feeling of unity on a solid basis. (Horney 1970 cited in Van Kessel and Haan 1993, p.9)

When considering the impact phase of the model a supervisor again may ask themselves:

Exploration: Impact

- *How has the supervisee located themselves in this situation?*

- *What are the tacit beliefs and assumptions which the supervisee brings to this situation?*

- *What are the predominant feelings which the supervisee is expressing about this situation?*

However, for professional practice, expression, or knowledge, of the personal self is not sufficient but must be understood in the context of the 'professional' role.

> Through this integration of personal competence and the professional role profile, the professional worker comes to acquire the different facets of the required professional ability in such a way that they are united in a whole of a higher order and s/he can function as a professional self. (Van Kessel and Haan 1993, p.9)

In order to assist the development of this integrated 'professional self', the 'exploration' stage of supervision includes consideration and review of external points of reference from the broader fields of practice.

Implications

In the implication stage, a wider consideration of the supervision issue occurs. There is an opportunity to balance the emotive with the cognitive. The supervisee is encouraged to consider the supervision issue from the perspectives of professional practice, values and theory; organizational policy and protocols; and cultural and socio-political contexts. The broader base and assumptions of practice and policy can be examined and tested for congruency while roles, plans and interventions can be scrutinized for effectiveness and viability. There is a possibility here for intellectual rigour and for meaningful debate which tests professional values, assumptions and theory. In an active supervision relationship, meaning can be made of the connection between theory and practice and new ideas and practice can be germinated. Discussion may also identify areas for development with regard to knowledge, skills or resources and ways in which these can be addressed. For newer practitioners, links can be made to the key theory and research that underpins their practice or the supervisee can be guided to search for recent evidence. This is the place where the supervisor may share knowledge and experience in order to assist the supervisee to broaden their own knowledge base and so arrive at new possibilities and solutions. It is, however, important for the supervisor to ensure that the sharing of wisdom and knowledge is to enhance the supervisee's practice rather than to dictate action. In specific situations of safety and policy there may be reasons for supervisees to be 'directed' to take a course of action but these should be rare. The task of supervision is to develop the repertoire of the supervisee, not to clone the supervisor.

■ SCENARIO 4

With the insights gained in the first part of the session, Jackie and the supervisor considered how Jackie could change her response in future sessions with the mother. The supervisor encouraged Jackie to review the purpose of her work with the client and the contract which had been drawn up between her and the client and to identify how the mother contributed to that work. They considered Jackie's position as therapist in the situation and discussed issues of power and control. From this, Jackie was able to clearly articulate her role with the client and the boundaries of that work. She was able to define where the mother fitted into that work and understood the limits of her authority as a therapist and potential areas of conflict. The next step, she decided, was to organize a meeting with the mother to clarify their different roles.

The exploration stage is the place where the supervisee is assisted to arrive at new understandings or actions and to do so with an accompanying clarity of their own self and actions. The supervisor may ask themselves:

Exploration: Implications

- *What is the bigger picture?*

- *What other information, theory, research and perspectives can the supervisee consider here?*

- *What are the socio-political, professional and organizational contexts?*

- *Is there a teaching/information sharing moment here?*

Experimentation

When a supervisee has reached some form of decision or understanding it is important that this is tested to determine if it is possible and realistic and whether there are sufficient resources available for the decision to be successfully implemented. Thus the task for the supervisee in the experimentation stage is to examine the solutions or understandings they arrived at and to determine whether or not they are viable in practice.

When the identified outcome of supervision is in the form of an activity or strategy it is important that the proposed action is considered and tested. What are the possible consequences of the proposed action(s)? How might these plans be sabotaged and by whom? What contingency plans are possible? What strategies can be identified to address any resource deficiency? Future scenarios can be identified and significant conversations rehearsed and/or role-played so that new roles, approaches and interventions can be trialled in a safe environment.

The importance of this stage of the supervision cycle is that it allows the 'solution' to be examined and tested to ensure that it is robust and that the supervisee is confident and has the required skills and knowledge to implement the plan. The detailed examination of the 'plan' or 'solution' not only tests its viability but also provides an opportunity for the supervisee to integrate new learning into their practice repertoire. This integration is vital if the supervisee is to be successful in the implementation of new skills and methods. When a supervisee is familiar with an action plan, has identified strategies to deal with possible obstacles and has a contingency plan of action should the original plan fail they are able to move forward. Many excellent strategies and plans are lost when the supervisee leaves supervision without the confidence, clarity or skills to follow through the next step.

It is in this stage, therefore, that the transformative potential of the model is evident. The model encourages supervisees not only to identify their reflection and learning but also to take responsibility to put that learning into practice. 'Reflection becomes reflective practice when the critical reflection shapes future practice' (Scaife 2010, p.2), and as Carroll (2014) notes, 'learning in supervision is ultimately transformative and not just transmissive' (p.19). One of the acid tests of the effectiveness of supervision is 'What are you (the supervisee) doing differently now that you were not doing before supervision?' (Carroll 2010, p.1).

In some situations, particularly in the supervision of experienced practitioners, the exploration of an issue may bring insight and understanding rather than an 'action plan'. Where this occurs, the experimentation stage allows these understandings and insights to be considered and integrated into practice theory and wisdom. Supervisees are encouraged to review their new understandings against established practice, existing ideas and theories and to identify where they may need to make adjustments and how they will do so. As with 'action plans', new 'understandings' can also be sabotaged, particularly if the new insight is accompanied by feelings of discomfort.

■ SCENARIO 5A

Sandra had had a good supervision session. She had brought two issues to supervision and she and her supervisor had clarified and established a clear goal for each issue starting with the first priority. They had reflected on the impact of the situation, Sandra's role and interventions to date, and through discussion had determined a course of action. Sandra was pleased with this and they moved onto the next issue. When she was on her way home, however, Sandra began to have doubts as to the usefulness of the agreed action. She could think of several things which could go wrong and in view of her busy workload doubted that it was worth the effort.

When the supervisee has ownership of a strategy and through practice or discussion has integrated this into their repertoire, then follow-up action will be clear and can be approached with confidence.

■ SCENARIO 5B

Sandra had had a good supervision session. She had brought two issues to supervision and she and her supervisor had clarified and established a clear goal for each issue starting with the first priority. They had reflected on the impact of the situation, Sandra's role and interventions to date, and through discussion Sandra had determined a course of action. Sandra was pleased with this and suggested that they moved on to the next issue. The supervisor, however, suggested that before they moved on they spent a bit of time on establishing how Sandra was going to carry out the agreed course of action. 'What was the next step?' 'How and when and where was she going to do it?' 'What could go wrong and what would she do then?' The supervisor encouraged Sandra to formulate how she was going to raise the issue with the person concerned and Sandra and the supervisor engaged in an impromptu role play. As she sought to find the 'right' words Sandra became increasingly clear about her stance and the issue she wanted to convey to the other party. When she was on her way home Sandra felt very confident about her ability to follow through with her plan. She had identified what she needed to do. She knew she could do it and had considered her options if it all turned to custard.

It is important to clarify how the supervision issue will be recorded and reviewed. This not only establishes accountability but also provides additional encouragement to the more tentative or reluctant supervisee to follow through on the action. This process in the supervision cycle also provides the opportunity for any identified gaps of knowledge or skills to be recorded and linked to specific training opportunities.

The supervisor's own reflections at this stage could include:

Exploration: Implications

- *How able/ready is the supervisee to put this learning into practice?*

- *What resources/coaching/support might be useful?*

- *How will this supervisee transfer knowledge/skills to this situation?*

Evaluation

The evaluation stage of the cycle marks the completion of the 'work' on the 'issue' which has been under discussion. The questions posed are: 'has the issue raised by the supervisee been addressed and resolved? Has the supervisee got what they wanted from supervision regarding this issue? The supervisor and the supervisee may reflect on the 'process' of the discussion and identify specific learning and any additional issues which have arisen as a result of the discussion and identify future action. There is an opportunity for feedback. This opportunity for the supervisee to review whether they have met the identified goal allows space for reflection and prevents both the supervisor and the supervisee from prematurely moving on to the next issue. The supervisor may mentally consider:

Evaluation

- *Has the supervisee got what they wanted?*

- *How able is this supervisee to articulate their learning from reflection?*

- *What future learning experiences might be helpful here?*

The supervisor and the supervisee will then return to the agenda and address the second item, repeating the cycle once more.

The conclusion

The supervision session ends when the agreed time has elapsed or when all agenda items have been addressed. As noted earlier, good beginnings create the space for learning and good endings enable the learning to be retained and integrated for future use. The conclusion of the supervision session is very important, creating an opportunity for both parties to attend to the ongoing supervision relationship. As we discussed in Chapter 3, the medium through which supervision is conducted is the supervision relationship. The conclusion of the supervision session allows the time spent together to be considered as a process from start to finish. It is an opportunity for each party to reflect on the session and to give and receive feedback. This can be conducted in a formal structured manner or through informal review. What is important is to ensure that over time both supervisor and supervisee have the opportunity to comment on each other's participation, the usefulness of time spent and techniques used, and to identify any changes which would improve the sessions. This review allows the supervision relationship to grow as well as the individual participants. Lizzio *et al.* (2009) refer to this process when they promote a regular monitoring of the supervision relationship which 'prevents' or at least 'mitigates misunderstandings and assumptions' (Lizzio *et al.* 2009, p.137).

The conclusion is also the time for the nuts and bolts of the session to be noted: the confirmation of any tasks set, time frames for completion, issues for follow-up and the date of the next meeting. Increasingly, supervision dyads comprise practitioners and supervisors who come from different ethnic or cultural backgrounds and for some the session may end with a ritual. Rituals of beginning and ending are often the time where difference can be respected and acknowledged and where the supervision space can be affirming of the 'professional self'. When the session has concluded, the supervisor may also take time to reflect on the entire session and consider:

Conclusion

- *How well did I listen, support and assist the supervisee in their reflection and learning?*
- *What could I consider doing differently in future sessions?*
- *What learning, consideration, questions am I taking away from this session?*

Professional practice in the current practice climate of the 21st century is experienced as uncertain, ever-changing and anxiety laden. To survive, the practitioner requires a strong professional self and an ability to critically analyse and assess themselves in a range of diverse situations. The old 'truths' of practice no longer apply and professionals are being called on to make rapid decisions and take action in ever-changing professional landscapes. The Reflective Learning Model of Supervision provides the basis for supporting and developing critical awareness. When a supervisee internalizes the processes of reflective learning, this can be accessed as a tool for 'in action' reflection.

Critique

As described in Chapter 1, our engagement with study, research and teaching of supervision began in the 1990s. At this stage, we were familiar with, and taught, a number of models and approaches to supervision, but were challenged to find a model which moved the supervisor and supervisee from 'hello' to 'see you next time'. It was from here that the Reflective Learning Model of Supervision developed and was first published in 2001 (Davys 2001). We wanted a straightforward model, or stepped framework, which could form the basis of a guided structure for supervision practice from which supervisors and practitioners could also comfortably consider a range of theoretical approaches to practice and approaches to supervision (see Figure 2.6). As has been well articulated by Gordon (2012), 'supervisors need a bridge to link the complexities of guidelines and models of supervision to their moment-by-moment facilitation of the supervision meeting' (p.72).

The Reflective Learning Model as an early model for this approach to supervision, has formed the basis of, and contributed to, further development of supervision processes (Watkins, Callahan and Vîşcu 2019). Constructing a model for the development of the skills and competence of new supervisors, Watkins *et al.* (2019) developed the Supervision Session Pyramid (SSP), which has incorporated an integration of the structure and process of the Reflective Learning Model (Davys and Beddoe 2010).

The four component processes in the SSP: 'the event/issue identification and clarification; exploration and elaboration, experimentation and collaboration; review and resolution' (Watkins *et al.* 2019, p.3), mirror the four stages of the Reflective Learning Model. The 'event/issue identification and clarification' form the base of the pyramid while the 'review and resolution' sit at the apex. The configuration of the processes as a pyramid we feel, however, distorts the representation of the significance of the individual stages of the supervision session. The position of the 'event/

issue identification and clarification' at the base of the pyramid, although emphasizing the importance of this stage, visually suggests that this stage is of more importance than the 'exploration and elaboration' process, where the major work of supervision occurs. However, Watkins *et al.* (2019) note the cyclic nature of the supervisory process for each issue which is presented by the supervisee. Further, on the basis of their examination of the literature and of supervision transcripts, they endorse our own belief that this approach to supervision spans theoretical perspectives. Regardless of the questions or perspectives reflected in the detail of the supervision session, they conclude that 'the same four component process remains on trans-theoretical display' (2019, p.5).

Within an acknowledgment of the boundaries, expectations and the power dynamic of supervision, the Reflective Learning Model allows for independence of process and of relationship. The model, with its emphasis on supervisee-led agendas, supervisee-directed goals and supervisee-focused learning, supports a supervision relationship based on mutuality, and accommodates multiple meanings and understandings. This postmodern social constructionist understanding of the plurality of truths mirrors the contexts faced by many practitioners as they consider the complex fields in which they practise.

Social constructionism in supervision has been described by Hair and O'Donoghue (2009) as inviting:

> supervisors to shape a supervisory relationship that encourages transparency, collaboration, and an exchange of ideas… This does not mean that supervisors deny or ignore their own ideas or experiences, but rather acknowledge that learning is a shared adventure. Supervisors, therefore, are encouraged to be tentative about their own knowledge, and curious about the knowledge of the supervisee…this means that all knowledge…can be valued and vulnerable to critique so that the potential is present for dominant beliefs and practices to be challenged and alternative narratives constructed. (p.76)

The goal of the Reflective Learning Model is for supervisees to find their own meaning and their own solutions and resolution to their own issues and dilemmas.

Notwithstanding the Eurocentric origins of the theories of reflection and learning, the Reflective Learning Model has been considered well suited to the supervision of supervisees from different cultures and ethnicities. Wilson (2015), testing the appropriateness and effectiveness of this model for the supervision of Māori and Pasifika who worked in the helping professions in Aotearoa New Zealand, reports that the participants found the model 'highly effective and strongly appropriate' (p.134). The Reflective Learning Model was seen by the participants to be respectful and to accommodate and value their world views and culture; reflection was encouraged and the participants valued the opportunity to consider different ways forward and to develop their own solutions. Participants also commented on the importance of supervisor competence and so, with the proviso that the model was correctly used, Wilson (2105) concluded that it was an appropriate fit for Māori and Pasifika supervisees regardless of the ethnicity of the supervisor.

It has been suggested that supervision models such as the Reflective Learning Model are appropriate for beginning supervisors (Watkins *et al.* 2019), and it is certainly our experience in providing supervision training and education that the Reflective Learning Model is a very useful starting place for new supervisors. We contend, however, that, given the flexibility offered by this trans-theoretical process, the Reflective Learning Model remains applicable for supervisors of all levels of experience. When reflection rests as the basis of learning in supervision, the Reflective Learning Model provides the structure to keep that learning on track and accountable. Further, it is suggested that the process of the model, with its emphasis on connection and mutuality, acts as a buffer against the possible hijack of Middleman and Rhode's (1980) collusion and collusion.

Developing Expertise: Becoming a Critically Reflective Supervisor

Chapter 6 will address the development of supervisory expertise and explore the role of supervision in promoting reflective practice, critical reflection, social justice and the core values of the helping professions. This chapter will explicitly promote career-long critical reflection on practice, with supervision as one means to facilitating this. This is not to assume that supervision alone can enable ongoing professional excellence. It needs to be accompanied by other means of professional renewal: postgraduate study, research mindedness, and a spirit of critical inquiry. Four topics will be explored in this chapter: six key tasks of becoming a supervisor; supervising ethical practice ethics; exploring critical reflection; and culture and diversity in supervision.

Becoming a supervisor

When we first began teaching supervision to social workers in the early 1990s we were surprised at the lack of material which clearly identified the core skills for effective supervision. As Schindler and Talen (1996, p.110) expressed it, 'the prevailing assumption [was] that new supervisors knew how to supervise because they had been supervised. Learning supervision by osmosis seems to have been the underlying belief'. There is still surprisingly little research conducted that explains the process of becoming a supervisor and how the supervisor role fits in to a career path. A recent study in Western Canada asked supervisors how they came to be supervisors (Schmidt and Kariuki 2019). Participant responses revealed 'three pathways to supervision: task exposure, supervision by happen chance, and deliberate decision' (p.326). None of Schmidt and Kariuki's participants described any specific policy or educational programme designed to recruit and develop supervisors from within their employment organization. While supervisors and managers supported their involvement there was no systematic pathway. This recent small study confirms an observation made by Watkins and Wang (2014) that despite professional commitment to the education and development of practitioners in counselling and therapy no such commitment is made to educate supervisors:

> Across the history of supervision, such rigorous, vigorous training has by no means been the norm: (a) training in how to supervise has generally been less recognized as *sine qua non* for supervisory practice; (b) being a supervisee oneself or gaining seniority have been seen as sufficiently qualifying supervision credentials. (Watkins and Wang 2014, p.178)

While in some professions there has been a change, Borders (2010) states that 'today, the need for supervisor training is widely accepted'; she also notes that mandating and providing supervisor education still varies 'rather substantially across disciplines' (p.130).

The role of supervisor, carrying as it does associations of expertise, knowledge, power and experience, is easily confused with similar roles (teacher, consultant, manager) where these attributes are central. For many new supervisors, assuming the role of supervisor requires conscious shifts in role, particularly when they aspire to facilitate supervision which is critically reflective. These include shifts from:

- teacher to facilitator

- expert to co-explorer

- being didactic to being relational

- providing answers to asking questions

- a focus on 'doing' to a focus on 'thinking'

- a position of knowing to a position of curiosity and openness to other possibility.

How do supervisors learn? How do they integrate new knowledge and incorporate new skills into the practice of supervision? A brief review of the international literature on supervisory training reveals a significant emphasis on developmental models of supervisory competence (Brown and Bourne 1996; Heid 1997; Hess 1986). A study of counselling supervisors found little evidence that supervisors improved greatly with experience alone (Worthington 1987). Supervisors need training and good supervision for themselves in order to continue to grow in their practice. More recently, Watkins and Wang (2014, p.180) note that supervision and therapy, 'although similar in some respects, are different processes and should be treated as such; furthermore supervision is a pre-eminently an educational process... and supervisors would do well to foremost treat supervision as an educational enterprise and accordingly align their efforts with an educational role'. We would add to this assertion, that where supervision is lifelong, not just for professional practitioner training, critical reflection is of equal importance. Supervision has its own special skills and processes, though these will reflect aspects of the learning required to become a practitioner. Many supervisor education approaches represent an extrapolation of developmental theories of practitioner development to the building of competence in new supervisors (Hess 1986; Loganbill *et al.* 1982; Watkins 1990).

Neukrug (2008) discusses the stages of theoretical integration for practitioners in the human services. This framework can be usefully recounted here as it incorporates many aspects relevant to the development of new supervisors. Neukrug describes a four-stage developmental process where practitioners begin at Stage 1 with *Chaos*, where practice is informed by rapid and haphazard responses and decisions (p.80). New supervisors often feel pressured to attend quickly to supervisee concerns. Stage 2 of worker theoretical development is characterized by *Coalescence*, where theory is learned and one particular theoretical perspective may be favoured with the integration of techniques from other approaches. For beginning supervisors, comfort may be gained from developing a thorough knowledge of one approach to supervision and being able to practise it. At Stage 3, practitioners demonstrate *Theoretical integration*, where one theory or approach is predominately used with the integration of one or more alternative approaches. At this stage, the supervisor becomes at ease with an integrated approach and their practice is more fluid. The fourth and final stage of this process is characterized by *Metatheory analysis* (p.80), where practitioners have an 'appreciation of many theories and begin to explore the underlying commonalities and themes'. At this stage, workers seek to understand the connections and effectiveness of combining discrete parts of differing theoretical perspectives to inform intervention strategies (Neukrug 2008, pp.80–81). Supervisors will also draw from a range of approaches in their repertoire, being able to flexibly change approach to meet supervisee needs. We have suggested such flexibility of approach to supervision in Figure 2.6.

In our experience, new supervisors initially focus on the anxiety-provoking aspects of the supervisor role and often feel that they need to be experts and 'fix' the supervisee's problem or issue. There is ambivalence about the power and authority inherent in the role and the dominant question is 'Will they like me'? Table 6.1 sets out some common preoccupations and associated behaviours of new supervisors. Echoing Neukrug's formulation, supervisors experience a middle stage where they aim to adopt changes in their practice and experiment with new approaches, settling where there is a fit with their practice orientation. Finally, their own unique style develops as they integrate new learning, build their own practice wisdom and, like Hawkins and Shohet's 'process-in-context-centred' stage of development (2012, p.80) supervisors have applied their 'helicopter skills' (2012, p.79). Here supervisors are able to be 'with' the supervisee but simultaneously be thinking about promoting learning and supporting practitioner resilience. The phases of learning are summarized in Table 6.1.

Table 6.1: Phases of learning for new supervisors

Phase	Preoccupations of supervisors	Supervisory behaviours
Becoming a supervisor	• Ambivalence about taking responsibility • Focus on role rather than process • Hoping to impress and be in control • Fear of supervisee's critical gaze • Focus on relationship building • Focus on own competence 'Will they like me?'	• Uncertainty about readiness • Focus on facts and premature problem solving • Avoidance of *or* over-reliance on authority • Limited range of interventions but enthusiastic about learning • Focus on own world view and style
Making connections	• Less emphasis on maintaining control • Anxiety about supervisee competence • Recognition of cultural differences • Adoption of the supervisory approach with best fit for their own theoretical orientation and practice style • Deepening skill in supervision process 'Do they respect me and am I helpful?'	• Increasingly consistent handling of power and authority • Greater range of interventions and willingness to experiment • Active curiosity about different world views

Integrating theory and style, promoting change	• Critical reflection on own practice • Learning to trust judgement and practice wisdom • Conscious monitoring of cultural maps of self, supervisee and service users • Finding courage to work with difference • Seeking deeper learning 'Are they practising ethically and are they learning?'	• Use of relationship to intervene and explore clinical issues • Awareness and comfort with own limits • Authority used appropriately within ethical domain. • Greater ability to contain and interpret supervisee distress • Utilization of 'helicopter skills' to use process effectively

The development of expertise in supervision: six key tasks

There are six key tasks facing a new supervisor. The first task is to develop the ability to work with the perceptions and reactions of the supervisee, keeping the service user focus at arm's length. A second key task is understanding teaching and learning as central to effective supervision, in the sharing of practice knowledge. A clear separation of the process of supervision from the role of the supervisor is the third key task. The fourth task is to manage the new authority that comes with the role. The fifth task is to facilitate the safe expression of emotions in supervision. The sixth and final task is to maintain a balance in supervision with respect to managing risk, which in some professional contexts may be a pervasive focus.

Task 1: Working with the service user at arm's length

The process of becoming a supervisor involves developing the ability to stand back from using one's own knowledge and clinical skills in direct practice and instead to facilitate transformative learning in the supervisee. There are benefits for both supervisor and supervisee in this process. Urdang (1999) found that new student supervisors' self-esteem increased both through mastery of a new skill and the validation, through teaching and supervising the student, of their own knowledge base and practice. Most supervisors indicated that supervising increased their self-awareness and capacity to analyse their own work, much of which had become automatic (Urdang 1999). The supervisor identifies the boundaries between their own knowledge base, assisting the supervisee to develop their own unique and separate professional knowledge.

Task 2: Knowledge for practice: supervisor expertise

The acquisition of formal knowledge for professional practice is considered to be a prerequisite for expertise as a supervisor, and while focusing on the supervisee's learning, a new supervisor often calls on their own practice experience plus formal professional or disciplinary knowledge. As Valkeavaara puts it, 'the knowledge which we all have about our own profession, and which lies behind how we function but which we have difficulties in conceptualizing explicitly, has been termed as tacit knowledge' (Valkeavaara 1999, p.178). Citing Argyris (1991), Valkeavaara notes that 'learning to be an expert in one's own domain takes more than a string of successes, it also requires problematic situations in practical settings which trigger the processes of the construction and reconstruction of expertise' (Valkeavaara 1999, p.178).

Expertise comes from repeated instances of encountering problems for which routine solutions and responses do not exist and for supervisors, their experience makes this process easier. Solving problems in professional life includes various phases of examining and defining the problem, finding and implementing potential solutions, trying these in action and evaluating the outcomes. Engagement in such processes of course doesn't occur in a vacuum as practitioners work in complex cultural and social contexts, which are rich in both resources and challenges. In the 21st century, the protocols surrounding many professions require discussion, reporting, evidence and a return to formal knowledge, before action is taken, and in the organizational context, professionals at all levels may contribute to communities of practice where knowledge is shared (Plath 2013). Knowledge for practice is in this way transformed. Supervision that holds and examines problems, and draws together practice knowledge which utilizes research findings, contributes to the development of research-minded critical practice by modelling the spirit of inquiry and not simply repeating the 'what works' mantra or 'do as I say'.

The professions vary in terms of their degree of focus on formal knowledge, the utilization of research findings, critical inquiry and the extent to which theory forms part of the supervisory process. We have seen in Chapter 1 that there is consistent inclusion of education and professional development in the major definitions of supervision, but interpretation of this is wide ranging. Certainly, in the supervision of pre-service professional education, learning is paramount. Here there is commonly an explicit focus in supervision on the integration of theory, evidence and 'practice' in a clinical or practical setting and considerable agreement that supervisors should model the integrated approach. Baxter argues that the oft-described theory-practice gap in nursing means that 'if students do not have theory-based practice modelled for them then it may actually result in "de-professionalization"' (Baxter 2007, p.104).

Task 3: Defining process and role

The third task facing a new supervisor is to distinguish between the process of supervision and the role of the supervisor. In many organizational settings this is made difficult because of the blurring of clinical supervision and management functions. As supervision educators we have found that new supervisors struggle when this dual focus is present and have often been hindered by supervision literature which privileges function over process. Seeking certainty, many supervisors have found the safety in a prescriptive model. We know from the countless conversations that we have had with supervisors and practitioners that supervision, in times of stress and risk-consciousness, often reverts to checklist approaches that smother reflective practice. In a risk-averse professional environment, practice may become reactive and mechanistic rather than reflective and creative. 'Checklist' supervision may indeed ameliorate against the anxiety practitioners and supervisors feel but it does not necessarily improve the practice (Beddoe 2010; Gillingham and Bromfield 2008). Smythe, MacCulloch and Charmley (2009) also caution against over-reliance on technical approaches and suggest that 'the real mark of excellence can only come when we allow ourselves to become lost in the unfolding of each unique moment of a supervision relationship... Some of our most precious moments have come when that process has in some magical way taken flight and given wings to all involved' (Smythe *et al.* 2009, p.19).

Task 4: The management of authority and power

A major issue in the development of new supervisors, and our fourth key task, is the management of the authority and power that comes with the role. As we noted in Chapter 3, the ability to recognize and acknowledge the power dimensions of supervision and develop collaborative relationships is crucial to effective critical reflection and decision making. The demonstration of respect and humility is central in supervision relationships (Hair 2014; Hawkins and Shohet 2012; Watkins *et al.* 2018).

Richmond (2009) suggests that traditional approaches to individual supervision have embedded a 'formally structured process of individual development' in which power relations are embedded through both managerial power and professional authority (p.544). Richmond cites McNamara, Lawley and Towler (2007, pp.79–84), who consider that power can be asserted through empowerment, 'power with', or disempowerment, 'power over'. They also describe 'power within, ' in which peer and group models enable supervisors to relinquish power to develop mutual supervision processes (Richmond 2009, p.545).

Key to the effective and non-oppressive use of power and authority in supervision is the clear understanding of the differences between the role of supervisor and the process of supervision. The supervisory role, whether or not it is embedded within line responsibility functions of an organization, is imbued with authority and power. Both supervisor and supervisee also bring in to the relationship their own ideas and beliefs about authority along with the 'baggage' of previous experiences, good and bad. There may be ambivalence about the extent to which the participants want to see power exerted within this complex relationship, in which knowledge itself is a major source of power. Both may fear being 'found out' as having less knowledge than they should. Both need to be able to create a place where it is all right not to know. Supervisors often fear that they will be expected to be 'all knowing' and the authors have seen hundreds of videos of supervision sessions and witnessed the struggle many supervisors have to resist 'telling' rather than facilitating, and the anxiety felt by new supervisors when a challenging situation is presented in supervision.

Pack (2009b) describes a personal experience of supervision in which she felt the underlying subtext in the relationship was 'do as I say':

> Here was the supervisor who defined my role as being one of unerring compliance for the common good of all. I was reminded in supervision constantly that she was sharing her years of experience with me to save me from what she considered to be my own incompetence. ... My identification with her judgment that was highly critical of my not being 'good enough', led to cycles of demoralization, shame, retroflection and withdrawal. (Pack 2009b, p.66)

Later, writes Pack, 'I [could] empathize with the supervisor who was struggling to find her voice within the team and was anxious about her professional identity and authority as a new manager'. There was no process in place to support 'the kind of dialogical engagement that would have allowed both of us to explore the process of what was occurring between us, or so it seemed from my perspective' (Pack 2009b, p.67). The adoption of a collaborative approach and a conceptualization of supervision as a learning activity, rather than a managerial process, enables supervisors to 'acknowledge that learning is a shared adventure' (Hair and O'Donoghue 2009, p.76).

Power and authority, previously discussed in Chapter 3, have been considered in a similar formulation by Hughes and Pengelly (1997) who distinguish three sources of authority which are useful to consider in the supervisory relationship. These are 'role authority' conferred by the organization, 'professional authority' earned through credible practice of knowledge and skill, and lastly, 'personal authority'. This latter form of authority comes from the individual's ability to exercise the other two without challenge (Hughes and Pengelly 1997, pp.168–169). Too much reliance on any of these sources of authority leads to distortions in supervision relationships. Too little exercise of legitimate authority can undermine accountability and lead to the collapse of safe practice (Morrison 2001). Supervisees need to know that their supervisor has the confidence to exercise authority if needed in order to challenge unsafe practice.

There are some tensions to be resolved in the transition to becoming a supervisor. First, new supervisors need to explore their thoughts and feelings about the change in status from full-time direct client work to supervision or to a 'management' role if this applies. Second, there may be some concern over the abandonment of service users for personal promotion. There are new relationships to be forged with colleagues, managers and supervisees. New supervisors often feel that they are exposed to a 360-degree critical gaze. It is helpful if educational opportunities for new supervisors explore these tensions within the social and cultural contexts in which they work. It is also helpful for new supervisors to explore these issues in their own professional supervision.

Task 5: Facilitating safe expression of emotions

The fifth key task is to facilitate the safe expression of emotions in supervision. This topic will be discussed in more detail in Chapter 8. As we have noted earlier, supervisors support practitioners to manage the anxiety and uncertainty generated by the work. The emphasis on risk management and increasing regulation and proceduralism in health and social care creates tension and uncertainty and thus the political context of practice ensures that anxiety levels remain high (Beddoe 2010). In response to this risk-induced anxiety, supervision scholarship has returned to the use of self, and explored concepts such as 'mindfulness' in practice (Andersson, King and Lalande 2010) which are seemingly miles apart from 'evidence-based practice'. On the one hand, practitioners can feel pressure to be 'scientific' and objective and turn to empirical models of practice, on the other hand, practitioners are urged to trust their feelings and listen to hunches. Supervision provides a space in which these competing voices can be heard and attended to. And this means making room and creating safety for feelings to be exposed. If supervision provides opportunities for the safe expression and exploration of feelings they may be a source of potential evidence about the degree of risk present:

Reflective supervision can provide an opportunity for containment of practitioner's anxieties resulting from the raw experience of the work. Through close listening to the case material, the supervisor takes in the rawness and transforms it into thoughts and ideas which are reflected back to bring understanding of the client's situation. (Harvey and Henderson 2014, p.345)

It is important in supervision to value the emotional responses of practitioners as contributing to reflection and therefore safe practice. Ruch describes how the 'linking of feelings and thoughts generates emotional development and cognitive development – thoughtfulness – and contributes to the construction of structures for thinking' (Ruch 2007a, p.662).

Facilitating the expression of feelings in supervision requires careful listening and observation to assess supervisee emotion, what they might be holding back, and the ability of the supervisor to understand their own feelings and to manage these in the supervisory relationship. Morrison (2007, p.255) notes that emotions are 'deep level signals about information that demands attention, as to whether a situation is to be approached or avoided. The rapid appraisal of such signals conveys the meaning of the situation and is often a trigger for action'.

Emotional competence on the part of the supervisor facilitates the expression and management of feelings in supervision. It is interesting to note how often 'support' is included as a function of supervision with little attention given to the nature of the support offered. Most practitioners seem fairly clear that what is required of their supervisors is more than empathetic 'hand-patting'. As Carroll and Gilbert (2011, p.151) state, 'emotions are not just internal reactions but connect us – in ways we sometimes cannot even imagine – to like and others. Far from being simply a distraction to tolerate or accept passively, feelings become the 'inner rudder' of our lives, personally and professionally'.

The highly charged crisis mode of operating in many health and social care environments, however, frequently mitigates against healthy expression of uncomfortable feelings. As Ruch states, 'paradoxically, the ability to admit to one's subjective position, uncertainties and ability to "not know" is a crucial ingredient in the reflective process' (Ruch 2007a, p.644) and yet is often undervalued or seen as unprofessional in the workplace. Approaches to dealing with the emotional content of supervision can include one in which feelings are subject to a technical focus. A contrasting, and more collaborative, reflective, approach focuses on feelings and can foster more reflective and effective practice. The features of these contrasting approaches are outlined in Table 6.2.

In an exploratory process, feelings can be both accepted and valued as a rich source of information and ideas. If only the accommodation of feelings is required, then the supervisor will rely on prescriptive approaches in which reflection is minimized to avoid close attention to the use of self in practice. For many supervisees, learning about the self in practice is the greatest challenge. Heath and Freshwater (2000) note that:

> when processes to encourage learning about self are used, the necessary high challenge must be accompanied by high support, and it should be noted that the creation of a therapeutic environment and the therapeutic use of self are not synonymous with therapy and should not be approached as such. (p.1303)

What may often be ignored is the extent to which supervisors feel under-skilled to cope with supervisee emotion, and their struggles with their own feelings. It is in this regard that training in some process-focused supervision model, such as the Seven-Eyed Model of Supervision described by Hawkins and Shohet (2012), can assist supervisors of all professions. The building of greater facilitation skills will develop confidence in supervisors who may not have been exposed to the development of interpersonal skills in their previous training. In a safe environment, especially learning with other beginning supervisors, it is possible to experiment widely with a range of strategies which can be constructed, challenged and rehearsed (Davys and Beddoe 2008).

Table 6.2: Feelings in supervision

Technical focus	Reflective focus
Managing uncertainty through seeking and applying rules	Greeting uncertainty as opportunity
	Open exploration of feelings
Low tolerance of feelings	High emotional support
Feelings to be tidied away	Nurturing self-awareness
Prescriptive interventions	Valuing feelings as information in practice
Task-oriented practice	Facilitative and challenging interventions
Blueprints to determine action	Critical reflection on other voices
Focus on limited outcomes	Experimentation and creativity
Over-emphasis on risk	Exploring reasoning about risk
Supervisor retains authoritative stance	Supervisor's feelings can be expressed
Relationship is more hierarchical	Relationship is more collaborative

Task 6: The management of risk

As noted in Chapter 4, a risk-averse stance has become a significant feature of contemporary professional practice in health and social care. Our sixth key task for beginning supervisors is to achieve balance in this environment of risk awareness. Parton (1996) has argued that in this climate both services and professions are judged in terms of how they assess and respond to risk. There are a number of background themes to this. First, since the 1980s a heightened community intolerance of professional 'misadventure', along with greater awareness of social problems has led to greater scrutiny of health and social care professionals. Knowledge of the phenomenon of abuse of service users, fear of harassment, fears of being harmed, privacy concerns, failure in duty of care, violence in the workplace and the effect of over-exposure to awful situations are among the many highly charged issues faced by practitioners. All of these issues create a sense of health and social care work being like a 'minefield'.

Second, the removal of the 'paternalistic, benevolent cloak' worn by previous generations of health and social care providers leaves practitioners less secure in their identity (Parton 1996, pp.103–104). In services subject to high levels of media scrutiny, such as statutory social work and mental health services, one of the consequences has been a narrowing of roles. Practice emphasis has shifted from preventive and development-focused practice to 'management' of those most vulnerable client groups deemed to be 'high risk'. Risk has in itself become a criterion for targeting scarce resources. Alaszewski and Coxon (2009) suggest that large bureaucracies (such as health and social care institutions) adopt formal risk approaches which involve collecting and analyzing information. This reflects 'the aspiration to control the world and its uncertainties… The required investment of time and resources means that the formal rational approach tends to be restricted to contexts in which such investments are worthwhile, i.e. the threats and potential benefits are high' (Alaszewski and Coxon 2009, p.204). Demonstrations of trustworthiness are seen in technological assessment and other work practices, shifting attention away from reflective development and on to risk management (Beddoe 2010).

For supervisors, the management of risk can become a constant source of stress. The feared outcomes may range from simple 'botch-ups', which threaten the team's reputation, to serious harm to service users, staff or the public. Carried to extremes, this can stifle practice. Innovation may feel too risky. In one sense, risk is about the probability of 'winning' and the estimated costs of 'losing' and it is vital for supervisors and their supervisees to retain a strong sense of hopefulness to balance the sense of imminent danger that pervades their practice world.

Exploring critical reflection

Contemporary education for the professions has been greatly influenced by reflective learning approaches to practitioner development (Bond and Holland 2010; Gould and Taylor 1996; Johns and Freshwater 2005; Redmond 2004; Scaife 2010). In this shift, good practice is promoted by teaching a framework for continual self-evaluation and improvement rather than a traditional master/student relationship. Much pre-service education for nursing, social work and the allied health professions encourages the development of reflection skills during preparatory education. Chapter 5 has outlined the Reflective Learning Model of Supervision which provides a process-oriented framework to foster reflective learning in supervision sessions by making reflection central, rather than peripheral.

A reflective practice process fosters the development of an 'internal supervisor'. 'Reflection on practice' occurs with a professional supervisor and reflects on action which has already occurred. On the job reflection is 'reflection in practice' and applies to learning in the field of professional practice. Fook and Gardner (2007) sees a reflective approach as affirming other ways of knowing, such as personal experience and its interpretation in supporting a holistic understanding of the complexity of experience that practitioners encounter in their day-to-day work. A reflective approach 'tends to focus on the whole experience and the many dimensions involved: cognitive elements; feeling elements; meanings and interpretations from different perspectives' (Fook and Gardner 2007, p.25). Such an approach facilitates the discovery of the kinds of knowledge relevant to the unpredictability of practice. Bond and Holland (2010, pp.131–135) offer some intuitive methods of reflection as a starting point for reflective practice as they have found nurses can struggle to make the shift from activity to reflection. They also stress the importance of supervisees 'using an experiential learning cycle while you work, rather than only waiting for your clinical supervision sessions [as an] ultimate aim in building these reflective skills' (Bond and Holland 2010, p.141).

The Critical Reflection approach (Fook and Gardner 2007, p.27) is 'a model for improving practice' which involves a bottom-up understanding of theory and practice, the intent being to close the gap between espoused theory and enacted theory in practice. Fook and Askeland (2007) acknowledge the contribution of Brookfield (1995) when they state that what 'makes *critical reflection* critical is the focus on power...which allows the reflective process to be transformative... In this latter sense, critical reflection must incorporate an understanding of personal experiences within social, cultural and structural contexts' (2007, p.522). The vignette *Lisa* which follows illustrates Johns' point that reflection is:

being mindful of self, either within or after experience, as if a window through which the practitioner can view and focus self within the context of a particular experience, in order to confront, understand and move toward resolving the contradiction between one's vision and actual practice. (Johns 2005, p.2)

◼ VIGNETTE: LISA

Lisa, a counsellor in her fourth year of practice, starts a new job in an infertility treatment clinic. She works mainly with couples considering specialized IVF treatment who are obliged to have counselling prior to making decisions about treatment. It is hard to get on to the programme. Couples find it very stressful, and face financial, emotional and social challenges. The 'rollercoaster of emotions' for couples in infertility is well reported.

Lisa comes to supervision following a very busy first few weeks and seems stressed and quite agitated. She tells her supervisor she often finds that the male partners in the couples she sees are very hard to engage with in counselling. She calls them 'resistant', 'angry', 'defended', 'rigid'. She says their behaviour makes her suspicious and the more she notices that they 'resist' counselling the more she thinks they are probably 'control freaks' or abusive.

Lisa is not a novice and her supervisor decides to unsettle her implicit assumptions using probing and challenging reflective questions. The dialogue below is a summary of key questions and responses.

Supervisor	Supervisee
What is it that tells you that these men are control freaks and abusive?	Well I don't really know – but I assume they are by the way they behave
What sits behind these assumptions?	Men are difficult Men don't want to deal with emotions Men aren't supportive Men have too much power in these situations
What knowledge, values and beliefs might sit behind these ideas?	My feminist beliefs My awareness of women being oppressed My understanding of coercive control
Do these feelings and concerns seem similar to other experiences?	On my placement, I worked with couples who were struggling with difficult pre-school children and the men were always really angry

How do these emotions affect your use of knowledge in your practice? Can you name these feelings? (deeper level reflection)	I forget why I'm doing the counselling and just want to fight them I become frightened that the woman in the couple is being abused I feel angry when men argue with me I feel less powerful than them when I should feel more powerful because I am the professional here
How do you conceptualize your use of power in this practice?	Male clients come to counselling because that's the policy and they have to, but they should just accept it and support their wives. Just get on with it if they want the treatment. I need to use my professional authority to probe and challenge if necessary
Having discovered these beliefs and thoughts what are your feelings?	I feel shocked that I have such a long list of negative thoughts about clients
What is that feeling of shock about?	I feel that I shouldn't be negative about clients. But then I'm a feminist and I see women so often disempowered by controlling men about fertility issues

Next steps:
There is a disjuncture here between Lisa's idea of professional neutrality and the emotions generated by her instinct to offer feminist advocacy.
At this point what does she want to change? What does she see as the appropriate way to manage this disjuncture?

How would you want to act/feel differently? Can you reconcile these two parts of who you are as a practitioner?	I want to be able to understand where those feelings come from and consider all the options, including the possibility of intimate partner violence But I do need to remember that men in this situation may be acting from a place of vulnerability I need to stay mindful of my potential to make precipitate judgements I can look out for the women I work with without assuming their male partners aren't vulnerable too
What might be happening for the men in these couples?	Lack of power for men who feel vulnerable and exposed People who are dealing with infertility face many intrusive discussions and tests Counselling may feel like another invasion of privacy
What's your learning here?	I need to remember that people have multiple and complex reasons for behaving in particular ways I need to acknowledge that power in professional encounters is not always clear cut

Next steps:
Lisa has started to resolve the disjuncture. Her supervisor guides her to consider alternative ways of engaging the men in the couples she works with. She rehearses some possible interventions. She decides that her 'homework' is to locate some research about men and infertility and to make a time to consult a male counsellor in a similar service.

Through the conflict of contradiction, the commitment to realize one's vision, and understanding why things are as they are, the practitioner can gain new insights into self and be empowered to respond more congruently in future situations within a reflexive spiral towards developing practical wisdom and realizing one's vision as a lived reality. The practitioner may require guidance to overcome resistance or to be empowered to act on understanding. (Johns 2005, p.2)

Exploring culture and diversity in supervision

In the conclusion to their supervision handbook, Watkins and Milne (2014, p. 674) argue that an exploration of culture within supervision, via 'deliberate and studious consideration is vital for supervision's future' (Watkins and Milne 2014, p. 681). The last decade has seen a flourishing of scholarship on culture and supervision. In their rich collection, *Multiculturalism and Diversity in Clinical Supervision*, Falender, Shafranske and Falicov (2014) explore key issues in the development of supervisory cultural competence. The opening chapter notes that much of our understanding of cultural competence has been grounded in the work of Sue and colleagues (see for example Sue and Sue 1999) which emphasized competence as stemming from knowledge, skills and attitudes in the domains of practitioner awareness of values and biases, 'understanding the worldview of the "culturally different"', and developing culturally relevant interventions (Falender *et al.* 2014, p.5).

There have been challenges, however, to the idea that cultural awareness, knowledge and skills are in themselves sufficient to lead to a more proactive stance that is grounded in social justice. Danso (2016) notes that:

The stream of literature still coming off publication lines underscores the popularity of cultural competence in cross-cultural discourse. Within this vast scholarly terrain are two opposing strands of thought, one extolling the virtues of cultural competence, the other questioning its effectiveness as a model for cross-cultural work. (p.415)

Indeed, the concept of cultural competence itself has been criticized as tokenistic, focusing on knowledge about 'other' cultures, assuming that practitioners and supervisors are always from the dominant culture, and for the weakness of the analysis of power relations (Hernández and McDowell 2010). Space does not allow a full discussion of the complexity of the debates. In the following section, a brief consideration of how supervision is being interpreted in other than dominant white contexts serves to illustrate the limits of cultural competence (Beddoe and Davys 2016).

In countries with a colonial past, such as Australia, Canada, and Aotearoa

New Zealand, professional practices came pre-packaged with inherent dominant cultural frameworks that cascaded into our models of learning and supervision. Given the understanding of the importance of isomorphism in supervision practice that has been explored in Chapter 2 (Edwards and Chen 1999), as new approaches to professional practice have developed, we have required new thinking about whether traditional models of supervision work for all supervisors and supervisees in all contexts (Beddoe 2015a; 2015b). Such exploration necessarily considers that supervisors and supervisees may well be from communities and cultures that are not dominant. Webber-Dreadon (1999, pp.7–8) writes: 'supervision primarily reflects the cultural values and aspirations of the typically monocultural dominant Pākehā [NZ European origins] group' and the development of alternative indigenous models has 'suffered the impact of subtle continued colonization through the process of avoidance and non-encouragement' (Webber-Dreadon 1999, pp.7–8). Social service agencies are keen to employ indigenous workers to ensure that cultural values and perspectives are present but then do not always 'have a process for inviting them in and ensuring they are part of the practice process' (Bradley, Jacob and Bradley 1999, p.6).

In recent research Wallace (2019) explores the interconnectedness of ngā aroro (key concepts) from Te Ao Māori (the Māori world) that influence the depth of critical reflection in supervision and enhance the cultural effectiveness of supervision. Her research challenges supervision to take a fresh view of supervision theory and practice, considering the strengths of supervision provided by those outside disciplinary boundaries, and explores the cultural significance of supervision being developed and evaluated with indigenous aspirations at the centre.

New supervisors (of all professions) are advised to recognize the limiting nature of one world view, which tends to be the one we have been socialized to, both personally and professionally. We note how extraordinarily hard it is to ensure that another view is able to be freely expressed and incorporated into thinking about the professional practice work we do in health and social care. Bi-cultural supervisors, and those who have experienced and reflected on cultural differences, may be more sensitive to the different cultural frameworks present in their supervisees' practice. Hernández and McDowell (2010, p.29) have urged supervisors to engage in critical analysis of the dynamics of power and to demonstrate 'critical social awareness and cultural humility' in order to build effective supervision relationships.

Supervisors from dominant cultures are particularly vulnerable to unconsciously perpetuating institutional racism through adopting models of supervision that are grounded in the dominant culture with associated unawareness of privilege. Leavy (2017, p.1) writes:

privilege, power, oppression, and domination operate in complex and insidious ways, impacting groups and individuals. And yet, these forces that affect our lives so deeply seem to at once operate in plain sight and lurk in the shadows, making them difficult to discern.

In cross-cultural relationships in supervision there is often a great deal of unspoken 'talk' happening that impacts on the formation of an open relationship with a high degree of trust. Participants often talk about feeling that there are unstated challenges around competence and that there is the potential for collusion around issues of poor practice. It is simply too scary for either party to ask for or give uncensored, thoughtful and constructive feedback, and this fear may be exacerbated by anxieties about unspoken differences. Supervisors and supervisees who ignore or minimize the differences between them risk mirroring the tensions and micro-aggressions inherent in the oppressive worlds in which users of services struggle.

Ultimately, reflection on cultural assumptions leads practitioners towards an empowering openness which challenges and renews vision. Within reflective supervision a space is created where questions can be asked and cultural differences are valued. Unpacking the nature of cultural identity suggests that supervisors unpack their own cultural narratives in considering both their relationship with their supervisees and the professional work that all are engaged in (Hair and O'Donoghue 2009, p.78). This means recognizing the journeys by which we all arrived in our current circumstances: our heritage, our migration stories, our different social, cultural and political lens and the ecology of how and where we live and work.

Critical inquiry in supervision

Applying a critical lens in supervision requires supervisors to 'explore and reflect on the way the supervisors, the supervisees and the agencies work with the service users/clients' thus ensuring that 'practitioners' actions and those of the organization are more explicit and conscious' (Noble and Irwin 2009, p.354). As noted in Chapter 2, Hair and O'Donoghue (2009) have addressed how power, culture and gender influence relationships and yet they are not explicitly addressed in most supervision models. These authors, from Canada and New Zealand respectively, argue that social constructionist supervision differs from traditional approaches to supervision in several important ways. First, following the principles of the strengths-based approaches to supervision described in Chapter 2, it is important for supervisors to develop a collaborative approach and ensure that supervisees manifest agency in a co-constructive process in 'supervision conversations' (p.77). Recognition of plurality and diversity of knowledge requires supervisors educated in the dominant western models of supervision to practise 'continual critical self-reflection'. As Tsui, O'Donoghue and Ng (2014, p.240) express so succinctly: 'when your worldview is relative and multiple, when you understand that how the world is perceived comes from different sources, and when you recognize that you are not the center of the world, you are becoming more culturally competent'.

Hair and O'Donoghue's (2009) approach brings to the foreground issues of social justice in practice and how supervision sessions can address 'structural barriers such as poverty, legislative policies, and suitable housing alongside clients' relational conflicts and distresses' (p.78). Social constructionist supervisors 'ask "*curious*" questions about idiosyncratic descriptions of local community knowledge of the supervisees and clients, including the influence of dominant socio-political and economic contexts such as national laws, tribal expectations, and spiritual understandings' (p.78). Similar questions as those used in the Reflective Learning Model of Supervision are used here, for example: "'I wonder..." or "I am curious about..." can help to create a transparent stance and stimulate collaborative knowledge production' (Hair and O'Donoghue 2009, p.79).

Ethics

'The essence of ethical supervision is creating a good "home" for ethical decision making' (Beddoe and Davys 2016, p.89). Professional ethics can ideally be explored in confidential, supportive and learning-focused supervision. Ethical principles offer a framework for thinking through the challenges of practice, stating that explicit consideration of these principles 'gives a degree of assurance that, whatever the actual outcomes, decisions have been taken from an ethical standpoint' (Scaife 2001, p.125). In this era of risk management, 'documenting the thought processes that underpin a decision can also protect the professional in the event of subsequent litigation' (Scaife 2001, p.125). Schön (1987) suggested that professionals are critically aware of ethical and moral choices and the implications of decisions when faced with problems in situ. He challenged the notion that professional competence was largely linked to the application of specific technical and/ or theoretical knowledge which was gained primarily through preparatory education. Rather, he suggested that competent professionals think, reflect, experiment and act within practice situations, thus constructing a more fluid notion of competence. Competence includes the ability to enter into dialogue about difficult situations, to apply thoughtfulness, open-mindedness and moral reasoning to those problems.

Supervision is often seen as the site for this continuing development of practitioners' ethical competence. Supervisors ensure ethical competence, a major part of the actual 'oversight' component of the role, through questioning actions, seeking the other point of view, considering alternative responses or interpretations and, most importantly, encouraging and challenging practitioners to think critically.

Of course, all of this would be easier if ethics was a simple thing. Banks (2008, p.1239) explains that the 'postmodern' turn in sociological and philosophical thinking has contributed to a questioning of universal values, all-embracing foundational theories (including ethical theories) and the legitimacy and roles of 'expert professional practitioners'. This complicates ethical thinking in professional practice, requiring us to reflect on the decisions we make and importantly understanding the cultural, social, political and economic milieus in which we live and work (Carroll and Shaw 2013). Bagnall (1998) argues that professions are less confident and sure of their legitimate authority in the full gaze of a critical media and public and that the 'rulebook' of ethical codes is no longer absolute. He suggests that enhanced tolerance and understanding of difference and diversity in our society mean greater contradiction in the moral dimensions of our professional and personal lives. Situational ethics tend to be grounded in a particular cultural context in contrast to the past 'universal claims' for moral rightness (Bagnall 1998).

Paradoxically, the professionalization of those professions more recently regulated has seen a proliferation of codes. New supervisors may feel a very deep sense of insecurity about how to guide ethical decision making. Scaife (2001) suggests that traditional ethical principles offer a framework for thinking through the challenges of practice. She suggests that explicit consideration of these principles 'gives a degree of assurance that, whatever the actual outcomes, decisions have been taken from an ethical standpoint' and in this era of risk management, 'documenting the thought processes that underpin a decision can also protect the professional in the event of subsequent litigation' (p.125).

Conclusion

What is required of supervisors is the development of an essentially reflexive practice incorporating the following qualities: an empathetic responsiveness to the subjective experience of others; sensitivity to the diversity of knowledge and world views; and the recognition that each professional encounter is unique. In complex multi-professional, multi-agency contexts a supervisor may also need to negotiate contested realities. Awareness of one's own limits of knowledge and competence also underpins a willingness to accept that you cannot meet all the professional needs of each supervisee, and to seek further consultation when indicated.

Ryan (2004) notes that 'Supervision is an inquiry into practice. It is a compassionate appreciative inquiry... In supervision we re-write the stories of our own practice...supervision interrupts practice. It wakes us up to what we are doing. When we are alive to what we are doing we wake up to what is, instead of falling asleep in the comfort stories of our clinical routines' (p.44).

CHAPTER 7

Skills for Supervision

The key task of the supervisor is to provide the space within which a supervisee reviews, reflects on, develops and refines their practice within the boundaries mandated by professional and organizational standards, knowledge and policy. The Reflective Learning Model of Supervision describes a path to this development and refinement through reflective learning. Reflective learning is learning which emerges through exploration of a supervisee's experience. It is a process of discovery rather than instruction.

A supervisor who works from this model of supervision must have certain attributes if they wish to develop and maintain this context for learning. To ensure that the supervisee is free to explore, the supervisor must encourage exploration. In order that the supervisee makes new connections, the supervisor must be open to and be able to recognize and validate these connections. To this end, the supervisor must value exploration, tolerate uncertainty, accommodate difference and remain open and curious about possibility. 'Curiosity' and 'not knowing' are connected concepts (Ruch 2009, p.352) which assist supervisors and supervisees to avoid the traps of linear thinking and understand that there is more than one truth and reality. When a supervisor exhibits these attributes, the supervisee is encouraged and able to express ideas, to explore values and beliefs, to examine assumptions and judgements and to acknowledge and express feelings. 'Interest prompts a person to explore new things, and to be open to new ideas, experiences and actions. These broaden a person's options' (Gazzola and Theriault 2007, p.191). The supervisor must also approach the work of the supervisee with good faith. By good faith we mean the belief that, until indicated otherwise, the supervisee is behaving to the best of their ability and has the capacity to learn and develop.

A good supervisor however brings more than attributes to the supervision forum. Although there are claims to the contrary, neither experience as a supervisee nor competence as a practitioner are adequate or sufficient preparation to become a supervisor (Watkins and Wang 2014).

Skill and competence are required, and training, as mentioned in Chapter 3, is an important prerequisite for those taking on the role of supervisor (Bernard and Goodyear 2014; Carroll 2014; Watkins *et al.* 2019). Despite this endorsement for training we note that such preparation and training are not universally available or required by professional bodies or health and social service organizations (Watkins and Wang 2014) and accounts of harmful supervision point to inadequacy in this area (Beddoe 2017, p.99). Having addressed the process of supervisor development in Chapter 6, in this chapter we focus on the interventions and skills of supervision.

Supervision is a skill-based activity where conscious and intentional use of 'interventions' is necessary in order that purposeful and quality reflection and learning occur. Heron (2001, p.3) has defined an intervention 'as an identifiable piece of verbal and/or non-verbal behaviour that is part of the practitioner's service to the client'. Within supervision, an intervention can therefore be described as an identifiable piece of verbal and/or non-verbal behaviour that is part of the supervisor's service to the supervisee.

In supervision, as in most if not all human service work, interventions are exercised in the context of a relationship. The qualities brought to the relationship by both parties, and the manner in which the relationship is developed and maintained, as discussed in Chapter 3, will influence the success of the interventions.

Several useful frameworks of interventions, identified in counselling literature, have been adapted for supervision. The framework which we continue to find the most useful describes five categories of intervention – facilitative, catalytic, conceptual, confrontative and prescriptive – and is based on that of Loganbill *et al.* (1982, pp.31–36). Each of the interventions comprises a subset of 'skills' and these are set out in Table 7.1.

Table 7.1: Overview of interventions and skills for supervision

Facilitative interventions	Facilitative interventions provide the conditions of supervision – the base on which the supervision process can rest (Loganbill et al. 1982).
	Skills of facilitative interventions: core listening, engagement and attending skills, paraphrasing, reflecting, silence, positive regard, attention to comfort and needs of space and privacy.
Catalytic interventions	Catalytic interventions, along with confrontative interventions, are aimed to promote growth, development and learning. Catalytic interventions are intended to promote change through assisted self-examination and self-discovery.
	Skills of catalytic interventions: open question enquiry, feedback, reframing.

Conceptual interventions	Conceptual interventions provide the supervisee with information and knowledge. This knowledge can range from empirical research findings to procedural information and to shared practice wisdom from the supervisor. The aim of conceptual interventions is to provide information which will assist the supervisee in their understanding and problem solving.
	Skills of conceptual interventions: information giving, prompts for procedural and formal knowledge.
Confrontative interventions	Confrontative interventions are designed to confront the supervisee with aspects of themselves of which they may not be aware or which they have not considered to be important but which are limiting their practice or understanding. Confrontative interventions often involve 'home truths' and are also, alongside catalytic interventions, intended to promote change.
	Skill of confrontative interventions: challenge, corrective feedback.
Prescriptive interventions	Prescriptive interventions are used when it is imperative that a supervisee behaves or acts in a certain way. This may be at a time of crisis, where there is potential risk or because of prescribed policy or protocol.
	Skill of prescriptive interventions: directives.

Supervision interventions and skills

Facilitative interventions

Facilitative interventions include the baseline skills which underpin all supervision. They are the foundation from which the other interventions can be made and help to create an open and accepting environment for supervision where reflection and introspection can occur.

Skills

Listening, attending, engagement, paraphrasing
This cluster of 'basic' skills provides the underlying conditions of supervision and supports the supervision relationship. The skills demonstrate positive regard, interest and the importance of the supervisee as the central player in the supervision process. Smythe *et al.* (2009) describe listening as 'the how of supervision that perhaps also tends to be taken for granted, yet sets the play in motion' (Smythe *et al.* 2009 p.18).

Listening in this context is not a passive activity but requires the supervisor to be present and engaged. Miller and Rollnick (2013) identify six traps to engagement and listening in motivational interviewing (pp.40–45) which can be equally well applied to supervision. The focus, in many of these 'traps', is on the listener (supervisor) who, assuming a position of control, pursues their agenda with scant attention to the agenda and desired outcomes of the speaker (supervisee). The ensuing exchange is neither collaborative nor negotiated.

- The assessment trap: the supervisor, in control, may question the supervisee to gather considerable (unnecessary) information before any discussion can develop and before establishing the supervisee's issue for supervision.

- The expert trap: when the supervisor believes they have elicited sufficient information from the supervisee, the supervisor will formulate and announce the solution.

- The premature focus trap: without establishing or hearing the supervisee's views and understanding of the issue, the supervisor directs the discussion according to their own perception and opinion.

- The labelling trap: the supervisor in listening to the supervisee's story draws their own conclusions and formulates a conclusion or diagnosis without discussion or exploration of the supervisee's views.

When caught in either of the following two traps, rather than asserting control in the supervision session, the supervisor may be seen to collude with the supervisee:

- The blaming trap: when a supervisee presents a situation where fault is identified, the trap for the supervisor is to collude with the supervisee and attribute blame, rather than exploring responsibility, professional accountability and a possible way forward.

- Finally, Miller and Rollnick (2013) identify the 'chat trap'. In supervision, this represents supervision which is unstructured, has no clear issues or goals and where supervisees are not encouraged to explore and consider their practice. A meandering conversation ensues.

Listening in supervision promotes engagement when the supervisor's focus is indeed on listening and not on their own agenda. Careful listening and accurate paraphrasing of the ideas and actions which the supervisees share and describe both contribute to the authenticity of the supervision relationship and convey support for the supervisee (Bond and Holland 2010).

Silence
Silence provides a space for the supervisee to internalize and consider what has happened in the session to date. Exchanges between the supervisee

and the supervisor, insights which have occurred, the supervisee's internal response to issues raised and general private reflection on the issue under discussion are all examples of what can be considered in moments of silence. Silence also provides a space in which the supervisee can determine their response. Moments of silence are particularly important for supervisees who have an 'introvert' learning profile and who require time for internal processing of information. Farmer (1988), for example, found that when supervisors paused for approximately three to five seconds after a supervisee spoke, a number of changes were observed. These included increases in: 'supervisee confidence, shown in fewer inflected responses'; the 'incidence of supervisee speculative thinking'; supervisee questions; a 'variety of supervisee utterances' and perhaps most importantly, an increase in the 'contributions by "quiet" supervisees' (Farmer 1988, pp.34–35).

Self-disclosure

When using the skill of self-disclosure, the supervisor draws from their own experience and practice to share thoughts, feelings and learning with the supervisee. These may be thoughts and feelings that have occurred during the supervision session or experiences from the past. Importantly, this sharing of information, when it includes doubts, uncertainty and mistakes, has been shown to increase the value of the supervisor in the eyes of supervisees (Krause and Allen (1988) reported in Lizzio *et al.* 2009, p.130). Lizzio *et al.* (2009, p.130) suggest that 'supervisor openness may initiate a virtuous cycle: supervisor openness leading to increased trust, promoting, in turn, supervisee openness, providing the basis for authentic learning'.

As with all interventions, supervisors need to be purposeful and economical with the use of self-disclosure. The risk is that supervisors will hijack the session and deflect the focus from the supervisee on to themselves. A supervisor may well ask themselves: what is my purpose for sharing this information? How will it facilitate the supervisee's exploration and reflection?

Closed questions

Closed questions are those which can be answered by 'yes' or 'no' (*Did you visit the family by yourself?*) or, may ask for a fact (*How may children are in the family?*). They are used to verify or confirm situations and to gather and clarify information. Closed questions can be used to provoke quick answers and to shape, define or identify details of situations. In general, closed questions do not generate reflection and so should be used sparingly.

Positive feedback

Feedback is a central and important skill which is woven throughout supervision. Because of its importance, we have discussed this in a separate section later in this chapter.

Catalytic interventions

Catalytic interventions are aimed to promote growth, development and learning through self-discovery and exploration. The skills of catalytic interventions include: open question enquiry, logical consequences, feedback and reframing.

Open-question enquiry

Open-question enquiry is central to the Reflective Learning Model of Supervision. Open questions allow exploration of all aspects of practice and lead to new and revitalized work through insight and understanding. The art of open-question enquiry requires the supervisor to have the capacity for meaningful engagement in the supervision relationship, the humility to put self-preoccupation aside and listen, curiosity and a versatile framework of questions.

Logical consequences

Logical consequences are aimed to alert the supervisee to the probable, or possible, results of their actions and to assist them in decision making.

Feedback

(See the section on feedback later in this chapter.)

Reframing

This is a skill where the supervisor employs a combination of practice wisdom and professional perspective to present the supervisee with an alternative framework through which to view their supervision issue.

■ VIGNETTE: DAMIEN

Damien, a new team leader, was distressed that two of his best team members had, with very little warning, resigned. He discussed this with his supervisor and shared his concern that, although he had done his best to support and extend their work experience, he had obviously not done enough to keep them interested in their roles. His supervisor suggested that, rather than not doing a good job, Damien had done an excellent job and had provided the two team members with confidence and skills which enabled them to expand their professional horizons into new areas.

This reframe encouraged Damien to view these team members from a different frame of reference and allowed him to consider how he could offer more opportunity for development in his team in general and so move forward rather than remain 'stuck' in his preoccupation with his own 'incompetence'.

Catalytic interventions, in conjunction with confrontative interventions, can be considered as the power house of supervision. By unsettling and disturbing ways of thinking, being and doing, these interventions deepen and provide a critical lens for reflection. New understanding, new insights and new learning are promoted. Ryan (2004) captures this in her description of supervision as a process which interrupts practice, alerting us to our automatic routines so that we can create new ways. Similarly, Fook and Gardiner (2007) consider that it is the 'unsettling individual assumptions' in the process of critical reflection which bring about 'social changes' (p.16).

Conceptual interventions

Conceptual interventions provide the supervisee with information and knowledge in order to assist their understanding and problem solving. This knowledge may be empirical research findings, procedural information or it may be shared practice wisdom from the supervisor. A clear distinction needs to be made between information giving and education. Supervision is educative but it is not formal teaching. When a supervisor finds that they are spending significant supervision time 'providing information' it is important to consider whether the supervisee has professional development needs which are beyond the learning that can occur in supervision. Has the supervisee become 'dependent' on receiving information rather than seeking it themselves and has supervision 'blurred' into an education session? (See Figure 2.2.)

Lizzio and Wilson (2002, p.29) consider that the purpose of developmental approaches to supervision is to support 'the supervisee's progression towards autonomous mastery'. They also note that practitioners may vary in their motivation and capacity for increasing self-management. Invitations to supervisors, to offer advice to supervisees, may mean several things.

Supervisee	Meaning
I have no idea what to do:	...and I haven't thought about it
	...I have thought about it and I still don't know what to do
I don't know what to do:	...I have thought about it, but I am not sure. I am not confident that I have the right answer
	...I have thought about it and I have some ideas that I want to check out with you
	...I have developed a plan/strategy which I want to critique

Before offering advice, supervisors may therefore wish to consider how the advice, and the process of giving it, will assist the supervisee to develop ownership of the problem. Giving advice too readily may mean that:

- the supervisee doesn't have to think

- the supervisee's self-doubt is reinforced

- there is a lost opportunity to examine what the supervisee has thought of already

- there is no validation or shaping of the supervisee's problem-solving ability

- there is no recognition, confirmation or validation of the supervisee's good ideas

- there is no critical discussion of the issue.

When supervision is considered as a collaborative exchange, requests for advice can be an opportunity for both affirmation, and building and developing the supervisee's own problem-solving ability. The process of responding to requests for advice, when accompanied by reflective enquiry and dialogue, allows for the knowledge and thinking which the supervisee has already applied to this question to be acknowledged, explored and validated.

Lizzio and Wilson (2002) recommend a focus on the skills of self-regulation: 'self-organization, self-evaluation, information seeking, goal setting and planning and self-monitoring of actions' (p.29). To avoid supervision becoming dominated by didactic interventions, supervisors might set 'takeaway' tasks that foster self-directed learning and active problem solving. Bond and Holland (2010) also offer a useful suggestion: 'a general rule of thumb is that the more technical a problem is, the more relevant it is to offer information or advice' (p.184).

Confrontative interventions

Confrontative interventions are designed to present supervisees with aspects of themselves of which they may not be aware, or which they have not considered to be important, and which are limiting their practice or understanding. 'A confronting intervention unequivocally tells an uncomfortable truth' (Heron 2001, p.59). Despite the name, confrontative interventions are not adversarial but rather aimed to promote change and movement. When faced with aspects of themselves of which they have not been previously aware, supervisees typically will become unsettled and feel a degree of discomfort. As similarly provoked by some catalytic interventions, it is through the process of resolving the unsettled state or discomfort that the supervisee discovers learning and change occurs. When handled well, confrontative interventions can be exciting (if at times uncomfortable) moments when supervisees see new possibilities and gain new understanding about themselves. The skills of confrontative interventions are challenge and feedback.

Challenge

In supervision, moments for challenge can arise when a supervisor hears or sees the supervisee limiting their understanding and effectiveness in practice through beliefs, attitudes or actions. Most often, these behaviours will be outside, or on the edge, of the supervisee's awareness. The process of challenge is to draw the supervisee's attention to these aspects in order that the supervisee becomes aware of the behaviour and can consider change. Lizzio et al. (2009) identify four ways in which a supervisor may challenge a supervisee: 'Inviting critical reflection of their assumptions and ideas... identifying their inconsistencies or "blind spots", or by providing critical feedback or raising uncomfortable issues that have emerged in supervision' (Lizzio et al. 2009, p.129).

■ VIGNETTE: HONORIA

Honoria was considering options for an elderly service user who was in the terminal stages of her illness. Her supervisor noticed that all Honoria's options included some form of residential care. When the supervisor pointed this out to her Honoria argued passionately against the proposition that the service user might want to die at home.

With the supervisor's help, Honoria recognized that she had a belief set about the needs of the elderly who she regarded as having little voice to assert their rights and who, as a consequence, seldom received the care they needed and deserved. Dying at home without 24-hour nursing care was, in Honoria's view, an example of this type of neglect. She had never considered that there was an alternative view.

The behaviour 'challenged' by the supervisor may include discrepancies between different aspects of the supervisee's behaviour or discrepancies between the supervisee's assessment of a situation and the assessment of that situation by others. These discrepancies can be between:

- what a supervisee says and what they do

- what a supervisee says and their non-verbal behaviour

- how the supervisee assesses a situation/client and how the supervisor assesses or experiences that client or situation.

■ VIGNETTE: RICHARD

Richard was describing a practice situation which he found very frustrating when his supervisor asked him how he would describe his approach to working with this particular service user. Richard was quick to reply that he was taking a very supportive and accepting role encouraging the service user to plan and initiate her own course of action. Given the preceding supervision conversation, the supervisor challenged Richard on this: 'I am very puzzled about what you have just said. On the one hand, you tell me that your approach has been supportive and allowed the service user to act in her own time; on the other hand, you have just spent ten minutes expressing your frustration that she has not followed your plan for her.'

By juxtaposing the two contradictory aspects of a supervisee's story or presentation, the supervisor provides the supervisee with the opportunity to consider and explore these incongruities.

Challenge is possibly one of the most potent and useful of the confrontative intervention skills: 'confronting is about consciousness-raising, about waking people up to what it is they are not aware of in themselves that is critical for their own well being and the well being of others' (Heron 2001, p.60). However, challenge is a skill which is not independent of support. Lizzio *et al.* (2009) describe an orthogonal relationship between challenge and support and caution that while a 'supervisor's goal is to provide sufficient challenge to stimulate growth and development', this challenge needs to be balanced by appropriate support so that the supervisee will not 'retreat' from the learning forum (Lizzio *et al.* 2009, p.130).

Corrective feedback
(See the section on feedback later in this chapter.)

Prescriptive interventions

Prescriptive interventions provide the supervisee with a specific plan of action for a particular situation. These are generally situations where there are no options. Apart from crisis situations, where client or supervisee safety is at risk and which apply to practitioners at all stages of experience, prescriptive interventions will most often be used with new practitioners, or practitioners who are new to a particular practice setting. The main prescriptive skill is a directive.

A directive may be used in three ways. It may be informative in that it provides the supervisee with precise instructions about how a certain procedure must be carried out: *'When this situation occurs you must ensure that form 362a is completed and given immediately to the lead practitioner.'*

It may be instructive about how the supervisee must act now (usually in a crisis or where safety is an issue): *'You must immediately phone the crisis team and alert the emergency services'* or *'I want you to immediately report what you have just relayed to me to your manager.'*

Finally, it may be corrective and require a supervisee to address a particular situation: *'It is not appropriate to receive gifts of that nature. You must return it immediately.'* Situations where directives are corrective may at times lead to performance issues and a supervisor will need to consider their position regarding the supervisee, the service user, the profession and the organization.

In most supervision relationships, prescriptive interventions will be rarely used and when they are it will be in situations similar to those above. If prescriptive interventions are the norm, it is probable that supervision has slid into performance management.

Giving and receiving feedback

As Carroll says, 'We all have blind, deaf and dumb spots. Listening to another speak into our lives through feedback, when done in the right way and with the right intention, is invaluable as a source of, and springboard for, new learning' (2014, p.54).

Feedback is 'a central activity of clinical supervision' (Bernard and Goodyear 2014, p.233), and while definitions of feedback vary there is general consensus that feedback is 'the process of telling another individual how they are experienced' (Hawkins and Shohet 2006, p.133). Reports from practitioners, however, suggest that feedback is often poorly handled in supervision (Ladany *et al.* 2013) and at times experienced by supervisees as 'highly critical and shaming' (Beddoe 2017, p.92). Feedback that 'hurts, wounds, shames and humiliates…does little to contribute to learning' (Carroll and Gilbert 2011, p.130). Conversely, positive or affirmative feedback can be limp, generalized, at times patronizing, or worse, rarely given. In the absence of positive feedback, Gazzola and Theriault (2007) found that supervisees 'felt overly criticised and did not feel appreciation for what they may have done well' (p.197).

To be effective, feedback needs to be present at all stages of a supervision session. The giving and receiving of feedback both enhances and tests the supervision relationship and is a skill which can be employed by both the supervisor and the supervisee. To build relationships requires work from all parties concerned. To maintain a relationship also requires work and includes the opportunity for needs and feelings to be expressed and for feedback to be given and received. When, within a supervision relationship, giving and receiving feedback is a regular and accepted practice there is opportunity for honesty and integrity to occur. Giving and receiving honest feedback requires courage which in turn contributes to a robust and trusting relationship.

Corrective or negative feedback, which provides information on behaviours that are not helpful, is possibly one of the hardest skills to master. Corrective feedback is often accompanied by associations of reprimand and powerlessness from past experiences, particularly from childhood when powerlessness was more often the reality and reprimand frequently the case. Within supervision, feedback is intended to assist learning. Corrective feedback, as a confrontative intervention, may not be a comfortable experience but when handled well is a catalyst for learning. In a study designed to explore effective and ineffective supervision, Ladany *et al.* (2013) found that supervisees 'can handle challenges, and in fact, may welcome challenges, especially within a positive supervisory relationship' (p.41).

Confirmatory or positive feedback may also be problematic if it becomes distorted by cultural or familial messages about praise and self-glorification. In these situations, positive feedback may be dismissed, minimized or critiqued to find ulterior messages. The art of giving feedback includes preparation, appropriate timing, thoughtfulness about context, and clarity of purpose. When feedback is given with respect, honesty and with an opportunity for discussion, learning can occur.

Preparation for feedback in supervision

The groundwork for creating a base for safe and purposeful feedback occurs during the initial phase of the supervision relationship when the supervision contract is negotiated, as discussed in Chapter 3. Here the purpose for regular feedback is explored and expectations are clarified. The supervisor and supervisee will discuss and agree how feedback is best given by the supervisor in order that it can be heard and considered by the supervisee. This groundwork may also include how feedback will occur in situations where practice is observed. Importantly, the mutual and individual responsibilities for the feedback process can be discussed and understood. Feedback, we believe, is a shared process where both parties have a role and hold responsibility.

The positioning of the feedback process as a two-way responsibility is illustrated by Hewson and Carroll (2016) through a very useful analogy. Employing a sporting metaphor, they describe three types of feedback: killer, cricket and collaborative. Killer feedback describes the process when 'the supervisor throws a ball that shatters the practitioner, eliciting humiliation and shame' (p.130). Cricket feedback 'occurs when the supervisor keeps bowling balls in the hope that they will get past the practitioner's defences' (p.130). Finally, collaborative feedback allows the supervisor to throw feedback balls to the practitioner which the practitioner is both able and willing to catch. 'Getting feedback', Hewson and Carroll observe, 'is not a passive process of being given something, but an active process of receiving' (p.129).

▓ VIGNETTE: RUSSELL

When they were negotiating the supervision contract, Russell and his supervisor discussed how Russell would like to receive feedback in supervision. Russell was pleased to be asked this question. He was excited about the idea of receiving feedback from his supervisor but he knew that in reality it may not be so comfortable. Russell was able to identify his ambivalence and his concern that he might become defensive and not hear what his supervisor had to say. Together, Russell and his supervisor discussed ways to minimize Russell's possible defensive reaction. Russell knew that he appreciated the opportunity to be his own critic in the first instance. They agreed therefore that the supervisor would ask Russell to give his own assessment of any situation before the supervisor gave her feedback. They also agreed that, if it were not possible or appropriate for Russell to provide his own critique, the supervisor would announce that she was going to give feedback before launching into it. 'I want to give you some feedback...' would be a cue to Russell and allow him to hold himself open to hear what the supervisor had to say. Russell also realized he would value opportunities for specific feedback on aspects of his practice which he identified himself. His supervisor was very happy to give him this feedback and suggested they could also arrange for her to directly observe his practice and give feedback if he wished. They agreed to review this particular aspect of supervision after six months.

Russell's supervisor then asked Russell how he would like to give feedback to her about their supervison together...

This exchange during the negotiation of the supervision contract not only prepared the relationship for moments of feedback, it also placed the supervisee in a position where he was responsible for his behaviour and took shared responsibility for the feedback process.

Noting that there are a number of pitfalls into which a supervisor may stumble when giving feedback, Hewson and Carroll (2016) reinforce the importance of understanding that the feedback process is relational, negotiated and attuned to the uniqueness of each individual supervisee.

Having established the ground rules for the feedback process, the supervisor may also consider how they can best compose and frame the feedback. Employing the acronym 'CORBS' Hawkins and Shohet (2012) provide a clear structure which helps the feedback provider to organize both their thoughts and their words. Table 7.2 provides a summary of CORBS, and brief guidelines follow.

Table 7.2: The CORBS feedback framework

Clear – be clear about what feedback you want to give and why you want to give it.
Owned – use 'I' statements, as you are describing your own perception of the behaviour.
Regular – remember that feedback needs to be threaded through all, or most, supervision sessions not something that happens once or twice a year.
Balanced – a range of feedback needs to be given: corrective, confirmatory and reflective (wondering).
Specific – the feedback needs to be concrete and relate to specific behaviour or events.

Hawkins and Shohet 2012, p.160

Feedback must be clear

The first important step before giving feedback is to be clear about what feedback is to be given and why. If the feedback is particularly confronting, when in the session will it best be given to ensure that the supervisee has sufficient time to reflect and respond? If a particular supervisee is grappling with a range of issues, it may be helpful to prioritize feedback and spread it out over time in order that they are not overwhelmed. Even the most robust practitioner has only so much capacity to hear and integrate corrective negative feedback. Similarly, when the feedback is confirmatory, care needs to be taken to ensure that the supervisee has space to 'hear' and appreciate the affirmation.

The relationship between feedback and change

When giving feedback, it is important to be clear about the intended outcome. Feedback, according to the earlier definitions, does not include a request for change. Feedback is the process of 'telling' a supervisee or 'informing' a supervisee about how their behaviour is experienced or perceived in order to bring it to the supervisee's awareness for consideration. Feedback thus provides an invitation to consider an aspect of behaviour which includes an opportunity, and an invitation, to change.

Before giving feedback to a supervisee, it is therefore important for the supervisor to consider whether the supervisee has the option not to change. If the intent is clearly for the supervisee to change their behaviour, then the supervisor needs to make an explicit request to that effect. If change is required, what are the parameters around that change?

When change is the required response, the feedback needs to be followed by a prescriptive intervention. The DESC script, in Table 7.3, which had its origins in assertiveness training and literature (Bolton 1979, p. 153) of the 1970s and was later developed by Bower and Bower (1991, pp.87–96), continues to be a most useful formula for moving from feedback to a request for change.

Table 7.3: The DESC script

Describe the behaviour you want changed: *When you speak to family members I hear you giving out a lot of very detailed information with no checks to see if the family understands what they are agreeing to.*
Express your concern (feelings): *I am really concerned that this important information is not being absorbed by the families.*
Specify the change in behaviour you want: *In future, I want you to spend more time and to check that the family understands what you are saying. I also want you to give the family a written summary of the discussion.*
Consequences – explain the reason you want the change: *In that way, we will know what information has been given and that the family has a record of the discussion.*

Feedback must be owned

The use of 'I' statements is a basic tenet of good communication. When the person giving the feedback uses the first person pronoun 'I', the feedback is firmly located as the perception, experience or assessment of that person and allows the recipient a space in which to consider the information. 'I find your behaviour disrespectful when you talk over your colleagues.' This statement identifies the behaviour and the speaker's response to it, but avoids labelling and generalizations; whereas 'Everyone thinks you are rude and disrespectful' is generalized, non-specific and may provoke defensiveness and denial.

Feedback must be regular

Feedback needs to be a regular and normal part of the supervision process. Earlier in Chapter 5 we talked about feedback as being a routine process in the supervision cycle of the Reflective Learning Model of Supervision. If feedback is not integrated as a regular part of the supervision process, then when it does occur the 'moment' of feedback may be overwhelming and accompanied by anxiety. Feedback is most effective when it is given as close to the event as possible. This allows both supervisor and supervisee to explore 'fresh' moments which are readily retrieved from memory, and, it is hoped, unhelpful behaviours will not have been reinforced by repetition and will be more easily addressed.

Feedback must be balanced

Feedback needs to be a balance of the corrective, confirmative and reflective types. Different thoughts have been expressed as to how this balance should occur. The 'sandwich approach' recommends that corrective feedback is sandwiched between two confirmative pieces of feedback. The 'trade-off approach' suggests that every piece of corrective feedback needs to be balanced by one piece of confirmative feedback. A variation of the 'trade-off approach', in recognition of the power of corrective feedback, recommends that two pieces of confirmative feedback are needed to balance the effects of every one piece of corrective feedback. We do not subscribe to any of these approaches.

When confirmatory feedback is coupled with corrective feedback it loses its potency and is often dismissed, not heard or treated with suspicion. The confirmatory feedback is frequently accompanied with a 'but': 'I really liked the way you introduced the service user to the possible treatment options *but…*'. The 'but' sits as a potential qualifier for the affirmation, a segue to the critical feedback, and supervisees are often unsure which feedback to focus on and believe. It is important that supervisees know and can trust what their supervisors think of their practice and can trust that positive feedback does not come with a proviso. Supervision is a professional practice and as such there is an expectation that professionals will accept and use corrective or negative feedback without the need for sugar-coating. That being said, it is important that there is a balance of all types of feedback and particular generosity given to confirmatory feedback. Many practitioners work in extremely stressful situations where feedback from either the community or service users may seldom be positive. Supervision is the place where work, effort and commitment can and should be recognized, validated and celebrated without being tied to conditions.

Our model for balancing the confirmatory and the corrective feedback is to provide them separately. All of the confirmatory together and all of the corrective together. Whether the confirmatory feedback should precede the corrective or vice versa is a matter of personal choice which can be negotiated between the parties – the supervisor and the supervisee.

Feedback must be specific

Finally, feedback must be specific. It must be factual, concrete and behavioural. The supervisee needs to know what it is that they are doing well or could do differently.

When giving feedback to another person it is a useful exercise to reflect on what we have said and wonder how we would have felt if we had received that feedback delivered in that particular way. Would we understand what behaviour was being commented on? Would we have felt free to comment and discuss the feedback without defensiveness?

Reflective or 'wondering' feedback

Carroll and Gilbert's (2011) inclusion of a category called reflective feedback is a most helpful addition to the feedback skill group. They define reflective feedback as moments where behaviour is held 'up to the light to review it' (Carroll and Gilbert 2011, p.132). We call this 'wondering' feedback, which is often the moment in supervision when the supervisor shares their thoughts about, or responses to, the supervisee's practice with a 'wonder', or a tentative interpretation, that can hang in the air for consideration: 'I wonder what [the patient] was thinking when you made that comment. I noticed she drew a big breath and looked frustrated.'

During supervision, the supervisor will encounter situations where the supervisee has behaved in a manner which is 'interesting'. This may mean that they have behaved in a manner which is different from the way the supervisor would have behaved or the supervisor may be unsure about what is the best way to act. Reflective feedback is the opportunity for supervisees and supervisors to consider situations with 'wondering'. It is important to distinguish this from giving information, sharing practice wisdom or self-disclosure. It includes the opportunity for the supervisor to share their own processes or thoughts with the supervisee as a resource which may add to the information and data being considered in supervision. In this regard, it includes elements of Hawkins and Shohet's (2012) Seven-Eyed Model of Supervision where in mode 6 the supervisor is 'tentatively bringing this material into consciousness for the supervisee to explore' (Hawkins and Shohet 2012, p.102).

◼ VIGNETTE: HENRY

Henry was describing an exchange with a service user. One aspect of this exchange caught the supervisor's attention. She was uncertain what she thought about this exchange and in particular Henry's approach, so brought it forward to be 'wondered' about. 'When I heard your response I was initially concerned that it was too sharp and abrupt – but I am wondering now if it might be the best way forward...'

These moments allow the supervisor to be a co-explorer with the supervisee, sharing and debating possibilities and options.

Receiving feedback

Giving feedback in a constructive manner requires care, preparation and thought. Receiving feedback likewise requires thought and preparation. It is easy to hear feedback as an attack, and despite an understanding of the value of feedback, it is easy to take it personally. We have already outlined the importance of early discussion, negotiation and agreement about how feedback will occur in any particular supervision arrangement, but the actual experience of receiving feedback is nevertheless often shaped by how individuals are feeling about themselves and their practice at any particular time. When practitioners are feeling confident and competent in their professional roles, feedback can be exciting and stimulating. They may be looking for challenge and to be extended in their work. At other times, for instance when practitioners are new to positions or roles, confidence can be low and they look for support and reassurance rather than challenge. Acknowledgement of this, either privately or in the supervision session, is useful preparation for receiving feedback. The following are some guidelines to assist with receiving feedback.

- Take the initiative and ask for feedback.

- Negotiate with the other person how you want to receive feedback.

- Evaluate yourself first – how do you think you performed/behaved in a given situation? What would you like to do differently next time? What aspects are you pleased about?

- Remind yourself that feedback is another person's perception of you and not the 'truth'.

- Request clarity if feedback is non-specific or unclear.

- Separate positive and negative feedback so that you hear each clearly.

We include here two useful guidelines for receiving feedback from Hawkins and Shohet (2012):

- 'Listen to the feedback all the way through without judging it or jumping to a defensive response…

- Try not to explain compulsively why you did something or even explain away positive feedback.' (Hawkins and Shohet 2012, p.160)

Use of interventions in supervision

During the course of supervision, supervisors will employ interventions and skills in a manner which reflects the supervisee's developmental level and experience of the practice context.

As discussed earlier, facilitative interventions, particularly the skills of attending, engagement and listening, are fundamental to all supervision. They are the medium through which the other interventions are woven and will be used consistently throughout all sessions, regardless of the experience of the supervisee. The frequency of the use of other interventions will, however, be influenced by the experience or developmental level of the practitioner.

New practitioners, and those new to a particular field of practice, will generally require more structure and active intervention in supervision than experienced practitioners. Le Maistre, Boudreau and Pare (2006) studied the school-to-work transition' of teachers, social workers, occupational therapists and physiotherapists. Drawing on situated learning (Lave and Wenger 1991), Le Maistre *et al.* describe a journey that addresses the needs of beginning practitioners thus:

> By engaging newcomers in authentic but not critical or central tasks, by gradually increasing both the difficulty of the work and the autonomy of the learners, and by the subtle application of just-in-time teaching and assessment, oldtimers create a centripetal force that pulls these newcomers toward capable, central participation in the community's activity. (LeMaistre *et al.* 2006, p.345)

New practitioners will need information, they may need assistance to identify consequences of actions and often require a high level of reassurance and support. Supervisors may also find that new practitioners ask for, and need, regular feedback and require challenge as they develop their own practice competence and wisdom. They also need to be encouraged to recognize and affirm what they already know and bring to the work context, and how to critique its application to practice.

Conversely, experienced and competent practitioners generally have developed practice wisdom and require little procedural information. These practitioners will use supervision to target, develop and hone their practice. Of interest to this group is the opportunity to critique and develop new practice options. Challenge, particularly feedback, is welcomed and seen as stimulating and providing interesting new perspectives. The supervision of experienced practitioners is usually rewarding, though can at times be challenging, for supervisors. Reflective feedback offers a chance for in-depth discussion and debate, and supervisors' own practice can develop through these ponderings.

It is useful to note the distinction between experience and competence. In their seminal developmental model of supervision, Loganbill *et al.* (1982) identify a category of practitioners who are 'stuck' in their practice. This group may be experienced in service but their practice has become limited. These practitioners will need confrontative (feedback and challenge) and catalytic interventions (open-question enquiry) to create the insight and understanding to change.

The above section provides a brief overview of the interventions and skills of supervision. We refer readers to other texts (Bond and Holland 2010; Hawkins and Shohet 2012) for more detailed information. The focus for the remainder of this chapter is how the interventions and skills relate to the Reflective Learning Model of Supervision.

The Reflective Learning Model of Supervision
Open-question enquiry in supervision

> Great supervision is about asking the right questions. Through careful facilitation of a reflective process, utilising the learning cycle, each supervision session can build the practitioner's skills in self-supervision. For it is this ability to 'do' and 'know' and 'be with' clients while simultaneously reflecting on process and future intervention that is at the heart of professional excellence. (Davys and Beddoe 2000, p.449)

The Reflective Learning Model of Supervision, presented in Chapter 5, describes a model of supervision which positions the supervisee as the central figure in supervision and the supervisor as the facilitator or guide. This model relies on the supervisor having both the skills to create an accepting environment for supervision and the skills to invite and facilitate an exploration of practice by the supervisee which leads to discovery, insight and understanding. As we emphasized in Chapter 3, the key to creating the environment or context for supervision is the establishment of the supervision relationship. The effective facilitation of a supervisee's exploration of their practice, however, requires the supervisor to have command of open-question enquiry.

Open-question enquiry, Socratic questioning, which prompts a supervisee to explore their practice, encourages them to open sensitive areas for consideration and to unpack feelings and motivation, will only be useful if the discussions are candid and truthful. The importance of establishing a trusting relationship is thus once again evident. A supervisor who is genuinely engaged in the supervision process and who is interested in the opinions and experiences of their supervisees will be an instinctive 'good' listener. A good listener attends, clarifies and asks open and expansive questions and so provides the encouragement and safety for their supervisees to take risks and explore their practice. Questions allow supervisees to find their own answers or solutions to their own problems and places them in the position of responsibility for their work. 'Questioning thus follows attentive listening that looks for understanding rather than claims to know' (Smythe et al. 2009, p.22). Who we see in the reflective mirror of supervision and what we learn will depend on what questions we ask and how we frame those questions.

The questions which assist supervisees to consider their work in depth are open questions. Open questions most commonly begin with who, what, where, when and how, and invite supervisees to review situations and to deepen the 'telling' of the supervision story. Questions which begin with 'why' are also open questions but can easily become interrogatory and, rather than encouraging reflection, can provoke defensiveness and justification from the supervisee. 'Why' questions therefore need to be used judiciously.

It can be useful for the supervisor to have a framework around which they can consider which questions to pose. Most practice can be defined by three parameters: action or doing, knowledge and thinking, and awareness of self and feelings. These three parameters also represent the reflective learning cycle. The work which a supervisee presents in supervision can be reviewed in terms of what did the practitioner do (or not do), what were they thinking (what knowledge, assumptions or judgements informed the action) and how or what was the practitioner feeling. This level of review, however, is not sufficient to transform practice. In order to uncover meaning and understanding, and so promote change, a higher order critique is required. Thus, it is not sufficient to 'know'. Understanding and change come from the critical examination and questioning of what lies behind this knowing, the implications of 'knowing'.

The art of asking 'good questions' inexorably begins with facilitative interventions, in particular the skills of good listening, and develops through the application of open-question enquiry. Questions will follow the narrative of the supervisee rather than the internal meanderings of the supervisor. In this way, each supervision session will be unique and particular to time and place. 'Such an approach must release both parties to a process of "play" where a question finds response and response provokes a more searching question' (Smythe *et al.* 2009, p.20). To promote critical reflection, the supervisor is attentive to the supervisee's story and actively curious. The supervisor listens for moments of choice in the narrative and notices inconsistencies, assumptions and incongruities. The supervisor listens for balance in the supervision 'story'. Does the supervisee speak of actions and knowledge but avoid feelings or does the supervisee become absorbed by their own processes and so overlook the connections between knowing and theory?

Supervision stories are also located in time and place. Consideration of the past in relation to the present assists supervisees to notice movement and change both in themselves and in their clients. Similarly, anticipation of, or hopes for, the future provides opportunity for planning new strategies and developing resources and skills. However, once again, simple review is not sufficient and past, present and future need to be examined for meaning and an understanding of the patterns and threads that connect them.

If we draw together all these elements, a matrix for the questions of supervision can be constructed (see Figure 7.1). Two overlapping triangles, one of doing, thinking and feeling, the other indicating past present and future are held in tension by the central imperative of critical reflection.

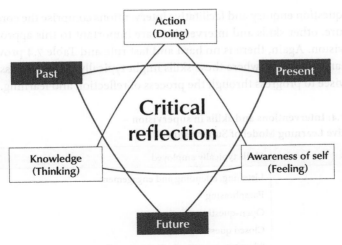

Figure 7.1: Reflection matrix

At the end of this chapter, we provide a list of questions for supervisors. These questions have been arranged according to the four stages of the Reflective Learning Model of Supervision. This ordering is not hard and fast and many questions can be asked in more than one stage of the model. We see the list as a 'starter pack' and encourage readers to create their own list of questions to reflect the uniqueness of their own practice style and that of their supervisees. The questions here come with a warning. Supervision is more than the posing of questions. The questions need to be relevant to the dialogue and the context. This is not supervision by numbers!

While questions may be central to the Reflective Learning Model, the interventions listed earlier in this chapter are also relevant and in the dance of supervision are essential to good footwork. Open-question enquiry, when used as critical reflection, is a skill of catalytic intervention. Questions, however, are not always appropriate or necessary in every supervision exchange. Bond and Holland (2010) offer a useful warning in this regard. Questions can be overused. 'Compulsive non-directiveness,' they say, 'may occur when the clinical supervisor continues to use support and catalytic interventions when some information or advice may be more appropriate' (Bond and Holland 2010, p.189).

Interventions and the Reflective Learning Model of Supervision

The above discussion of open-question enquiry describes in some detail the use of questions within the Reflective Learning Model of Supervision. While open-question enquiry and facilitative interventions comprise the core skills structure, other skills and interventions are important to this approach to supervision. Again, there is no hard and fast rule and Table 7.4 provides a summary to identify where these skills might typically be used to assist the supervisee to progress through the process of reflection and learning.

Table 7.4: Interventions and skills in supervision –
Reflective Learning Model of Supervision

Stages	Skills typically employed
Event	Listening, attending and engagement
	Paraphrasing
	Open-question enquiry
	Closed questions (minimal)
	Silence
	Information giving (minimal)
Exploration: Impact	Listening and attending
	Open-question enquiry
	Feedback: confirmatory and reflective
	Reframing
	Challenge
	Silence
Exploration: Implications	Listening and attending
	Open-question enquiry
	Feedback – confirmatory, corrective and reflective
	Reframing
	Challenge
	Information giving
	Logical consequences
	Directives
Experimentation	Listening and attending
	Open question enquiry
	Feedback – confirmatory, corrective and reflective
	Challenge
	Directives
Evaluation	Listening and attending
	Open-question enquiry
	Feedback – confirmatory and reflective

One hundred and more questions

Event

What have you brought to supervision today?

What is your top priority for today?

What is it about this particular situation that has your attention?

What is your supervision question?

What would a successful outcome look like?

Where do you want to start?

How can I assist you with this?

What would be helpful?

What don't you want from me?

What is the goal for the issue?

How will you know you have got what you want?

Tell me about it...

How much do I need to know in order to understand the situation?

Exploration

Impact

What have you done so far?

What did you see?

How are you feeling right now about this situation?

How were you feeling at the time?

What, if anything, has changed since this happened?

Have you been in a situation like this before?

What has helped you on previous occasions?

How is this situation different from others in the past?

What stops you from...?

If there were no consequences, what would you like to do/say now?

If you were to give yourself wise counsel, what would it be?

How do you see your relationship with this person/client?

Who do they remind you of?

How much of yourself do you see in the client?

Have you discussed this with the person/client?

What do you like about this client/family?

What do you think the client/family like about you?

What do you not like about this client/family?

How do you think the client sees you?

What is your greatest concern?

How important is it for you that the client...?

How does this situation affect you?
Who have you been able to talk to about this?
What is your greatest fear?
When this happens, what are you thinking?
When this happens, what are you feeling?
What do you do with your feeling of...?
How do your feelings about this impact on your work in this situation?
What do you think might be going on for the client?
How might the client be feeling?
What prevents you/makes you hesitate/ignore...?
Whose problem is this?
What is your gut feeling about this situation?
What assumptions have you made?
What is the basis of your assumptions?
What values or beliefs have guided your thoughts and actions?
What is the most challenging aspect of this situation for you?

Implications
What have you thought of so far?
What were you thinking at the time?
What do you think now?
What did you say?
What has guided your approach so far?
What have you done on previous occasions?
How is this situation different?
How has your presence/intervention changed the situation?
Who else could have done what you have done?
When did this...start?
How do you determine your priorities?
How did you come to that conclusion/decision?
What is the advantage of what you do now?
What are the disadvantages of what you do now?
What would happen if you stopped...?
What is your role?
Who is your client?
Who are you accountable to?
When you do x what is the client learning?
What are the tasks associated with your role?
What is your goal?
What do you need to remember to say, do or look out for?
What other approaches could you take?

Do you know about…?
Have you considered…?
What other knowledge or resources could you apply here?
What do you know about…?
What is your area of strength?
What are your limitations?
Why might the client be behaving as they are?
What are the implications for you/the client/the agency, etc?
What is the purpose of your thinking on this matter?
From what perspective are you thinking?
What assumptions are you making?
What information are you using?
How are you interpreting that information?
What conclusions do you come to?
What is the theoretical base of your interventions?
Why have you taken this approach?
If you were the client, what would you have noticed?
If you were to give yourself some wise counsel, what would it be?
What do you think you have done well?
What strengths does this family/client have?
What changes have you observed in this client/family?
What goals does this family/ client have?
How might you ascertain what the client/family thinks/wants?
What expectations does the client/family have of you/agency?
Are the client's goals realistic?
What are the limitations of your role?
What would you have liked to change about this situation?
If this situation was resolved what would it look like?
What do you wish you had done differently?
What are the policies, procedures which direct your work?

Experimentation

So, what are you going to do now?
Where are you going to start?
When are you going to…?
How might you approach this person?
How are you going to say that?
What is the most likely response from the client/family?
How will you respond to the client's/family's response?
What response are you most concerned about?

How would you deal with resistance/refusal/aggression/denial, etc?
What are the possible consequences of your plan?
Who needs to be there?
What resources might you need?
What would happen on a future occasion if this occurred?
How could the decision be sabotaged – by whom?
What would you need to give up to make the changes/put the plan in place?
What if there is no change in this situation?
What contingency plan do you have in mind?
Who else needs to know?
How will results be measured?
What will you notice different about your/your client's behaviour?
What have you learned?
What areas do you need to work on here – skills, knowledge attitude?
What do you need to record about this session/client/family?
Are there issues of safety involved?

Evaluation

Given where you started, where are you now?
How has the issue been addressed?
At the beginning how would you rate…?
How would you rate…now?
What other issues have arisen?
How will we follow up, review, evaluate, debrief?
What is the timeframe?
How has this process been?
How could it have been different?
What have you discovered/learned?
How are you feeling?
Any issues remaining about the issue or with me?

CHAPTER 8

Communication and Emotion in Supervision

In Chapter 2, we indicated that support was a core condition of effective supervision. In Chapter 6, managing the emotional content of supervision was described as a key focus for learning for beginning supervisors. In this chapter, we will explore the place of strong emotion in professional practice and supervision and the relevance of this to the understanding of and responding to challenging moments in practice.

> To become wiser is to stay tuned to the insights bred of challenge, tension, joy and breakthrough 'felt' within the experience of being there. Such glimmers of insight are brought to understanding by reflection and somehow embodied into discerning judgement. (Smythe *et al.* 2009, p.20)

Working in health and social care can be emotionally stressful regardless of the context. At every interface, and often on a daily basis, practitioners are engaged with other human beings who are at various stages of critical decision making, distress or crisis. Many practitioners will be required to assess client situations, make decisions and intervene in ways which can have far reaching effects on their clients' lives. These engagements will, on occasion, create a level of stress, doubt, anxiety and, sometimes, despair for practitioners regardless of that practitioner's level of experience or training. All too often there is no clear way forward and situations are characterized by changing circumstances, new and contradictory information and uncertainty. In order to deal with these recurring practice situations, practitioners need to be strong and confident in themselves and to have a place or a space where they can attend to this distress and anxiety. Supervision has been identified as one of those safe spaces (Ruch 2007a; Winter *et al.* 2019). 'To feel good about others we need to feel good about ourselves. Our own feelings of inadequacy, anger or distress get in the way of how we relate to others, or get projected onto colleagues or clients' (Hawkins and Shohet 2006, p.21).

Overlaying the individual challenge for many practitioners are the broader influences on both the practice environment and supervision. Supervision, Turney and Ruch (2018) suggest, has been colonized by 'new public management' (2018, p.126). This observation, though specific to social work in Britain is, we believe, valid for many professionals in many countries. Neo-liberal political agendas, which subject health and social service providers to budgetary constraints and focus on service outcomes, performance indictors and audit, make it 'difficult [for practitioners] to retain a balanced relationship-based professional stance' (Hingley-Jones and Ruch 2016, p.235). This shift in relational engagement in turn shapes supervision environments and conversations, and relational austerity becomes a risk.

> In a financially austere climate professionally-informed practice shrinks in response to what might be referred to as 'relational austerity' – practice that is increasingly authoritarian rather than authoritative and combative rather than compassionate – emerges as an unintended consequence of this ideological manoeuvre. (Hingley-Jones and Ruch 2016, p.237)

The importance, and indeed the necessity, of acknowledging and exploring feelings in supervision is clearly stated by Hughes and Pengelly (1997) who argue that practitioners cannot avoid being emotionally affected by their work with clients and that these feelings will, in some form or another, be present in supervision. These feelings hold important information about clients and about the practitioner–client relationship (Hughes and Pengelly 1997; Turney and Ruch 2018). If these feelings can be expressed and examined in supervision, this information will become available to help inform the current and ongoing work with that client. Such examination and expression are essential, indeed a prerequisite to safe practice (Hughes and Pengelly 1997, p.82).

Nordentoft (2008) found that group clinical supervision with a focus on 'emotion work' seemed to both 'introduce and legitimize a different emotional vocabulary and a different organization of talk' at case conferences in a palliative care team (p.924). In addition, she found that treatment beliefs and practices within the team were questioned in group supervision by including the views of those who didn't usually contribute in the case conferences. Nordentoft observed that the supervisors became role models and less participative practitioners became more willing and confident in leading challenging discussion (Nordentoft 2008, p.919).

Nordentoft's findings highlight the dual nature of care in the emotionally demanding work of palliative care where the needs of both the patients and the staff should be addressed. From the research, it is suggested that the promotion of an exploration of feelings in supervision for these health professionals increased 'moral thinking and ethical reflections on care and treatment' (Nordentoft 2008, p.924). The connection between emotions and reasoning is important. 'Remove emotions from the ethical equation and you have effectively removed the relationships involved, and created an ethics involved solely with problem solving' (Carroll 2014, p.93).

Despite this recognition of the importance of emotions and that a central role of supervision is to 'hold and support the supervisee in times of crisis and doubt' Hawkins and Shohet (2012, p.254), not all supervision arrangements offer the required safety for such expression and exploration. A number of factors are identified as contributing to the creation of barriers to this emotional work and include the personal views and personalities of both practitioners and supervisors, the culture of the organization and of the profession, and the degree to which it is safe to expose one's vulnerability (Hawkins and Shohet 2012; Lewis 2005; Ruch 2007a; Winter *et al.* 2019). In addition, a current focus on evidence-based practice, which urges practitioners to seek rational answers to practice situations, does not encourage an examination of the uncertainties and hunches of emotional responses. Turney and Ruch (2016), for example, note reports which consider emotions in professional assessment and decision making as 'problematic and a source of bias that needs to be kept under control' (p.674). Where such professional objectivity and detachment are valued, subjectivity is regarded as a weakness rather than applauded as awareness (Bond and Holland 2010). In this type of professional climate, practitioners require considerable self-confidence, assertiveness and a sense of safety if they are to expose the more uncertain aspects of their practice.

The barriers which prevent an exploration of feeling in supervision by a supervisee can be regarded as stemming from three fears: fear of being overwhelmed by feelings, fear of the judgements of others and fear of distortion in the professional encounter. These fears are detailed in Table 8.1.

Table 8.1: Barriers to the expression of feelings in supervision by the supervisee

Fear	Contributing factors
Fear of being overwhelmed by the feelings	• Feelings may be too painful and distressing to be acknowledged • The act of reflection may open a deep well of unexplored scenarios from the past which threaten to overwhelm • Practitioners under stress often feels very vulnerable and any acknowledgement or expression of feelings could be 'out of control' • Accessing feelings may risk experiencing shame and failure • Feelings may be suppressed when practitioners are too busy and task focused to take time to listen and reflect
Fear of the judgements of others	• Feelings may be perceived as a sign of weakness and evidence of 'over involvement' • In work contexts where public opinion is critical, any exposure of a practitioners' own vulnerability and feelings may be too risky • Practitioners may feel uncomfortable about strong negative feelings about service users when unconditional respect is the professional norm • Practitioners may feel uncomfortable about strong positive feelings, particularly of sexual attraction, towards clients • In organizations where supervision is viewed as 'hand holding', 'soft' or emotional babble, practitioner may not feel safe to expose feelings in supervision
Fear of distortion in the professional encounter	• Practitioners may wish to be perceived as scientific and objective • Practitioners may believe that the expression of strong emotion belongs to the counselling realm and has no place in supervision • Practitioners may not trust the ability of the supervisor to 'hold' the emotional content • Practitioners may believe that an expression of feeling may prejudice a client's rights

In the same way that supervisees may repress expression of feelings in supervision, so can supervisors deter exploration of the emotional content of the supervisee's work. Like supervisees, many supervisors are caught up in the expectations and limitations of professional and organizational culture and feel exposed and vulnerable to public criticism. Supervision at the interface of risk (also see Chapter 11), and in a practice environment characterized by austerity (Hingley-Jones and Ruch 2016) may prioritize risk management over attention to the practitioner's own process and affect: quite simply, the supervision session runs out of time to deal with this aspect of practice.

Table 8.2 summarizes the barriers for supervisors to encourage and promote the expression of feelings in supervision.

Table 8.2: Barriers to the expression of feelings in supervision by the supervisor

Fear	Contributing factors
Fear of being overwhelmed by the supervisee's feelings	• Supervisors may fear becoming overwhelmed by the supervisee's pain • Supervisors may hold old unresolved practice issues which are triggered by the supervisee's emotions and threaten to resurface • Supervisors' own burnout and vulnerability may limit their capacity to deal with emotion • Supervisors may fear they will share the supervisee's sense of shame and failure
Fear of exposing inadequacies as a supervisor:	• Supervisors may lack the skills and confidence to 'hold' the supervisee and deal with the feelings • Supervisors may fear that they will not be able to 'make it better' • Feelings may be perceived as a sign that the supervisee is not coping, and reflect badly on the supervisor • Supervisors may feel conflict between responding to and acknowledging feelings and traditional practice norms where feelings are held at a distance • Supervisors may be caught between the need to balance priorities of risk and the expression of feelings
Fear of criticism	• In organizations where supervision is viewed as 'hand holding', 'soft' or 'emotional babble', supervisors may not encourage practitioners to expose feelings in supervision • In work contexts where public opinion is critical, the focus of supervision becomes task and compliance centred • Where the practice ethos is evidence-based, feelings are not valued or regarded as contributing to fact • Where performance issues are evident and require urgent attention, feelings can be regarded as a distraction

The challenge for supervisors and supervisees is thus to create a supervision space where there is sufficient mutual trust and respect to withstand an examination of the multi-layered emotional work of human service practice. This space will need to be secure enough to both resist the pressure of risk-management perspectives and hold at bay the criticisms which can arise from particular organizational and social contexts. In order for this to happen, both participants require a clear understanding of the boundaries of supervision, the courage to face the fears of exposing feelings and willingness to value moments of uncertainty. When the opportunity to explore the emotional impact of practice is not available to practitioners, the feelings surrounding practice do not cease to exist and practitioners are left to manage the emotional impact of their work alone (Dwyer 2007, p.53).

Emotional intelligence

The ability for either the practitioner or the supervisor to attend to the 'emotional' business of supervision will depend on a number of factors, the most critical of which is their emotional capability or level of emotional intelligence.

> It is not personal intellectual intelligence alone that enables us to successfully navigate life's various situations, either as direct workers or as supervisors our emotions also play a part. The skill of self-awareness helps us to counter our biases and reach for greater objectivity. (Dolgoff 2005, p.7)

The relevance of emotional intelligence to practitioners Morrison (2007) notes, is well captured by Shulman (1999) who states that 'the capacity to be in touch with the client's feelings is related to the worker's ability to acknowledge his/her own. Before a worker can understand the power of emotion in the life of the client, it is necessary to discover its importance in the worker's own experience' (Shulman 1999, quoted in Morrison 2007, p.251).

Emotional intelligence is generally seen to comprise four interrelated domains. Two of these domains – 'self-awareness' and 'self-management' – can be considered as intrapersonal domains while 'other awareness' and 'relationship management' are interpersonal domains (Morrison 2007 p.25). The interrelatedness is circular. Thus, the awareness of one's own emotions leads to the understanding of and ability to monitor and manage those emotions. Awareness of one's own emotions also facilitates an awareness and understanding of the emotions of others. The management of one's own emotions, and an awareness of the emotions of others in turn, assists the management of relationships.

Emotional intelligence is recognized in competent practitioners whose understanding of, and facility to address, both the emotional and practical/technical components of practice are 'inextricably connected' (Morrison 2007, p.247). Applied in practice, emotional intelligence, Morrison says, contributes through five core activities: engagement; assessment and observation; decision making; collaboration and cooperation; and dealing with stress, building resilience and coping strategies (Morrison 2007, pp.253–258). Although originally thought to be a relatively stable trait, emotional intelligence has been shown to be able to be developed and improved, but opinions differ as to what activities will effect this change. Where Schutte *et al.* (2001, p.535) suggest that it is possible that training could influence an improvement in emotional intelligence, Clarke (2006) suggests that rather than training, 'team-based learning activities and supervision' (p.459) develop emotional ability. In his study, Clarke (2006) found that the process of reflection and discussion, both elements of supervision, enabled emotional abilities and experience to become visible and thus to be accessed. In this manner, tacit learning becomes more 'explicit'. Clarke (2006) also emphasizes the importance of the specific work context, and the surrounding cultural, social and organizational norms on the learning and demonstration of emotional abilities.

For supervisors, emotional intelligence is the ability that enables them to understand their own feelings and to manage these in the supervisory relationship. It is the ability to accurately read how their supervisees are feeling and to manage those feelings in relation to themselves within the supervision relationship. Emotional intelligence will enhance the supervisor's ability to maintain the tensions and balance between support and challenge within supervision and to manage the complexities of power, authority and any dualities of role. A person who has high emotional intelligence is someone who conveys warmth and respect and elicits those responses from others; communicates clearly and does not play power games; achieves a balance between personal acknowledgement of others and the formal aspects of professional relationships; has broad networks of relationships; is optimistic; examines mistakes for opportunities to learn and looks for solutions with mutual benefits (Dolgoff 2005, p.9). The capacity for meaningful interpersonal connectedness is thus seen to have a direct relationship to emotional intelligence. Howe (2008) suggests that emotionally intelligent people use their 'emotions to improve their reasoning' and typically 'cooperate and collaborate with others in mutually rewarding relationships' (Howe 2008, p.14).

As a relationally connected professional the first, and possibly most basic, requirement of a supervisor is to be capable of listening and being present. We are reminded in Chapter 7 that listening is an active process where focus and attention are necessary. When present and listening, the supervisor can be witness to, validate, and 'hold' the emotional energy, pain, distress or possible despair of a supervisee. 'How one listens and feels listened to underpins what is said. If a person does not feel safe to speak, what is "unhearable" becomes "unheard of". "All is well" may rather mean "all has not yet been spoken"' (Smythe *et al.* 2009, p.22).

In his study of the experience and handling of fear in supervision, Smith (2000) concludes that 'participants did not want clever or "helpful" interpretations of what they were feeling and why. They wanted to be allowed to rediscover their sense of self in the company of another' (Smith 2000, p.24). Smith describes the need for the listener to listen at a level which matches the intensity of the experience being recounted. Action, so often the panacea of discomfort, is not always required. In Smith's study, the participants welcomed 'acceptable attempts to "hold" and think about experiences rather than act as a result of them. "Don't just do something – sit there!" seems to be the message' (Smith 2000, p.23). The appreciation and importance of a supervisor's ability to 'meet' the supervisee's varied emotions is noted in other studies (Davys 2005b), and Toasland (2007) describes the role of the supervisor to 'receive, experience and make bearable' (p.200) the emotions generated in the course of a practitioner's work.

The emotional work of supervision, however, extends beyond validation and support. If professional practitioners (and their supervisors) 'can tolerate experiencing and thinking about' their emotional responses to client work 'they will find in them a rich source of information about the core issues in the lives of their service users' (Hughes and Pengelly 1997, p.82).

In reflective supervision, taking the lid off is essential, not to expose or make a counselling client of the supervisee, but in order to explore the impact and the implications of strong feelings on practice.

In this exploratory process, feelings are accepted, valued and examined for the information they hold and understanding they offer. With new information comes the possibility of choosing from a wider range of theories from which new strategies of intervention can be devised and reviewed. Possibilities for future action can be considered and rehearsed within a safe space where ongoing concerns and anxieties can be also be addressed. A consideration of the emotional threads of practice can lead to an identification of alternative motivations of both clients and practitioners, and contingency plans can be made to address the possible implications of these. The relationship between emotions and good reasoning is highlighted by others (Carroll 2014; Nordentoft 2008) and Turney and Ruch (2016) make 'the case for an approach to supervision that acknowledges the contribution of *both* cognitive *and* affective knowledge to assessment and decision making' (italics in the original, p.675).

Working with emotion in supervision

The emotional work of supervision is the dual responsibility of both supervisor and supervisee. Bond and Holland (2010) describe the two primary emotional skills as awareness and self-acceptance. Awareness involves the ability of the practitioner to notice, value and evaluate their feelings. Awareness thus promotes choice. When a practitioner knows how they feel they can decide how to respond to and behave in the moment. When situations are complex, this choice may be to 'hold' or contain the feelings in order that they are taken to supervision where they can be expressed and more closely and extensively explored for meaning and understanding.

Emotions can be identified by physical effects. Changes in body sensations, warmth and energy provide clues to underlying emotions both pleasant and unpleasant. However, awareness does not guarantee that practitioners will bring feelings to supervision for discussion. Practitioners must also be accepting and non-judgemental about whatever feelings arise in the course of their work: 'awareness and acceptance go hand in hand. The more you can come to accept your feelings non-judgementally, the easier it will become to be increasingly aware of your emotions and the energy that goes with them' (Bond and Holland 2010, p.149).

Containment

Containment of the feelings which arise from the content and context of practice is an important task for supervision, but a clear distinction is made between containment, suppression and accommodation. Hughes and Pengelly (1997) note that containment in supervision is often used as if it were a means of control – 'keeping the lid on' or as a form of 'collusive support' (p.176). While the 'keeping the lid on' approach to feelings can be a valid strategy of practice it needs to be followed up in supervision. Ferguson (2018) identifies such a process. Employing the term *'defended* self', Ferguson describes that aspect of self which is 'principally concerned with protecting itself from unbearable levels of anxiety' (p.418). Here 'suspension of feeling and self-preservation occurred at times by practitioners consciously turning reflection on and off, to meet the demands of the situation' (p.421). Such non-reflection, Ferguson continues, however, 'should only be a temporary state and needs to end with supervisors providing containment, and enabling critical thinking on what has been experienced' (p.424).

Containment in practice is thus employed by the practitioner 'in the moment' to 'contain' feelings until an appropriate time and safe place are available for expression and exploration. In this way, Bond and Holland (2010) describe containment as an emotional skill. At times in practice where, for valid professional reasons, it is not appropriate to express emotions, 'containment is about expanding your sense of your own personal strength so that you can contain the feelings, gently "holding" that part of you which is feeling emotional and postponing expressing the feelings until a more appropriate time '(Bond and Holland 2010, p.150). Containment in this sense is a postponement, not suppression, of expressing and exploring feelings.

Containment, however, goes beyond the 'holding' of emotional material. Again, as described above, it requires the supervisor and the supervisee to examine and understand the information brought to supervision. For the supervisor, containment is 'the process in which authority becomes translated into effective interaction' Hughes and Pengelly (1997, p.176). In this manner, containment 'provides a concept for the capacity both to be truly (rather than collusively) supportive and to challenge effectively' (Hughes and Pengelly 1997 p.178). In a similar vein, Gazzola and Theriault describe the need for supervisors to both create 'an atmosphere of safety and challenge the supervisee to go beyond his/her comfort level' (Gazzola and Theriault 2007, p.200). The process of containment supports the practitioner beyond the supervision session and provides an inner strength which the supervisee can carry into practice situations.

> Good experiences of supervision in turn support the further development of the internal supervisor and the worker's capacity to contain themselves in the difficult circumstances that threaten to stop them from thinking and feeling what as far as is humanly possible they need to be able to. (Ferguson 2018, p.425)

Importantly, Hughes and Pengelly (1997) distinguish between the container and the contained. Effective containment includes the capacity of the supervisor to know themselves as 'different' from the supervisee and thus to avoid becoming overwhelmed or wrung out by the emotional material which is brought by the supervisee to supervision. In this regard, it is important for supervisors to access their own containment through their own process of supervision.

Through supervision, the supervisee is resourced and supported to withstand the emotional content of their work on a day-to-day basis. As part of this task, and of particular importance, is the ability of the practitioner to manage the transferential processes which occur in all relationships, but in particular those between themselves and their clients.

Transference, counter transference and parallel process

The feelings which supervisees bring to the supervision room emanate from a variety of sources and are not always immediately identifiable or palatable. The situations and accompanying feelings are often a product of the distortions of transferential and parallel processes. As Hughes and Pengelly (1997) so aptly observe 'the significance of supervision lies... in the search for meaning in the "grime" of difficult work-related feelings' (Hughes and Pengelly 1997, p.87). Transferential material provides useful information about and understanding of client situations. Examination of this material is also necessary in order that it does not interfere with or distort the supervision process. In order to explore these processes, they first need to be identified and named (Page and Wosket 2015, p.94).

Definitions of transference describe a process whereby the feelings, attitudes and responses which belong to an earlier relationship are transferred or projected onto a person in the present (Bernard and Goodyear 2014; Hawkins and Shohet 2012; Page and Wosket 2015). In social service settings, transference may include the unwanted or painful feelings of the client which are projected onto the practitioner/supervisee. The transference, originating from the client's history, will thus intrude onto the client–practitioner relationship. Counter transference is the response of the person onto whom the feelings or attitudes have been transferred. Supervisees in turn may transfer feelings and attitudes onto their supervisors. It is possible that the supervisor may also have a counter response (counter transference) to the supervisee. The process can thus be multi-layered and complex.

Transference can be identified in a number of ways. Careful attention to a supervisee's language and the images and metaphors which accompany a supervisee's description and experience of practice can provide useful clues (Hawkins and Shohet 2012): 'I feel as if I am banging my head against a brick wall' or 'It is just like taming a wild animal.' These, often exasperated, comments by supervisees are metaphors which can reveal the hidden dynamics of relationship between the practitioner and the client. They provide a starting place for questions. 'In what way is this client like a wild animal?' 'How does this suggest the client views the relationship with you?' These are the sorts of useful exploratory questions which can begin to open discussion. In some cases, a supervisee may be first aware of a client's transference when they recognize their own counter transference.

Counter transference is also an unconscious response, in this case by the practitioner in response to the client's situation. The importance of exploring counter transference is twofold. First, as it is outside a practitioner's awareness, it brings this aspect of the relationship into consciousness in order that it can be 'known' and explored. Second, this exploration increases knowledge about, and understanding of, the client situation which will thus inform and assist in the 'work' with this client. Hawkins and Shohet (2012) name five types of counter transference, which can be summarized as:

- feelings/attitudes of the supervisee which have been stirred up by the client

- feelings/attitudes which have arisen as a result of the attributes assigned to the practitioner by the client

- the supervisee's (oppositional or counter) response to the role assigned by the client

- feelings, sensations and physical symptoms which have been projected by the client and which the supervisee has taken on

- the supervisee's desire for the client to change for their (the supervisee's) sake and not the client's own sake.

Transferential material is thus a rich source of information which can provide useful understanding of relationship dynamics. It is important, however, to delineate the boundary between supervision and therapy. Supervisee counter transference (or transference) may extend beyond the brief of supervision and require more than identification and naming for resolution. Page and Wosket (2015) refer to this when they advise supervisees to take any unresolved issues to other appropriate forums, possibly their 'own therapist, for further exploration and resolution' (Page and Wosket 2015, p.94).

Parallel process, sometimes called mirroring or reflection process, is a phenomenon considered to be unique to supervision (Bernard 2006, p.10). Parallel process is where the dynamics of the here and now or current relationship are unconsciously acted out in a second relationship. Thus, the dynamics of the client–practitioner relationship are repeated in the supervision relationship. A supervisor may discover that when discussing an equivocal 'yes but' client in supervision, a normally receptive supervisee presents as defensive and dismissive of any possible solution to their supervision issue. Parallel process is reversed when the supervisee behaves in client work in parallel to the relationship with their supervisor. In this manner, supervision can have a direct effect on the work and dynamics of therapeutic relationships. The following vignette demonstrates how the dynamics of a client situation become mirrored in the supervision relationship.

◼ VIGNETTE 1: SASHA

A practitioner and her supervisor were discussing the case of Sasha, a ten-year-old boy who had been admitted to a foster care home because he was withdrawn, not communicating and was assessed as very depressed. Sasha had lived with his elderly grandmother since the age of six after his mother, a drug user, had overdosed and died. The grandmother lived in a small rural community where unemployment was endemic and educational aspiration low. The grandmother, however, still grieving the untimely death of her daughter (Sasha's mother), was determined that Sasha would break free from the limitations of the town. She had high expectations of his behaviour and scholastic achievement and did not encourage him to play with local children.

In the foster home, Sasha flourished, participating in the activities with the other children, learning to play and responding to overtures of friendship. His grandmother was concerned with these changes which she interrupted as the first signs of the carefree lifestyle adopted by her daughter. She began making complaints against the foster home caregivers. The practitioner was working very hard with the grandmother and Sasha. She was concerned by this turn of events and was sensitive to the importance of their ongoing relationship.

During the supervision session, the supervisor made a number of critical observations about the practitioner's work with Sasha and questioned whether foster care was really the best option. The practitioner, normally articulate and confident about her practice and ready to discuss and provide a rationale for her actions, accepted these observations from the supervisor without comment and left the session feeling hopeless and inadequate. Afterwards, the supervisor was concerned by the critical attitude she had taken with regard to the practitioner's work. The practitioner was very capable and always thorough in her work.

After some reflection, the supervisor realized that she and the practitioner might be behaving in parallel with the dynamics of the relationship between Sasha and his grandmother. The supervisor had become anxious and highly critical of the practitioner's work and the practitioner, in response (and out of character) had become withdrawn and defeated. When she raised this with the practitioner both recognized the parallel process and were able to explore this new insight and discuss future plans for Sasha with optimism and a fresh perspective.

As demonstrated in the vignette, parallel process is seldom conscious and generally enters into supervision as a form of 'discharge' by the supervisee or as an 'attempt to solve the problem through re-enacting within the here and now relationship' (Hawkins and Shohet 2012, p.99). The task of the supervisor is to first 'notice' the process. In order to do this, the supervisor must be aware of, and value, their own responses in supervision and in particular notice when their response to a particular supervisee is 'different'. In this manner, a supervisor can make conscious, or bring to the fore for consideration, dynamics which have originated in the client–practitioner relationship and which have been transported into supervision. As in the example above, it may not be until after a supervision session that the supervision participants become aware of the 'altered' dynamics in the relationship. Unless the process is named it is not available for examination and the supervision process is at risk of hijack by the very dynamics it seeks to resolve.

Relationship dynamics in supervision

Thus far in this chapter, we have considered the emotional work of practice and the impact of this within the supervision relationship. We have emphasized the importance of reflection and the difference between accommodation and expression of feeling. We have also identified that containment is not 'suppression' and is more than support. Containment includes the ability to move beyond support to challenge and explore feelings for meaning and understanding.

We conclude this chapter with discussion of the 'drama triangle' in Figure 8.1, which in our experience is one of the most frequently played out relationship dynamics in both health and social service practice and supervision. Karpman's triangle, sometimes referred to as the drama triangle (Karpman 1968), comprises three roles: persecutor, rescuer and victim. We use the original language of this classic model and emphasize that what is being described is not the person, but rather the 'role'. 'Role is the functioning form the individual assumes in the specific moment he reacts to a specific situation in which other persons or objects are involved' (Moreno quoted in Greenberg 1974, p.122). This relationship dynamic or 'unhealthy process' (Morrison 1993) is frequently played out in situations where there are issues of inequality or power and is often transferred to supervision through parallel process (Hughes and Pengelly 1997).

The power of the drama triangle is in the switches or changes in role: each role has its own payoff. As such the drama triangle constitutes a game. 'Games are sets of ulterior transactions, repetitive in nature, with a well-defined psychological payoff' (Berne 1974). Morrison (1993, pp.92–93) provides a very useful checklist of the common features of psychological 'games'. In summary, this includes:

- non-specific, generalized and incomplete information is shared

- abrupt and inconsistent mood swings

- an avoidance of discussions about feelings or needs

- discussions become person rather than issue based

- incongruity between verbal and non-verbal communication

- feedback is unclear and indirect

- lack of resolution of issues
- pervasive sense of blame of self or the other(s)
- no acceptance of responsibility.

Morrison concludes that 'problems cannot be resolved when games are in action' (Morrison 1993, p.93).

The very nature of the health and social service professions, particularly at the critical interface of care and protection, leaves practitioners susceptible to an enactment of the drama triangle. Organizational arrangements and relationships can also trip practitioners into roles which generate their own momentum and race around the three points of the triangle as participants struggle to gain clarity. As represented in Figure 8.1, the drama triangle comprises three roles: victim, persecutor and rescuer.

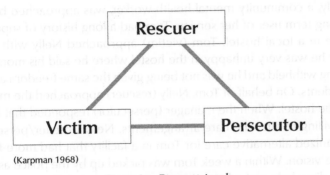

(Karpman 1968)

Figure 8.1: Drama triangle

A key to the drama triangle is to understand that it does not represent a whole person but rather particular roles which one person may assume in relation to another. The other key feature of the triangle is the absence of responsibility taken by any of the players.

Thus the victim eschews responsibility for events or actions and attributes blame to the persecutor. The victim seeks a rescuer to save them from this unfair and untenable position.

The persecutor likewise does not consider themselves responsible for their actions and locates a victim or scapegoat to blame for shortcomings and failure. The rescuer, meanwhile, finds in the victim a 'worthy cause' and, in order to 'save' the oppressed and attribute responsibility, identifies the persecutor as the cause of all this distress. Of particular significance to the 'helping' professions, where there can be a wish to assist the oppressed, the disadvantaged or the 'needy', is the role of rescuer. It is the role of rescuer that completes the triangle. The victim requires a persecutor and the persecutor requires a victim. But it is the rescuer who requires both a victim and a persecutor and thus ensures that all roles are filled. The very nature of the triangle, however, is that the roles switch and change, thus ensuring that the drama continues and no resolution is reached. The victim, having gladly welcomed the rescuer, is ultimately disappointed with their efforts and 'blames' (persecutes) them for failure. The roles are thus switched and the rescuer becomes the victim and the victim the persecutor. The new victim may look to the original persecutor for 'help' or rescue or may draw in a new player to fill that role and so on. In the following vignette, Nelly was readily hooked into the role of rescuer of the service-user only to find herself the victim of his criticism when things went wrong.

■ VIGNETTE 2: NELLY

Nelly, a community mental health worker, was approached by Tom, a long-term user of her service. Tom had a long history of supervised care in a local hostel. Tom (victim) approached Nelly with claims that he was very unhappy in the hostel where he said his money was being withheld and he was not being given the same freedom as other residents. On behalf of Tom, Nelly (rescuer) approached the manager of the hostel. When the manager (persecutor) responded that he was unwilling to alter the care arrangements, Nelly (rescuer/persecutor) organized alternative care for Tom in a facility that had more flexible supervision. Within a week Tom was picked up by the police as drunk and disorderly and admitted to the public hospital. Tom (persecutor) was very upset and blamed Nelly (victim) for not having sent him to an appropriate new care facility. He missed his friends and this is why he had got drunk. He now wanted to return to his original hostel. The original hostel was now unable to accommodate Tom as all beds were full. In supervision, Nelly (persecutor) complained about the inflexibility of the original hostel manager and (victim) expressed her hurt that Tom had not appreciated her help. The supervisor heard Nelly out and then asked her about her process of moving Tom in the first instance. Nelly (victim) saw this as an attack on her professional decision making and (moving to persecutor) accused the supervisor of being unhelpful and not open to allowing mental health service users any choice.

The victim, persecutor, rescuer role dynamic is one of the most common problematic interactions which is brought to supervision. While recognition of the process and identification of the interactions can be sufficient to break the cycle and open the way for creative resolution, there are other helpful models which can also be used here. In supervision, and all transactions for that matter, games can be initiated by any member of the interaction. It is important to remember that if a 'game' is in action then everyone is playing. In order to stop a game, one need only stop playing. In supervision, either a supervisor or a supervisee can be the initiator of a game. It is also important to note that many interactions during one's daily activities have elements of game playing, and family interactions in particular can often include 'gamey' exchanges. What is important is to recognize, acknowledge and stop those interactions which we do not want and which lead to unhealthy relationships and prevent the resolution of problems.

Morrison (1993, p.98) identifies a list of strategies which can be employed to stop a game. Among these he notes the importance of identifying how the 'game' starts, who starts it and how one gets 'hooked' into the exchange. Most significantly, Morrison recommends that participants identify what 'payoff' keeps them playing and the corollary, 'What would be the cost of stopping?'

Over the years, a number of variations have been applied to Karpman's triangle (Karpman 2007). One variation which we have found to be a most useful tool is the 'empowerment cycle' (Cornelius and Faire 2006). The 'empowerment cycle' identifies alternative roles which can be employed to break the repetitive cycle of the drama triangle. Essentially, the 'empowerment cycle' pairs each of the three psychological roles identified by Karpman with an alternative constructive role. The shift of roles brings with it an accompanying shift in behaviour and elicits a different response. Cornelius and Faire (2006) describe their model as a cycle but for consistency of structure here we have partnered the empowerment cycle with the drama triangle (see Figure 8.2). The roles are paired as follows: persecutor – educator/consultant; victim – learner; rescuer – mediator/facilitator (Cornelius and Faire 2006, p.106).

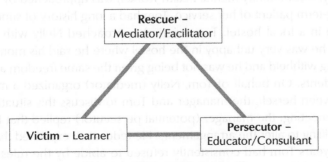

Figure 8.2: Empowerment triangle

Thus, if one finds oneself assuming a persecutor role the challenge is to become an educator or consultant. As an educator the task is to educate and provide information. An educator asks the question, 'What information would be helpful for others to know in this situation?' An educator or consultant is interested in the ideas of others and listens to and acknowledges their needs and considers differing views. When decisions are made, the process is open and, where possible, is collaborative and includes the views and needs of others.

If one finds oneself invited into, or if one assumes, the role of rescuer, the challenge is to become a mediator or facilitator. Implicit in the rescuer role is an assumption that the 'victim' is not capable of helping themselves and therefore needs rescuing. Questions which ask 'victims' to identify how they might themselves resolve the issue convey the belief that they are indeed capable. Similarly, assisting someone to take action rather than 'doing' it for them conveys respect. A discussion of the broader context of situations and the possible reasons for behaviour (which have appeared persecutory) can help a 'victim' to understand other perspectives and possible motivation for behaviour.

Finally, in situations when one feels like a victim it is useful to become a learner. What can I learn from this situation? What action can I take here? Can I approach this situation myself? What support might I need to do this? Why do I need to complain to others? How do I benefit from this position I am in? How willing am I to resolve this situation? What responsibility am I avoiding here? These questions generate responsibility and promote a sense of ownership for both action and inaction and create choice rather than passive acceptance and powerlessness.

◼ VIGNETTE 3: NELLY – THE ALTERNATIVE SCRIPT

Nelly, a community mental health worker, was approached by Tom, a long-term patient of her service. Tom had a long history of supervised care in a local hostel. Tom (victim) approached Nelly with claims that he was very unhappy in the hostel where he said his money was being withheld and he was not being given the same freedom as other residents. On behalf of Tom, Nelly (mediator) organized a meeting between herself, the manager and Tom to discuss this situation. At the meeting, the manager (potential persecutor) replied that he was unwilling to alter the arrangements. He (educator) explained that over the years Tom had consistently refused to abide by the rules of the hostel. Nelly (mediator) encouraged the manager (educator) to explain what Tom would need to do in order to hold the same privileges as other residents. Tom (victim) was very upset and (persecutor) blamed Nelly (potential persecutor) for not standing up to the manager. Nelly (educator) reiterated the reasons put forward by the manager. She (mediator) encouraged Tom to list the things he did like about the hostel and what specifically he (potential learner) would be prepared to change. Tom (victim) left in an angry huff.

In supervision, Nelly (victim) complained about Tom's lack of appreciation for her efforts and how she was fed up with working in this area where there were no resources and loads of frustrations. The supervisor heard Nelly out and then asked her (mediator) what she had learned from this episode. Nelly (persecutor) said she was not going to fall for that game and that she had nothing to learn. What had happened was not her fault and she had done her best. The supervisor (educator) summarized her view of the case and praised the work that Nelly had done, acknowledging the care she had taken to get both Tom and the manager talking and agreeing that this was hard and sometimes thankless job. Nelly, feeling heard and appreciated, began to plan for her next encounter with Tom.

Challenging moments in supervision arrive in various forms and will often be a combination of the situations and dynamics described in this chapter. At these moments, supervisors may feel overwhelmed, anxious, inadequate or just plain tired. What is most important is that supervisors take note and value their own responses in the same way that we have adjured practitioners to notice their responses from practice. It is through noticing and valuing these responses that the first clues about relationship dynamics and disturbances can be found.

The following checklist can be a helpful start for supervisors in these situations:

- What am I noticing in this situation?
- How does this differ from my usual feelings with this supervisee or in supervision?
- What are we not talking about here?
- What information is implicit, not defined or not available?
- Who is carrying responsibility for this situation and do I think that is reasonable?
- What am I feeling right now about this situation?
- How am I contributing to this situation?
- What can I do differently right now?

Good supervision is characterized by authenticity, immediacy and presence. Good supervision relationships allow supervisees to feel heard, valued and enabled to present themslves in all of the messiness (and glory) of their practice without fear, shame or embarrassment. For supervisees to do this they need to have some awareness and understanding of how they act in practice and a willingness to acknowledge their thoughts and feelings. Supervisors similarly need to have an awareness of who they are, how they behave, and what they think and feel in order to provide safety, containment and a way forward for the supervisees. As described by a supervisee in a study of good supervision: 'I can have a range of emotions. That person [supervisor] can meet me at any of those levels and really validate how I am feeling and find a way out of that' (Davys 2002).

CHAPTER 9
Promoting Practitioner Wellbeing

The functions of supervision have long included the 'supportive' (Kadushin 1976) and the 'restorative' (Proctor 2001) functions which essentially address those aspects of supervision where the personal and professional spheres intertwine. For example, research has determined that effective supervision is significantly associated with job satisfaction and maintaining commitment to the organization and is linked to employees' perceptions of the support they receive from their employer (Carpenter *et al.* 2013). Mor Barak *et al.* (2009) note that social and emotional support provided in the presence of a valued supervisory relationship is valued by workers. Although the role of personal support in supervision is sometimes contested due to ethical concerns about slippage across professional boundaries (Yegdich 1999), it is generally accepted that professional boundaries impose limits to the depth of 'personal work' that is undertaken in supervision. While there are tensions at the boundary of the personal and the professional, we agree that support is retained as a core condition of effective supervision, underlining the significance of the self in professional work (Hughes and Pengelly 1997) (see Figure 2.4). However, it is by no means straightforward to try to define the boundaries, and the nuanced accounts of much supervision practice demonstrate that the personal and professional do collide. In their 1998 review article, Yegdich and Cushing asserted that confusion was created by Butterworth (1994) when it was suggested that clinical supervision would:

> Promote both personal and professional development. That these areas are intimately connected is not in dispute…what is lost for refinement are the nuances of how professional development may feed into personal development and vice versa, while the notion that one will automatically bolster the other is naively accepted. (Yegdich and Cushing 1998, p.15)

In spite of this questioning whether supervision could address both professional and personal development, since our first edition it has been increasingly emphasized that exposure to demanding, stressful work and the impact of working closely with service users who have traumatic stories and are distressed by emotional, psychological and physical experiences can have corrosive effects on professionals (Koivu *et al.* 2012; Mor Barak *et al.* 2009) and that agencies need to provide supportive supervision as part of prevention. Increasingly governments, professional bodies and employers have developed responses to reduce the risk that professionals working in health, social care and justice settings will be harmed by their work. Western governments have acknowledged the obligation to ensure that workplaces and practices are safe and that workers have access to a range of mechanisms to prevent harm. Employee assistance programmes, monitoring workload and supervision are among these services. A body of research clearly indicates that supervision can provide ongoing protection from harmful exposure (Beddoe *et al.* 2014; Koivu *et al.* 2012; Mor Barak *et al.* 2009). In statutory helping, such as social work, there is an 'uneasy alliance' present, which Ingram (2012, p.16) describes as the 'balance between the rational and technical aspects of practice and how they sit next to the relationship-based aspects of practice' and the conscious and unconscious emotional responses to the work, as we have noted in the previous chapter.

For supervision practice, insights from supervision research (Mor Barak *et al.* 2009) and from studies in other fields such as resilience (Bottrell 2009; Luthar and Cicchetti 2000), emotional intelligence (Goleman 2005) and positive psychology bring increased awareness of the potential for supervisors to make a difference (Howard 2008). This chapter will review the research on problematic stress in health and social care and consider a range of useful strategies for both strengthening protective factors for professionals and methods for assistance when stress becomes a problem.

Stress in the helping professions

> Much of our work demands that we draw extensively upon our own personal resources, and these are likely to be worn down through constant use. ... The accumulation of stress may be gradual and insidious, and sometimes it arrives suddenly and overwhelmingly. (Brown and Bourne 1996, p.107)

In health and social services, the determination to reduce harm from stress and other detrimental effects of work on staff is particularly visible in fields such as child protection, mental health and the oversight of criminal offenders where 'high-stakes' risk assessment imposes greater accountability on practitioners and public expectations may often be experienced as overwhelming and unrealistic. As we have seen in Chapter 4, attempts to reduce workplace harm are often undermined by workloads and the impact of frequent organizational change.

Burnout is fully recognized as both detrimental to professional health and wellbeing but also potentially damaging to service users. Burnout is a multi-dimensional concept delineating three major components: emotional exhaustion (feeling emotionally over-extended), depersonalization (feeling detached from service users) and dissatisfaction with personal accomplishment (feeling reduced competence and satisfaction) (Maslach 1993). Kalliath and Beck (2001) note that each of these components need to be considered when examining the impacts of caring work (p.72). Burnout is corrosive of practitioners' engagement in their organization and work with service users as well as their overall wellbeing and capacity to remain in their profession.

After more than a decade of austerity, the demands of high-pressure environments have required practitioners to be highly skilled at rapid and accurate assessment of patient and service user problems and the application of evidence-informed interventions in an efficient and accurate manner. Workers feel pressure to be 'scientific' and objective and employ empirical models of practice, but somewhat paradoxically, practitioners are urged be mindful of their own feelings and interpret and reflect on these. There is increased understanding of the significance of emotion at work and, as discussed in Chapter 8, supervision is intended to create a reflective space in which these competing voices can be heard and attended to. The helping professions employ both science and emotion in everyday practice. Good practice requires the updating of knowledge for practice and the support of practitioners' emotional strengths.

The stress system

Collins (2008) describes stress 'as the product of complex interactions between environmental and organizational demands and the individual's ability to cope with these demands'. Problematic stress or 'distress' arises 'from a disparity between the perceived demands made on an individual and their perceived ability to cope' (Collins 2008, p.1176). Many factors in practitioners' personal lives also impact on work and vice versa (Kalliath, Hughes and Newcombe 2011; Thompson 2009). Most practitioners may experience role strain, where stressful working conditions and caring roles within their own families compete with time for rest and recreation. It is often acknowledged that professional cultures may encourage heroic narratives of strain and sacrifice that are unhealthy (Calvert 2014; Oates 2019). In health and social care, stress factors can be generated at numerous sites (Adamson, Beddoe and Davys 2012; Brown and Bourne 1996): in the practice itself, in teams and organizations and the other bodies encountered by professionals in their work, and specifically in supervision practice in some fields (Griffiths *et al.* 2019a). Relationships in these sites of practice contain myriad problems compounded by deficits experienced by practitioners in their agencies – lack of resources, inadequate supervision, insufficient debriefing after critical incidents and the acceptance of a high level of personal abuse from service users (Beddoe 2003) and colleagues (van Heugten 2009). Workplace exposure to verbal and physical abuse is an ever-present part of the job in health and social care despite the 'zero tolerance' rhetoric (Gabe and Elston 2008; Hunt *et al.* 2015). Supervision is a key component in the ongoing management of the impact of this traumatic exposure, although it must be seen as one part of an ecological approach to worker wellbeing in high-stress organizations and not the panacea for all problems (Adamson 2011; Adamson *et al.* 2012). We need to address the organizational barriers that may impact on help-seeking behaviour in hierarchical organizations (Oates 2019).

Table 9.1 maps how stress factors can emerge from all aspects of the stress system, starting with the personal life of the practitioner, including their health, personal and family relationships and obligations, social and cultural dimensions, practice strengths and challenges. All these factors collide with the demands of practice in professional life. Brown and Bourne (1996) took a systems approach to stress in social work that has utility across professions. Their model identified stressors at the following points: the practitioner's personal life, their current and past practice and the intersection of this with previous stressful or traumatic events, the team and agency context (pp.108–109). In our first edition of this book, we added the dynamics of community expectations and relationships, including the pressures of inter-agency and interprofessional work and the impact of rapid policy change and political agendas on professional practice as noted by Evetts (2009). For professionals working in services for children and vulnerable adults, general community and societal understandings and attitudes towards service, often voiced in news media, also impact significantly on practitioner stress (Chenot 2011). We note also the associated stresses of working with groups who may be stigmatized.

Table 9.1: A systemic perspective on stressors in health and social care

Systems		Stressors
1	Personal	Stress factors in the practitioner's personal life, for example: • relationship difficulties • health • addictions • loss or bereavement • financial difficulties • familial responsibilities • personal history of abuse or trauma
2	Practice	Stress factors arising from practice: • overly high proportion of high complexity 'cases' • abuse and violence in the field or clinical setting • racism, sexism, homophobia, religious intolerance, cultural stereotyping • being the subject of threats and vexatious complaints • large caseloads, minimal control over allocations • high profile cases where risk assessment is a major factor
3	Workplace	Stress factors emanating from the practitioner's team situation: • status and power issues and dysfunctional teams • personal conflicts • bullying and harassment • frontline staff feeling undervalued • involvement with other colleagues' work stress • moral distress arising from unpalatable policy
4	Agency	Stress factors arising in employment: • restructuring and redundancies • competitive environment, contracting and funding uncertainties • inter-professional conflict • poor physical working conditions • temporary staff, rapid turnover • unrealistic targets
5	Community	Stress factors emanating from the social environment: • attitudes towards illness (physical and mental) and social distress • attitudes towards service users • public ambivalence about intervention • care and control contradictions • unrealistic expectations • public critique of practitioners, rather than policy
6	Socio-political environment	Stress factors emanating from the socio-political environment: • low tolerance of mistakes and the crisis of trust • the political nature of public services • audit culture • media interest in exposing professional fallibility • for some professions, low status and poor public understanding of the professional role

Adapted from Brown, A. and Bourne, I. (1996)

■ VIGNETTE: JENNY – PART 1

Jenny was a 45-year-old nurse in a community health setting working in a child development team. She was the principal earner in her household, her partner was a part-time student and cared for their pre-schooler. Jenny's mother had struggled all her life with alcohol and Jenny was frequently called to her care home because her mother was drunk and aggressive; her father had not been in contact for 16 years. Jenny had always identified heavily with service users with family addiction problems and had been challenged before about her boundaries.

Jenny's department was very stretched – major budget cuts had led to staff reductions and restructuring. Despite the potential extra demands, such a move made Jenny plan to apply for a promotion to team leader. Her partner needed more money for his university fees and they really needed the additional salary Jenny's promotion would bring. She was suspicious that she wouldn't get the job because she felt strongly that the service manager didn't like her.

Jenny was working very long hours and struggling with one particular case. She had been working with the Grimm family; James (6), a child with fragile health, was currently very unwell. James's mother, Tamsin, had a serious gambling problem and her ability to cope with care of James was deteriorating. Jenny was in conflict with the family's child protection social worker who was insistent that James was better off with Mum. Jenny could see the household becoming dirtier and more chaotic and worried about the poor nutrition and personal care James was getting. Jenny had been visiting James's home virtually every day and a co-worker was shocked to find that Jenny had taken James out to medical appointments and even to the park at the weekend because she knew that Tamsin was regularly leaving James and his sister (aged nine) at home alone to go to the casino. Jenny had not reported these incidents to the child protection social worker.

Back at the office things were very difficult – Jenny was now the source of gossip and didn't get on with several people in the team and she was seen as shirking her share of caseload and focusing on her favourite clients.

Table 9.2 illustrates how Jenny's situation could be mapped out against the systemic stressors illustrated in Table 9.1. There is no expectation that a supervisor could or would address all of these but they would inevitably feature in supervision and the personal concerns may intrude more, as Jenny's distress increased.

Table 9.2: A systems approach to assisting stressed supervisees

Stressor systems	Jenny's story	Systems interventions
Personal	Financial Gambling Family history	Refer to employee assistance programme
Practice	Difficulties with service users with whom she over-identified Previous performance feedback Professional boundaries	Refer to employee assistance programme or personal counselling or treatment Supervision and links to appraisal
Team	Personal relationships Workload and equitable allocation	Team meetings Negotiation and transparent mechanisms to allocate work
Agency	Promotion Interprofessional relationships Restructuring Budget cuts	Supervision and support for personal professional development Team and agency meetings – open communication
Community	Inter-agency relationships and protocols	Regular focused meetings Clear expectations of staff relationships with other practitioners and developing partnerships
Socio-political climate	Gambling Substance misuse Resourcing for health and social services	Communication from 'the bottom up' to organizational hierarchy, professional action through membership of professional and community advocacy groups

The supervisor's approach to stress

In Table 9.2 we suggested supervisory interventions that could assist Jenny in her situation. A map of systemic sources of stress is useful and we suggest that supervisors follow Brown and Bourne's suggestion that mapping their own situation can be helpful to practitioners in understanding the complexity of their work environment (Brown and Bourne 1996, pp.109–110). In addition, this mapping helps supervisors to avoid the trap of placing responsibility on practitioners who are themselves struggling to cope with things outside their control, such as unmanageable caseloads and insecure funding. Self-care and managing workplace stress can be a standard supervision agenda item and starting a new supervision relationship is a good time to establish this. Supervisors can explore with supervisees their personal experience of any workplace stress that has become distressing. Questions might include:

- Can you tell me about a time that you were distressed and what strategies you employed to manage this?

- What do you think are the major triggers of distress for you in your job?

- How will I know when you're stressed?

- What can we put in place to assist you to avoid distress and strengthen your own good strategies?

- What are your ideas for improving the way we work in this team/agency in order to improve our workplace?

- Can we talk about how you want me to approach support for you if I notice that you are becoming distressed by work pressures?

- What's helpful for you when you're stressed?

- What is unhelpful for you when you're stressed?

Asking specific questions and focusing on the behaviours rather than the problems assists supervisors to develop an understanding with their supervisees about their coping styles and takes a collaborative rather than a problematizing approach to stress.

Prevention

Prevention of stressful workplaces may often need systemic changes, but supervisors can employ many skills and resources to aid them to work with supervisees: referral to employee assistance programmes for personal problems; referral to personal counselling or treatment; using transparent processes to discuss workload in individual and team meetings (where applicable); and developing clear expectations of staff relationships with other practitioners. At the organizational level, supervisors can model communication from 'the bottom up' to the organizational hierarchy, and support supervisees to find constructive ways to contribute to improving the workplace and processes. A constant source of stress in organizations is practitioner frustration with 'red tape' – compliance activities or procedures that pose barriers to good practice and their ability to meet the needs of service users. Supervisors can advocate for more systemic interventions. An example is provided by McDonald and colleagues (2012) who reported on a programme of workshops for nurses and midwives aimed at creating positive responses to a stressful workplace environment through the exploration of practical coping strategies. Finally, practitioners can be encouraged to develop their active participation in and leadership of advocacy for change through membership of professional organizations and community advocacy groups.

As noted above, there is evidence that supervisor support can make a difference to practitioner wellbeing at work. Kalliath and Beck (2001) had earlier tested the idea that low levels of supervisory support would impact on job burnout and the turnover intentions of nurses. The study tested a model against data from 250 nurses and found that 'low supervisory support results in higher levels of exhaustion, depersonalization and intention to quit' (Kalliath and Beck 2001, p.76). Kalliath and Beck's research strongly supports supervision as a support mechanism available to nurses to combat the negative impact of emotional exhaustion and depersonalization (p.76).

A meta-analysis study conducted by Mor Barak *et al.* (2009) found that 'effective supervision can delay or mitigate the effects of detrimental factors and can contribute to positive outcomes for workers in social service organizations' (Mor-Barak *et al.* 2009, p.25). Citing Kadushin and Harkness (2002), they assert that 'accumulating research on supervision indicates that the various dimensions of supervision may have protective, proactive, or preventive roles in ensuring a positive work environment that can contribute to worker effectiveness and potentially to quality service delivery' (p.25). With a focus on broad welfare and service organizations, Mor Barak *et al.* encourage organizations to provide supervisors with training that covers the three key supervisory dimensions emerging from the study: task assistance, social and emotional support, and strong supervisory interpersonal interaction (p.27). Andrea's story illustrates how supervision can support practitioners to develop an approach to their work that takes account of feelings.

■ VIGNETTE: ANDREA – PART 1

Andrea worked in a child health service as a community-based nurse with specialist skills in child development. The service was extremely overloaded, practitioners were stretched, workloads were high and a series of restructurings had meant that many practitioners had not had supervision for months.

In working with a four-year-old boy and his mother, Andrea had been monitoring Timmy's progress with a medication regime in which medication dosages were increased if improvements were not reaching a certain level at prescribed intervals. Timmy was not making progress and Andrea discussed the results of testing with the team consultant and they agreed to raise the dosage.

As Andrea drove away from Timmy's house the following day she was struck by an uncomfortable feeling that she was missing something. She felt nauseated and a little shaky. Timmy's mother Angela was very anxious and had been very reluctant to take on the medication regime as she felt that a 'good mother' should be able to make her child well with diet and loving care.

Andrea wondered if Angela was not giving Timmy all his tablets but dismissed this thought as silly. She fleetingly considered mentioning this to her team leader but he was more stressed out than she was so she moved on to their next task. As she got out of the car at the next house, she muttered to herself that this was not what she was taught in her nursing degree... As she knocked on the door the feelings of nausea returned.

In this situation, Andrea was suppressing her feelings about this potentially explosive case. The recognition that use of self is a key component of effective practice requires the commitment to be open about feelings – the ability to know when to stop and take the time for quiet reflection, to focus on the present moment and to explore what strong reactions might be telling us in such situations. As noted in Chapter 8, Ferguson (2018) observed instances of 'suspended self-preservation' where workers delayed addressing the emotional content of experiences they encountered in practice situations (p.420). In Chapter 8, we identified and discussed this as a skill of containment where practitioners may choose to delay reflection on their experience and feelings.

It is assumed that the more conscious practitioners are about the way they perceive, interpret and interact with phenomenon in their environment the greater the likelihood that they will be able to select responses that are effective in practice. Skills cultivated by mindfulness practice comprise: self-awareness, self-observation, self-care, emotion regulation, a deepened sense of empathy and a predisposition for personal responsibility (Baer 2006; Birnbaum 2005; Claxton 2005; Kondrat 1999; Lau et al. 2006; Morrison 2007). Each of these skills is pertinent to the development of an emotionally competent practitioner (Morrison 2007). In learning to be reflective, and take even just a few minutes to consider the importance of strong emotions in practice, practitioners create the opportunity to consciously use themselves to best effect in the complex and challenging situations encountered in professional practice. Some practitioners may use techniques to improve their self-awareness. Birnbaum (2005) used relaxation and guided meditation to focus on students' capacity to become 'observers of self' and to develop their inner voice in order to facilitate self-awareness and the use of 'self' as a tool in helping relationships. Birnbaum (2005, unpaginated) notes, 'The ability to observe ourselves is acquired and entails listening and tuning in to ourselves and the world around us. The observing self is better able to listen and identify the different voices that exist within and around it.'

■ VIGNETTE: ANDREA – PART 2

We return to Andrea, who noticed her symptoms and decided to stop for a few minutes to focus on her thoughts and feelings, rather than rushing off to her next activity. Andrea noticeably calmed and felt better as she focused on her breathing and relaxing her muscles. The nausea lessened. She returned to her busy role but noted that she should trust her own feelings and follow up on her concerns about Timmy and Angela. She made a mental note that she must take this experience to supervision. She wanted to urgently plan the next steps in ensuring that Timmy was safe.

Traumatic incidents and the role of supervisors

In 2018, following recognition of the limited literature available to guide supervisors of workers who were providing trauma-informed clinical services, a special issue of *The Clinical Supervisor* aimed to fill the gap. 'It is only when therapists have knowledgeable and supportive supervision that they can operate from a trauma-informed perspective' (Knight 2018, p.12). Knight (2018) contends that well-informed and supportive supervision requires the same elements that comprise trauma-informed practice and care, namely knowledge of trauma and its effects on clients, indirect trauma, core skills of clinical supervision, and core precepts of trauma-informed practice and care (Berger and Quiros 2016). Awareness of the effects of exposure to the corrosive impact of work with abuse and violence, alongside the skills of effective supervision relationship building, can create safety and trust.

It is not just the everyday experience of stress that challenges practitioners. All practitioners in the helping professions may experience either directly or indirectly a critical incident or traumatic event in their workplace or in a work-related context. Stressed practitioners are particularly vulnerable to traumatic or critical incidents. Adamson (1999) reminds us that 'our assumptive worldview relies on an ontological security that we are safe, that the sky is not going to fall in on us today' (p.30). Both serious incidents and the juxtaposition of stressful everyday events can propel practitioners into a situation where they may feel deeply distressed and unable to cope. It is not uncommon for people in such situations to use expression such as, 'I didn't see that coming' or 'It was like a bolt from the blue'. Their equilibrium is disturbed by the unexpected event or even the unexpected strong emotional reaction to an event.

There are numerous ways in which professionals can experience harmful exposure. Apart from the longer-term impact of stressful workplaces there are times when the boundaries of service user and work experience become blurred. Adams, Figley and Boscarino (2008) note that 'empathic engagement with traumatized clients often requires the professional to discuss details of the traumatic experience' (pp.239–240). As a consequence, health and social care workers may report symptoms connected to 're-experiencing the client's traumatic event, wishing to avoid both the client and reminders of the client's trauma, and persistent arousal' (p.240).

As noted earlier in this chapter, health workers also face the daily risk of verbal and physical abuse (Elston, Gabe and O'Beirne 2006), and to illustrate this we will return to Jenny's experience.

Fear in practice: Promoting practitioner safety

Jenny's story continues in order to consider the impact of critical incidents and to explore the supervisor's role:

■ VIGNETTE: JENNY – PART 2

As a result of feedback from James's school, Jenny and the child protection social worker decided to do a joint visit to address James's care and protection needs with Tamsin. They found her aggressively drunk and hard to engage. Tamsin's temper quickly flared up when James's wellbeing was questioned. She lashed out at Jenny, giving her bruises and an abrasion on the arm, before falling awkwardly and cutting her head open on the fireplace. There was a lot of blood: Tamsin was initially moaning and incoherent. At this point, the care and protection social worker froze and Jenny had to take charge and call an ambulance.

James returned from school, and as no family members could be located, he was taken into care. Tamsin threatened to 'get' Jenny as soon as she was out of hospital. 'I know where you live,' she said. Jenny returned to the office at 6.15pm. Everyone else had gone home except her supervisor.

The supervision literature tends to be somewhat silent on workplace violence, a notable exception being Brown and Bourne (1996), who emphasize that the skills for dealing with stress and traumatic events are essential components of a contemporary supervisor's repertoire. There may be some acculturation in supervisors' experience that has blunted their awareness of what might be happening for supervisees. Just as frontline workers may have reduced empathy in the face of constant human suffering, supervisors may become less responsive to supervisee concerns. In child protection and adult services, the stigmatization of service users adds to the critical attitudes of the public generated by practice failures. Supervisors may unwittingly be modelling unhelpful strategies (Beddoe 2003), unaware of the impact of hostile public attitude on their own approach to practice:

- *Being fearless: 'It's a war zone!'* This kind of practice involves defensive practice. There is a danger of internalizing negative expectations and being prescriptive and authoritarian. The message is 'this is how to survive!' (Beddoe 2003, p.22). Unfortunately, these practitioners are likely to be blamed if they are assaulted. This approach may place supervisees at grave risk through exposing them to unnecessarily dangerous situations (Smith 2006).

- *Being passive and avoiding conflict: 'It's a matter of survival – live to fight another day!'* This approach can signal a serious threat to competent decision making. The dangers are well documented, especially in the child protection literature (Goddard and Tucci 1991; Morrison 1997). Practitioners who strive to use verbal engagement skills to enable a positive relationship with service users may avoid conflict to the detriment of children and vulnerable adults, their own safety and that of colleagues. In addition, they may 'miss' vital information generated by their personal experience of the hostile and angry person (Beddoe 2003, p.22).

When social workers had experienced traumatic events, Smith (2017, p.127) found that one of the most unhelpful responses they recalled was when their supervisors 'under-estimated and "played down" the significance and repercussions of the event as they had experienced it'. After near misses, workers 'described responses like, "Well nothing happened did it? You're still here and OK aren't you?"' Such responses minimize the emotional and psychological impact of what might have happened. Smith (2017 p.127) argues that 'groundless re-assurance…serves no good purpose and leaves people feeling misunderstood'. In his earlier research, Smith (2000) had studied the responses of practitioners to the question, 'What responses would you like from an ideal supervisor to whom you took an experience of fear?' (p.18). What participants wanted was their supervisor to make time to 'listen to them without criticism', show 'a capacity to understand, acknowledge and recognize' the experience, followed by 'reflection, non-critical exploration, validation, affirmation and confirmation of the supervisee… Supporting the supervisee and taking action', where necessary (Smith 2000.p.18).

What then were Jenny's needs after the event described above, where as an already stressed nurse she then experienced a frightening incident and was injured herself? There are some essential differences between regular scheduled supervision and a supervisory response to a critical incident response (Adamson 2001). Supervision is planned while incidents are not. Intervention post incident may be directive, practical and time limited while supervision involves an extended engagement. There are multiple agendas in supervision (support, education, administration) and there are also multiple agendas within critical incident management (e.g. practical assistance, 'normalization', debriefing and reintegration); 'the demands of an incident make these tasks less parallel and more sequential' (Adamson 2001, p.41). Immediately after a critical event, the needs of the incident predominate. Where 'normal' supervision is essentially reflective, this is a crisis and premature reflection may be inappropriate' (Adamson 2001, p.38).

Where a supervisor also has organizational responsibilities, they may have to balance 'damage control' strategies in terms of service user safety issues with the needs of the practitioner in front of them. Adamson notes that the 'enabling' aspects of supervision may need to be balanced with any 'ensuring' components (p.40). In Jenny's situation, there may be compelling management responsibilities which would need to be addressed, such as follow-up with the hospital and alerting others who need to know.

Critical incidents will clearly affect more people than the people immediately involved and some effort may be needed to address this at both individual and team level. There is a level of additional stress generated in teams and workplaces after an incident such as Jenny's where post-incident reactions on the part of the survivor may include intense irritability and an apparent inability to acknowledge the impact of the event.

An additional issue to consider is that supervisors, especially if they work in the same service as an affected supervisee, may also face strong feelings (Adamson 2001). These may include feelings of inadequacy and incompetence, apprehension about the impact on the wider team, the supervisor's own fears and anxieties, concerns about 'victim's' competence and fears about consequences and organizational vulnerabilities (Bourne and Brown 1996).

Coping and resilience

Collins (2008) identifies two styles of coping strategy: problem-solving coping and emotion-focused coping (Collins 2008, p.1177). The former strategy involves active efforts to change the current negative circumstances: planning, seeking the involvement of others, communication and seeking practical advice, assistance and information. Goal-oriented strategies encourage a sense of control (Collins 2007, p.262). Emotion-focused coping includes seeking support for emotional reasons and seeking sympathy or understanding (Collins 2008, p.1180.) Opportunities to talk about stressful situations and distressing thoughts and feelings can help practitioners make meaning out of negative events and situations, which in turn aids integration and resolution of stressful experiences (Brown and Bourne 1996; Collins 2007, 2008). Supervision provides the space for the ventilation of emotion. Ventilation is important but there is some evidence that over-emphasis on venting emotion in supervision can be negative. Collins (2008) cites Carver, Scheier and Weintraub 1989 who suggested 'over-use of ventilation and sympathy seeking for long periods may not always be adaptive and can impede "adjustment", as it is believed too much focus on distress can distract people from active coping and movement beyond distress' (in Collins 2008, p.1180). An active engagement of positive emotions is important to avoid disengagement, depersonalization and anger or disillusionment with service users (Satymurti 1981).

Extensive venting of emotion in supervision can also be corrosive for supervisors, and this is perhaps exacerbated when supervisors and supervisees share stressful circumstances. At the lower end of intensity, this may mean supervisors can be over-exposed to the complaints and stress narratives of others and become desensitized and irritated. Under these circumstances, reflection is difficult and venting is easier. This passage by Busse (2009) about becoming a supervisor illustrates this well:

> At the beginning of supervision I was faced with dissatisfaction and a stream of abuse. Apart from spontaneous flight tendencies as a result of this scenario, I also felt a desire to reflect. The combination of issues…offered everything a supervisor needs to feel challenged. Initially it was difficult for me not to give in to the urge to offload, which time and again manifested itself in complaining and moaning by the supervised. (Busse 2009, p.166.)

Busse noted that over time he himself started 'to complain about these difficult and unprofessional people… [T]he situation that the supervised experienced in their everyday life threatened to reproduce itself in supervision' (Busse 2009, p.166).

At a level of greater intensity of stress, in circumstances that are more emphatically traumatic, Dekel and Baum (2009) developed the term 'shared traumatic reality' to describe where practitioners 'live and work in the same community as the people they serve' and are exposed to the same 'traumatising circumstances as their clients' (Dekel and Baum 2009, p.8). In crisis intervention, especially after major disasters, terrorism or violence, professionals are not only helping survivors to navigate through a stressful event and cope with the emotional consequences, but are also having to cope with their own circumstances and emotions, and, if in leadership roles, having a duty of care to look out for the needs of their teams (Dekel and Baum 2009, p.8). The concept of resilience enters the realm of professional coping from this understanding of 'bouncing back' from adversity.

'Psychological resilience refers to effective coping and adaptation although faced with loss, hardship, or adversity' (Tugade and Frederickson 2004, p.320). Resilient individuals experience the frustration and anxiety brought to the surface in adverse times but even at the centre of these experiences they are able to call on positive emotions and use humour, creativity and problem solving. Luthans, Youseff and Avolio (2007b) have used the phrase 'psychological capital', which is:

> an individual's positive psychological state of development and is characterized by: (1) having confidence (self-efficacy) to take on and put in the necessary effort to succeed at challenging tasks; (2) making a positive attribution (optimism) about succeeding now and in the future; (3) persevering toward goals and, when necessary, redirecting paths to goals (hope) in order to succeed; and (4) when beset by problems and adversity, sustaining and bouncing back and even beyond (resilience) to attain success. (Luthans *et al.* 2007b, p.3)

Promoting resilient practitioners: hope, optimism and balance

It is important to maintain a balanced view of the experiences of professional practitioners in the helping professions. A study of Canadian child welfare workers (Stalker *et al.* 2007) surprisingly found participants scoring high on a measure of emotional exhaustion and, at the same time, 'high on overall job satisfaction' (Stalker *et al.* 2007, pp.182–183). Individual characteristics, for example finding support in relationships with supervisors and colleagues, strong personal reward in helping others, 'having a commitment to the mandate of child welfare and believing that one's labour is making a difference, contribute to satisfaction with child welfare work in spite of work overload and emotional exhaustion' (p.182). A review of this research confirms that there are preventive strategies to promote continuing optimistic engagement with the work, although Stalker *et al.* sound a note of caution that the incidence of emotional exhaustion should not be ignored because of its potential to contribute to depersonalization (Stalker *et al.* 2007, p.189).

The flipside of examining burnout is to consider the factors that might mediate against exhaustion, depersonalization and real or feared reduced competence. Collins (2007, p.256) asks, 'What might enable some workers to persist, endure and thrive in their careers, compared to others who may become ill and sometimes eventually leave the profession?' Collins notes three kinds of coping strategies which relate to positive affect: 'positive appraisal, goal-directed/problem-focused work and the infusion of ordinary events with meaning' (Collins 2007, p.255). Literature over the last ten years (Beddoe *et al.* 2014; Delgado *et al.* 2017; Grant and Kinman 2014; Hunter and Warren 2013) has indicated that resilient qualities are important for workers in the helping professions and should be enhanced via supervision and other interventions.

'Hope, resilience, optimism, and efficacy' are linked constructs and research has shown 'that they are developable' (Luthans *et al.* 2007a, p.545). A study of nursing care assistants confirmed that 'supportive relationships, adequate resources, encouragement by others, and improving perceptions of self-efficacy (ability to achieve goals in their workplace) may foster their hope' (Duggleby, Cooper and Penz 2009, p.2376). In this current decade, research continues to support organizational interventions to provide support. In research undertaken in Northern Ireland, McFadden (2018) confirmed that managerial and supervision support, along with good peer relationships, was of critical importance to the retention of child protection social workers, confirming earlier research, for example Yankeelov *et al.* (2009). Coping skills, access to personal and social support and the fostering of individual characteristics such as hopefulness and self-efficacy are cited as beneficial in protecting practitioners from the potentially debilitating effects of their work through building their resilience.

A recent review of literature by Foster *et al.* (2019) reports, however, that there was a risk with the prevailing focus in the reviewed literature on personal resilience in mental health nursing where measurement of resilience was seen primarily as a trait-based or individual attribute. A focus on 'resilience as existing within the individual alone can be seen to place the responsibility for positive adaptation on the individual. There is potential to judge or blame the person if they do not respond positively following adversity' (Foster *et al.* 2019, p.81). In an article in *The Guardian*, Galpin, Maksymluk and Whiteford (2019) found that practitioner participant accounts from their recent research suggest 'that resilience is being used in professional settings as a metaphor to blame individuals for not coping with ever-increasing workloads, ever-diminishing resources and significant political, structural and organizational failings'.

Hopefulness, continuing commitment to the mission of their helping profession and self-belief in one's ability to make a difference are crucial to not just surviving but thriving in professional practice. Feudtner *et al.* (2007, p.187) cite Snyder (2000) in delineating three main components of hope:

> first, individuals who are able to anchor their thinking about the future to specific desired goals are more likely to be hopeful. Second, people who can imagine or plan ways to achieve these goals (step by step...) have greater hope. Third, individuals who think that they themselves as capable of pursuing goals successfully, who believe in their own capacity to get what they want, are more hopeful. (Feudtner *et al.* 2007, p.187)

Feudtner *et al.* also found that 'nurses' level of hope is associated with their self-reported comfort and competence regarding palliative care' (p.187). The vignette which follows illustrates Feudtner *et al.*'s view that 'hopeful thinking enhances personal performance and is pivotal in confronting the challenges that life-threatening illness and end-of-life care present' (p.191).

▪ VIGNETTE: MOANA

Moana, an experienced nurse, was working on the paediatric oncology ward in a large public hospital. There had been a recent increase in the number of admissions of severely ill children and associated deaths. Of particular concern to Moana was a child who had died very unexpectedly. To Moana it 'felt like the straw that broke the camel's back'. Normally robust and resilient, Moana felt overwhelmed by this latest loss. She felt vulnerable, unable to cope with her own emotions and had begun to doubt her ability to work any longer in this area. In supervision, Moana's supervisor asked Moana to talk about this child and why he in particular was causing her so much distress. What was different about this child? Moana was able to identify that the unexpectedness of the death meant that she felt that she had not been able to do all she could for this child. The supervisor asked Moana to describe what her aims were when working with children. She then asked her to identify how this applied to the child in question. Moana was surprised to realize that she had in fact been working within these aims with the child but had not had the time to formally detail her plans. It had been short and intense but Moana had offered this child all the very best of care at every step of his journey. The supervisor asked what Moana was learning from this. Moana realized that she had an internalized framework which she readily applied to all her work and that she could trust herself to adapt to different circumstances. Moana left supervision feeling sad but knowing that she had the knowledge and the skills to offer appropriate and competent care and in particular that she was able to adapt her work to accommodate different circumstances.

Thus, resilient practitioners 'use positive emotions to bounce back' from emotionally challenging experiences (Tugade and Frederickson 2004, p.320). The ability to find personal resources, including positive emotions, during periods of high stress or in the face of critical incidents is a key attribute. Each practitioner has a unique personal history, and many social workers, counsellors, nurses and other health professionals may have been attracted to their career because of their exposure to challenging personal, familial events. Supervision can foster a secure place where fears and anxieties can be named (Ruch 2007a) and explored but also where positive emotions can be called on (Howard 2008). This is of considerable importance in relation to stress 'where the dominant discourse has the potential to pathologise the individual' (Howard 2008, p.110).

We have explored the nature of stress and the impact on individuals but professional practitioners rarely work entirely alone, and increasingly work in teams, often multidisciplinary in nature. Ruch (2007a) notes the important 'potential of teams in general and co-working in particular', especially given the observation that 'increasingly individualistic' approaches to professional practice dominate and these 'emphasize the role and responsibilities of individual practitioners at the expense of collaborative interventions' (Ruch 2007a, p.666).

Supervisors as advocates

To what extent should supervisors be advocates for practitioners in health and social care? Morrison (1993), in adding the 'mediation' function to supervision, identified the role of supervisors as both a buffer and a conduit between professional practitioners and managers. Supervisors can actively lead the charge to foster safe and supportive workplaces, however Bogo and Dill found that:

> Supervisors do not view themselves as leaders or generators of change. Rather, they feel like conduits, like messengers, and like they are in the middle between senior administrators and frontline workers. Whereas staff might perceive them as having power, they experience an illusion of power. (Bogo and Dill 2008, p.151)

This middle position ('piggy in the middle' as Hughes and Pengelly (1997) put it) is often an extremely difficult place to be. For the external supervisor, who holds an ambiguous position in relation to their supervisee's organization, there can be a sense of powerlessness and concern about the degree of responsibility to report on serious stress factors. Where does the 'duty of care' begin and end? External supervisors require good supervision so they can explore the complex ethical dimensions of supervisory responsibility in relation to supervisee distress.

In 1996, Brown and Bourne noted that supervision is a very stressful activity. They noted that supervisors need their own supervision 'in managing…to strive to disentangle their own needs from those of supervisors' (Brown and Bourne 1996, p.181).

> The future fascinates us. With our insatiable desire to know the future comes an alternation between seeing the future as a fatalistic or deterministic given (que cera, cera – what will be will be), to viewing it as a series of possibilities over which we have some power. (Carroll 2007, p.237)

Michael Carroll provides a potent message in the passage above; being future oriented and having a belief in possibilities and a commitment to the search are key dispositions in the resilient practitioner. Supervision that models these dispositions and highlights successes and achievements can make a major contribution to better outcomes in health and social care.

CHAPTER 10

Supervising Students in Clinical Placements

The clinical placement brings the student into the rich and challenging world of professional practitioners. The beginning practitioner 'learns their conventions, their constraints, languages and appreciative systems, their repertoire of exemplars, systemic knowledge and patterns of knowing in action' through interaction with experienced practitioners (Schön 1987, pp.36–37). A student entering this world brings their own knowledge, understandings and beliefs; they are not an empty vessel to be filled. Teaching within the clinical placement can provide the basis for enduring professional dispositions by exploring new meanings for behaviour, enhanced interpersonal communication skills and a reflective and inquiring stance in professional practice. Placements also provide students with an understanding of the social, cultural and structural differences among health and social care social organizations. In the health and social care professions, student placements also provide students with the opportunity to test out their capacity to demonstrate the critical thinking and anti-oppressive practice that will be expected of them (Hutchison 2015; Lay and McGuire 2010; Scammell 2016). As we noted in Chapter 4, the organizational context of professional practice hugely shapes everyday work processes and relationships, for example a medical intern will find the working relationships in a busy rural GP practice quite different from the complex hierarchical arrangements in a major teaching hospital. A child protection social worker might struggle with practice in a women's refuge. Clinical placements give students an opportunity to experience different work contexts.

Why supervise students? There are benefits for both placement educator and supervisee in this process. As we noted in Chapter 6, Urdang (1999) found benefits for supervisors though mastery of new skills, enhanced self-esteem, increased self-awareness and the capacity to analyse their own work. Thomas *et al.* (2007, pp.S4–S5) found that responses from 132 field

213

educators of occupational therapy students rated the following benefits highest: future recruitment; developing staff supervision skills; developing clinical reasoning; organization and time management; promoting exposure of the service to university; updating clinicians' skills; and promoting diversity in workplace. Additional benefits associated with student supervision included:

> students conducting evidence-based practice, quality improvement and in-service activities, an improved ability to 'stay connected' with tertiary institutions, the tendency for students to indirectly promote the occupational therapy role within supervisors' work settings, and improved opportunities for running larger client group programs. (Thomas *et al.* 2007, p.S5)

The central aim of clinical education is to provide opportunities for workplace learning to enrich students' understanding of their profession and to foster beginning competence, including developing a reflective disposition (Stagnitti, Schoo and Welch 2013). Field education is valued as a major site for the integration of theory and practice, the development of professional identity and deepening of disciplinary socialization. Placement educators play an important role in shaping dispositions, including those about other professions, by modelling attitudes, behaviours and expectations (Arndt *et al.* 2009, p.19). Arndt *et al.*'s (2009) study found that students understood the specific roles of other professions in the classroom but did not appreciate how to communicate and complete tasks which required cooperation with other disciplines (Arndt *et al.* 2009, pp.21–22). Given the current emphasis on interprofessional working in health and social care, field education may need to play a greater role in preparation for work in complex environments.

This chapter addresses three main topics: the role of supervision in clinical placements in the health and social care professions and the potential for interprofessional learning; the tension between didactic instruction and the facilitation of reflective practice in placements; and the utility of a reflective learning process for supervision for students. Space does not permit exploration of teaching processes or the major issue of assessment.

A note on terms: There are numerous terms used in relation to the student placement and the participant roles in professional education for the health and social care professions. In this chapter, we will denominate the learner as the student, the teacher/supervisor as the placement educator and the context as the clinical placement.

Supervising in clinical placements

Supervision within the clinical placement is a structured, interactive and collaborative process which takes place within a purposeful professional relationship. McMahon (2014, p.333) offers four guiding principles for supervisors' engagement with supervisees, which are also vital to the student placement: 'offering emotional presence and sensitivity; valuing both vulnerability and competence; offering knowledge and experience with humility; and developing a relationship to support continued personal and professional growth'. The central principle here is the 'developmental relationship between supervisor and supervisee, the quality of the other principles either enhancing or limiting the quality of this relationship' (McMahon 2014, p.337).

Just as we discussed in Chapter 3, the centrality of the supervision relationship is crucial, particularly given the complexity of the placement educator's supervisory role. This relationship may involve some or all of these components: observation, monitoring, teaching, coaching, supporting and providing reflective supervision, and assessment for students during their placement. The placement educator has a dual role within this relationship (Beddoe 2000) to simultaneously motivate the student's professional development while often managing a busy clinical practice load. An effective working relationship must be established between the student and the fieldwork educator to provide a vehicle for learning, with a strong focus on the tasks of building professional identity, learning to work in teams and managing the demands of the workplace in professional practice. The placement educator also makes a significant contribution to the student's learning about supervision itself and more broadly about self-management within the complex web of professional relationships at work.

Within this student–placement educator relationship both parties will bring the sum of previous professional experiences. Where students have had previous negative experience of supervision and placements, they may be reluctant to participate. It will take time and positive exchanges to enable trust in the relationship to grow. Frequently, negative experiences have been related to conflict over power and student difficulty with critique. The dimensions of power and authority in the field placement situation are complicated by the potential for serious role conflict for the practice educator who 'must be guardian of standards and safe practice, friend, mentor and counsellor to the student, but also educational assessor and in part, gatekeeper to the profession' (King *et al.* 2009, p.142).

One of the key differences between student supervision and supervision of qualified practitioners is that the work of relationship building needs to happen very quickly because of the short timeframe of the fieldwork placement. There are several other key elements that differ and all contribute to the need to consolidate a positive relationship within a defined, often short, timeframe to support student learning. Figure 10.1 demonstrates the key differences between student and practitioner supervision.

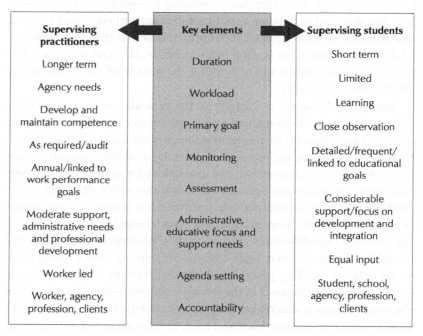

Promoting practitioner wellbeing

Supervising practitioners	Key elements	Supervising students
Longer term	Duration	Short term
Agency needs	Workload	Limited
Develop and maintain competence	Primary goal	Learning
		Close observation
As required/audit	Monitoring	Detailed/frequent/ linked to educational goals
Annual/linked to work performance goals	Assessment	
		Considerable support/focus on development and integration
Moderate support, administrative needs and professional development	Administrative, educative focus and support needs	
		Equal input
Worker led	Agenda setting	Student, school, agency, profession, clients
Worker, agency, profession, clients	Accountability	

Figure 10.1: Student and practitioner supervision

The agenda for interprofessional learning

Interprofessional education (IPE) is part of a substantial international movement to improve health and social care by reducing interdisciplinary barriers and encouraging collaborative work. Leonard and Weinstein (2009) acknowledge the many barriers to effective IPE at pre-registration level, citing structural barriers, cultural differences, logistical problems with programmes, timetables and the requirements of regulatory bodies (Low and Weinstein 2000). Added to this is an ongoing scepticism, lack of robust evidence for effectiveness and teaching challenges (Freeth *et al.* 2006). In spite of all these challenges, Leonard and Weinstein (2009, pp.215–216) feel that clinical placements, valued very highly by all stakeholders, provide an excellent pre-service experience of working together. Developing a programme of shared activities with other health and social care field educators can provide additional learning opportunities for both fieldwork educator and student.

While, as discussed in Chapter 3, it is generally accepted that it is not appropriate for students to be supervised by a supervisor from another profession (Davys 2019; Davys and Beddoe 2016), placement educators can provide opportunities for students to work alongside other disciplines and learn how each has a role, perspective, professional culture and expectations about how they will relate to service users and others (Beddoe 2010, p.261). This provides rich opportunities for learning both from other bodies of knowledge and also from the experience of teamwork (Smith and Anderson 2008). Placement educators from other disciplines can contribute to success with students both by providing peer support (for both students and educators) and by sharing learning activities.

■ SCENARIO

Robert and Wenli were two nursing students on placement in a busy special care baby unit with Rachel and this coincided with the fieldwork placement of Sunita and Philippa, who were social work students in the child development service. Both Rachel and Maria, the social work placement educator, were experienced educators who met regularly for peer support and had often talked about the possibility of bringing the students together. Before the students arrived, they planned some joint activities. When comparing notes about how the placements were going, Maria talked about difficulties in engaging Philippa in one-to-one supervision, as she was very reluctant to talk about the challenges of cross-cultural practice in the diverse local communities. Rachel and Maria used their peer supervision relationship to rehearse some ideas, and agreed to try a joint group supervision session to see if this was helpful. In this session, discussion of families of newborns known to all the students resulted in an interesting and lively debate about roles and approaches when working with families of different religions. It was noted that the six people in the room represented five religions, four different cultures and two professions! Wenli offered to meet with Philippa to help her better understand Chinese family roles. At the end of the session, the students agreed to meet without the placement educators to discuss their research projects. As Rachel and Maria debriefed over coffee later they considered this to be a highly successful joint supervision session and planned one more towards the end of the placements.

The experiences of Maria and her nursing colleague illustrate how bringing both students and placement educators together can demonstrate the important aspects of working together. The Leicester model of interprofessional education identifies the following advantages of interprofessional immersion during training: patient and professional experiences, deeper understanding of different professional perspectives, theory and policies and the provision of opportunities for joint work to find solutions to problems identified (Smith and Anderson 2008, p.769).

Attributes of excellent placement educators

The skills of placement educators are the same as those needed by supervisors of qualified professionals, with the additional focus on teaching and the integration of theoretical and ethical knowledge in practice situations and assessment. Kilminster and Jolly (2000) reviewed the literature across the health and social care professions and found a fairly stable and consistent set of characteristics of effective supervisors: direction and constructive feedback and opportunities to carry out procedures and review them (medicine); provision of advice, feedback, opportunity to reflect and being a role model (psychology); teaching skills, interpersonal style and professional competence (radiographers). In summary, effective supervisors have empathy, offer support, flexibility, knowledge, interest in supervision and good tracking of supervisees, and are interpretative, respectful, focused and practical (Kilminster and Jolly 2000, pp.832–833).

In social work, Barretti (2009) found that students want placement educators who are 'available, respectful, responsive, supportive, fair, objective, and that are knowledgeable and able to directly communicate their knowledge…and provide evaluative feedback'. Students also reported a preference for placement educators who 'encourage autonomy, provide the opportunity to be observed, and facilitate professional development' (Barretti 2009, pp.50–51).

Cole and Wessel (2008) found that a placement educator could enrich the learning experience of physiotherapy students in the following ways: good preparation, demonstration and time to obtain information, confirmation of learning through the provision of feedback and recapping, and the provision of 'hands on experiences appropriate to students' knowledge, skills and comfort' (p.163). Students appreciated respect and valuing of individual input, time and being allowed an appropriate level of independence. As in the case of Barretti's review, Cole and Wessel found that students valued clinical educators who demonstrated professional behaviour related to communication, evidence-based practice and continuing education (p.163). Summing up these attributes, it is apparent that field educators have a challenging set of expectations to meet, all the while demonstrating congruence with professional values through their behaviour and communications (King *et al.* 2009). The greater focus on teaching and learning in student supervision, and on both informal and formal assessment, differentiates it from the supervision of experienced practitioners. This role is not without tensions.

Conversely, Watkins (1997) found that ineffective supervisors of psychotherapy trainees demonstrated 'rigidity, low empathy, low support, failure to teach…being indirect and intolerant, being closed…lacking in praise and encouragement, being sexist, and emphasising evaluation, weakness and deficiencies' (Watkins 1997, p.168). Students and clinical interns are vulnerable because their 'clinical supervisors hold supervisees' careers and futures in their hands – the supervisor has all of the authority and nearly all of the power over the supervisees and their futures' (McNamara *et al.* 2017, p.140). This power is recognized by students and can be expected to impact on the relationship. Ensuring that the nature of assessment and formal feedback to the student's education institution is clear, with expectations spelled out, helps to dispel anxieties.

Tensions between teaching and facilitation in field placement supervision

It is our view that students on placement benefit from clear, structured facilitation of their experiences as reflection may not always come easily to every student. Three fundamental tensions (Davys and Beddoe 2009, p.920) are present in student supervision:

- The need to maintain balance between teaching (information giving and instruction) and facilitating review and reflection (Beddoe 2013).

- The fostering of reflection in situations where there is limited experience and which are overlaid by high levels of student anxiety. This anxiety may stem from a number of sources which include the nature of the work, interpersonal dynamics and the student assessment process (Gelman and Baum 2010; Maidment and Crisp 2010).

- The management of the dependence–autonomy continuum as students test their new knowledge and skills in 'real' work, recognizing that confidence may fluctuate over the course of the placement (Beddoe 2000).

A key focus of student supervision is the promotion of a sense of ownership, mastery and understanding in clinical practice. At the same time, the placement educator is charged to both facilitate reflection in beginning practice, and instruct and guide the student in practice activities in which they will be assessed. The balance of these two dimensions of supervision enables the focus on the student's experience rather than the supervisor's expertise (Davys and Beddoe 2009, p.920). The supervision process, undertaken with a clear contract and negotiated expectations of all the parties, provides an excellent vehicle for learning.

Key tasks for the student in placement include the consolidation of learning, managing both critical and complimentary feedback, and self-regulation in the workplace. During this phase, students may experience conflict between their need for their placement educator to be confidently in charge and their own emerging sense of professional competence and desire for greater autonomy. As King *et al.* (2009, p.140) have asserted, the 'journey from dependence to independence is both dynamic and contextual' and during this time students can be vulnerable and require assistance. For some, over-confidence may need to be tempered and for others, lack of confidence may mean they require considerable support to undertake even relatively simple tasks. Good preparation for undertaking clinical activities, with clear parameters, opportunities for reflection and regular review, is an essential component in building student confidence. Encouraging well-planned peer learning activities can also enhance experiences (Tai *et al.* 2017), while continuous opportunities for feedback and reflection can contribute to a growing sense of accomplishment, confidence and belonging in their chosen profession. Ideally during this phase, the student is able to experience some independence while appreciating constructive input and oversight of their work.

Students look to placement educators to assist them to manage and reduce anxiety (Gelman and Baum 2010; Ruch 2002) and to provide structure and teaching along with facilitative support (Lizzio, Stokes and Wilson 2005). Balance between the features of student supervision is important and we have found Butler (1996) useful in affirming the notion that students need to experience a 'mixture of interventions which are equally weighted at both ends of the didactic–facilitative continuum' (Davys and Beddoe 2009, p.921). The duty of care in relation to the safety of all participants requires relatively high levels of instruction and information (the didactic mode). This is necessary in order that students have a context and guidelines to begin to undertake the basic tasks of practice, and high levels of positive feedback and support interventions (the facilitative mode) are required in order that they can accept the challenge to reflect on the action taken and the consequences of that action (Davys and Beddoe 2009, p.921).

We have previously noted that the literature cautions that didactic supervision creates over-dependence on the instructions, experience and expertise of the placement educator and produces surface learning (Davys and Beddoe 2009, p.921). Surface learning focuses on content rather than underlying purpose and meaning, and Clare (2007), discussing the work of educationalists Marton and Saljo (1976), describes surface learning as 'extrinsically motivated, passive and reproductive' in contrast with deep learning which is an 'intrinsically motivated process of personalised meaning construction' (Clare 2007, p.434). Lizzio and colleagues (2005) have explored the didactic-facilitative tension in supervision in a study which investigated supervisee perceptions of the learning processes in professional supervision. Their study explored whether 'deep/surface learning, anxiety and self-management are salient to supervisees' perceptions of their approach to professional supervision' (Lizzio *et al.* 2005, p.243). Lizzio *et al.* did not find a polarized relationship between didactic and facilitative approaches; in fact, the use of the one did not exclude the other. Field educators who were perceived by their supervisees as helpful used a wide range of interventions, including didactic interventions to instruct and inform students on best practice. Where supervision includes a clear focus on learning and development then didactic interventions are not an obstacle to deep learning.

The placement educator's challenge to achieve the necessary balance is clearly indicated by Lizzio *et al.* (2005) who outline the need to find 'an appropriate balance between supervisory authority and supervisee autonomy, between evaluation and support and between transmission of required knowledge and the reflective engagement with the supervisees' experience' (Lizzio *et al.* 2005, p.240). While a perceived lack of supervisor support can negatively impact on supervision, Lizzio *et al.* (2009) note that 'too much support…can also inhibit the effectiveness of supervision. For example, if a supervisor is overly concerned with "being supportive" they may become too permissive and not address "touchy issues" such as supervisee competence or performance' (Lizzio *et al.* 2009, p.129). This can result in superficial engagement in supervision and if an incident arises in which the placement educator is obliged to be directive, or deliver critical feedback, this can elicit hurt and defensive responses. The student, who has interpreted the placement educator's support as unconditional support, may feel that any direction or critique is a retreat from that supportive stance, no matter how carefully the feedback or instruction is given. As in practitioner supervision, the development of a clear contract and mutual expectations about the nature and focus of feedback are vital.

Developmental approaches

Developmental models focus on the educative function of supervision, incorporating an assessment of the supervisee's level of experience. As noted in Chapter 2, most developmental models consist of three to five stages and range from 'novice' to 'expert' (Butler 1996) or describe the steps towards a mature integration of the self and professional competencies and foci (Hawkins and Shohet 2012, pp.77–82). The value of these models is that they take account of the student's level of experience and competence for their stage in their training. Developmental models are characterized by stages and assume that people will move through all stages over time, from novice or beginner to confident 'expert', and thus often subject to the criticism that they are rigid, and blind to cultural and social differences, difference, power and context. Prescriptive approaches to professional development can equate the norm with success and regard divergence as a deficit, minimizing factors of diversity and context (Gardiner 1989). Cultural assumptions implicit in developmental models therefore need to be considered for the information left out, such as lived experience of trauma and privilege and oppression related to race, class, gender or sexual orientation, as much as for the information which they provide. In particular stages of dependency, autonomy can vary widely and Nye suggests that developmental models 'recognize an early, time-limited phase of dependence in supervision as the norm, the ultimate goal...is to move supervisees out of dependence to an independent autonomous stance. These models reflect...U.S. culture and traditional clinical developmental theories' (Nye 2007, p.84). More recently, Stoltenberg *et al.* (2014) have reviewed the importance of taking into account cultural norms and communication styles within education and professional development.

Despite these notes of caution, developmental models can be useful for beginning placement educators in that they provide an explanation of how skills develop over time and therefore a guide by which to assess new practitioners' development and competence. The supervision model developed by Loganbill *et al.* (1982) has been highly influential in supervision, particularly because of the assessment framework it provides. Developmental approaches assist placement educators to understand the challenges in transitions that occur for students learning as they cycle through stages, always drawing on previous knowledge and skills and making meaning through interpretations of new experiences by reflection on earlier but similar or even contrasting events.

Stages of student learning

In Chapter 5, we noted the usefulness of Butler's 1996 work on reflective learning for professional practice. Butler rejected explanations of competence that suggested that it was merely the acquisition of an increased repertoire of skills and techniques (Butler 1996). Rather, he described a model of performance development based on reflection, asserting that, 'through reflection, performance is transformed. And it is this transformation that brings about improvement in the performance' (Butler 1996, p.277).

Novice, the first stage of Butler's model, describes a context where students are new to the work and have little real experience of the situations which might arise in practice. At this level, the student seeks rules and certainty. Rules provide safety and help to shape and guide practice. Butler describes the behaviour of novices as 'extremely limited and very inflexible' (Butler 1996, p.278).

The second stage of Butler's model, *Advanced Beginner*, is characterized by the student's belief that there will be a correct solution for every problem, and frequent expectation that the placement educator will hold most of the answers. At this point, dependence on others will be high. A field educator once commented, 'The students are like Lorenz's geese – every time I turn around they are there!' As we noted in Chapter 5, Nye (2007) has employed Vygotsky's ideas as helpful in re-valuing 'dependence' on the other as 'essential to learning and development across the life course. For Vygotsky, this is not a process with an end point...something to be outgrown...[but] inevitable if learning and development are to occur' (Nye 2007, p.84). Cultural difference, age and gender may have an impact on the degree of independence sought and previous educational experience may influence problem-solving approaches. At this stage, the student will draw on formal knowledge and previous experience to identify the main facts and issues in any given practice scenario but their repertoire of interventions will be limited. In a similar vein, Loganbill *et al.* (1982, p.17) describe a beginning practitioner as exhibiting 'naïve unawareness...narrow and rigid thought patterns' and as having a strong dependence on supervision but reflecting the cautions considered above. Lizzio *et al.* (2005, p.251) remind us that student dependence is appropriate behaviour to ensure safety. Deferral to the expertise of experienced practitioners also indicates the student's self-awareness of their limitations.

At this beginning stage, students may be resistant to reflection and seek clear solutions rather than complex answers or facilitation to think through practice issues in supervision (Butler 1996). Butler concludes that novice and advanced beginners 'can take in little of the complexity of their performance situation, it is too new, too strange, and they have to spend time remembering the rules they have set for them' (p.278). Three requirements need to be met to assist students: support to understand the performance setting, help to set priorities, and assistance to learn to reflect on their own performance and become less rigid and more flexible by developing and trusting their own personal practical knowledge (Butler 1996).

A note on student anxiety and stress

It is important to remember that students are not all the same – many will be young and still developing their personal skills and belief systems, some will be mature students and some may be training in a new profession and having to adjust to being a novice again. Student anxiety in placement is well documented (Gelman and Baum 2010; Sprengel and Job 2004) and studies have frequently reported specific worries, including lack of skills and experience, practical matters, safety, difficulty engaging service users and making mistakes. In addition, students are concerned about the quality of their placement and their relationship with colleagues and supervisors (Hay *et al.* 2019). Lizzio *et al.* (2005) have demonstrated that supportive, empathetic communication between a placement educator and their student reduces this anxiety. Students predict the challenges of field education, especially in direct work and in practice teams, and are often very anxious about exposing their lack of experience as they test out their skills in new situations. It can be helpful for fieldwork educators to share their own journey from student to seasoned professional. Being open to an exploration of mutual hopes and using empathetic self-disclosure can normalize these concerns and help build a constructive and trusting relationship (Beddoe 2010, p.261).

Developing critical thinking

Lietz (2009, 2010) explores critical thinking in child protection practice where outcomes of actions involve gathering data from multiple sources, reflective analysis of this data and 'ultimately synthesizing this evidence to support decision making'. This requires 'openness to considering multiple perspectives and creativity to uncover multiple options or responses' (2010, p.71). Deal (2004) suggests that there are specific strategies that clinical supervisors can use to encourage their supervisees to think critically (Deal 2004, p.11). Among these is the modelling by supervisors of a self-critical perspective, being able to share challenges and undertake transparent thinking and decision making (pp.11–12).

Placement educators can encourage students to continuously test their assumptions against research and good practice guides to ensure that in their clinical work they are able 'to differentiate between opinions (e.g., preferences and personal theories of causality or change) and data (e.g., facts about clients, relevant research findings)' (Deal 2004, p.14). Such practice protects against unchallenged stereotypes, cultural assumptions and poor reasoning and assists in the development of integrating a framework for addressing social justice issues in supervision (Chang *et al.* 2009; Hair and O'Donoghue 2009). For Deal, 'supervisors can best apply these strategies when their own critical thinking skills are well developed, they are comfortable with ambiguity' (Deal 2004, p.11), and do not attempt to expedite the process by over-simplifying it. Critical thinking essentially requires practitioners to ask questions of their practice and to examine the structural issues associated with any professional intervention. This can be seen as demonstrating a 'critical spirit'.

Why does critical thinking matter? Are service users in health and social services likely to receive better services if practitioners use critical thinking skills? Critical thinking skills are essential for effective practice in complex, ambiguous and uncertain situations. This especially applies to practice contexts where there is an element of risk assessment and management of ethical dilemmas.

As a consequence of the questioning of universal values (Banks 2008), discussed in Chapter 6, and the concomitant challenges to professional expert status, students and interns on clinical placements may find the lack of 'clear unequivocal ethical rules' unsettling (Beddoe 2013, p.374). Multiple perspectives can be confusing, and taken-for-granted values and assumptions may be challenged in practice with service users from diverse world views, thus requiring students to reflect honestly about their own biases and cultural assumptions. Fieldwork supervisors can foster the following relational attributes: 'valuing diversity; providing empathetic responsiveness to the lived realities of others; recognizing that each professional encounter is unique; and teaching skills for negotiating complex and contested decisions' (Beddoe 2013, p.374).

Beginning practitioners often struggle in their search for certainty and safety and need to develop the following critical thinking attributes: curiosity, the motivation to stay well informed, respect for reasoned inquiry, flexibility in considering alternatives, the courage to suspend judgement, and the ability to reconsider decisions in the light of new information (Facione 2013, p.9). A practitioner deficient in these attributes might be 'close-minded, inflexible, insensitive...unfair when it comes to judging the quality of arguments' and as a consequence 'never willing to reconsider' (Facione 2013, p.11). Placement educators can play a major role in encouraging critical thinking skills in their students through selecting tasks that draw on different perspectives, including, for example:

- seeking information about a mental illness by looking at formal codified knowledge

- reading narrative accounts of service experience, consumer websites

- talking to patient advocates, interviewing relevant health professionals prior to direct contact or observation in clinical work.

However, Deal and Pittman (2009) caution that to ensure that such experiences translate into skills, educators need to 'purposefully engage students in reflecting upon and evaluating their experiences' (p.98). Furthermore, field educators need to be open to their students' ideas and by 'sharing with students how they make decisions and evaluate their own work, and asking questions that require reflection and analysis, field instructors can help students use their new experiences to sharpen their critical thinking' (Deal and Pittman 2009, p.98).

The Reflective Learning Model for students on placement

The world of contemporary education for the health and social care professions is dominated by two major themes: reflective practice and evidence-informed practice. Each approach has at its heart the aspiration to deliver the most competent professional practice to service users. Evidence-informed practice utilizes positivist approaches to ensure that practitioners deliver services and 'treatments' that have been proved 'to be effective'. At the core is the desire to ensure that scarce resources are well used on 'what works' and the approach addresses the technical-rational paradigm of seeking certainty of outcomes in intervention. Reflective practice addresses the messiness of the processes and relationships in professional work, recognizing that practitioners work more often with uncertainty, emotion and contested understandings of what good outcomes are in the 'zone of ambiguity' (Brookfield 2009, p.294). As we noted in Chapter 5, reflective practice is driven by the desire to improve practice through thinking about experiences and teasing out the assumptions and perceptions that underpin practice.

Reflective practice is a major feature of pre-registration learning for the professions and is embedded in the many requirements within field education. Reflection is a core concept in the pre-service education of the health and social care professions. Black and Plowright (2010, p.246) offer a helpful definition:

Reflection is the process of engaging with learning and/or professional practice that provides an opportunity to critically analyse and evaluate that learning or practice. The purpose is to develop professional knowledge, understanding and practice that incorporates a deeper form of learning which is transformational in nature and is empowering, enlightening and ultimately emancipatory.

The literature on reflection and reflective practice is enormous and ever growing. Most authors acknowledge the intellectual debt to several key theorists: Schön (1987) for the concepts of reflection -in-action and reflection-on-action; Kolb (1984) for the cycle of experiential learning, and Mezirow (1981) for the critical thinking-generated perspective transformation. In a recent study, Marshall (2019) undertook a systematic review and thematic synthesis of the concept of reflection across professional contexts. Based on this analysis, a very concise and helpful definition, emphasizing that reflection produces new insights is proposed: 'reflection is a careful examination and bringing together of ideas to create new insight through ongoing cycles of expression and re/evaluation' (p.411).

Critical reflection is an extension of reflection to require reflective practitioners to address explicitly issues of power and justice in their work in order to promote critical thinking that goes beyond individualizing accounts of service user problems and concerns. Bay and Macfarlane (2011, p.746) neatly explain that 'the purpose of critical reflection is not just to improve practice, although that is certainly part of it, but to change and challenge dominant power relations and power structures'; Brookfield (2009, p.295) argues that pre-service education needs to place critical reflection at the core of practitioner development and what 'makes reflection critical is its foregrounding of power dynamics and relationships and its determination to uncover hegemonic dimensions to practice'. Critical reflection is a process that seeks to unsettle assumptions in order to change practice and helps us to understand the connections between our public (professional, organizational) and private worlds (Fook and Askeland 2007, pp.522–523). For Brookfield, a critically reflective practitioner retains a critical perspective on their profession, 'always asks whose interests are served by particular codes of practice, and stays alert to the way they are embracing ideas and behaviours that are subtly harming them' (2009, p.294).

Butler sees learning the art of reflection as crucial to the progress of the practitioner's competence (Butler 1996); however, students and beginning practitioners may be challenged by reflective processes. Yip cautions that premature encouragement to reflect can overwhelm the student and create resistance and distress (Yip 2006). Utilizing critical reflection in field education supervision requires preparation, an assessment of the student's readiness to examine assumptions and beliefs, and attention to a clear and understood process in which reflection occurs. Supervision is one occasion where reflection is 'guided' in order that learning may occur. The appropriate conditions for reflection include a 'supportive environment', 'readiness to undergo self-reflection, and awareness of one's limits and breaking point' (Yip 2006, p.781). Teaching techniques such as mindfulness may equip students with tools for self-management (Chinnery, Appleton and Marlowe 2019; Marlowe *et al.* 2015).

The Reflective Learning Model of Supervision described in Chapter 5 has proved equally useful in working with students on placement (Davys and Beddoe 2009). It is assumed that the placement educator and student will have spent time developing their placement contract and supervision agreement and have built an effective relationship in the beginning stages of practice learning (Beddoe 2000). This chapter finishes with an illustration of the Reflective Learning Model by a vignette describing in detail a significant supervision session involving social work student Keli and her supervisor Nancy.

Beginnings

Supervision starts with greetings and sharing any significant 'news' before beginning to focus on the agenda for the session (see Chapter 5). Taking time to reconnect also models the maintenance of ongoing professional relationships. The 'beginning' process includes agenda setting, with a major focus on issues generated by the student. In student supervision, it is important that the field educator is alert to what might be left out and comfortably introduces topics which require attention. When the placement educator and student have established and prioritized the agenda, the reflective learning process can begin.

The Reflective Learning Model for Students (see Figure 10.2) describes four stages – *event, exploration, experimentation* and *evaluation* – which are addressed sequentially but allow for the student and the supervisor to move back and forth between the various stages if necessary. The model utilizes the stages of experiential learning as described by Kolb (1984).

In the following vignette, Keli is experiencing the dilemmas of a novice and we specifically locate a reflective process approach to supervision. We focus on the micro-process of supervision rather than the more typical focus on the student's development over time. This approach was developed as a teaching model as the authors found that social work field educators were searching for approaches to supervision that provided a structure for action, rather than just an explanation of theoretical models (Davys and Beddoe 2009).

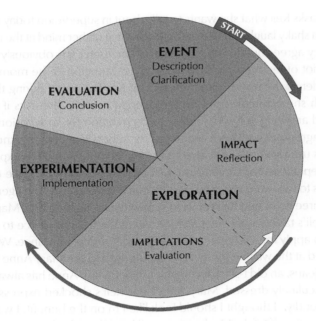

Figure 10.2: Reflective Learning Model for Students

▉ VIGNETTE: KELI

Keli is a social work student on her first field placement in a community parent support service. She is working alongside Nancy, an experienced worker, to provide counselling and supportive services to parents facing crises. Nancy also provides her supervision. Keli arrives late to supervision and her characteristic joie de vivre seems lacking. Nancy comments on Keli's flatness. Keli says she's really tired. After a few minutes catching up they start to develop an agenda for the session. First up for discussion is the recent work she has undertaken with Mary Anne, a 38-year-old woman whose life has changed dramatically due to a tragic accident in which her husband Owen was killed. Mary Anne and Owen had together run a successful family business that was largely dependent on his technical skills. Complex financial matters mean that for at least six months Mary Anne cannot gain access to any funds from the sale of the assets. Mary Anne is now a widow with four young children, one of whom has learning difficulties and very fragile health. Yesterday, Keli had arranged to meet Mary Anne at the welfare benefits office.

Keli launches into an account of her meeting and what went wrong. Nancy listens sympathetically to Keli's experience for few moments and then asks Keli what she wants to talk about in supervision today. Keli says with a shaky laugh that there is only one thing on her mind at the moment. Nancy agrees but comments that this encounter has obviously brought up a lot of feelings and is dominating her attention at the moment. She wonders if there were other things that Keli has noted during the week which she wanted to put on the agenda as well. She asks if Keli has noted anything in her notebook as preparation for supervision as they had agreed when they contracted for supervision. Nancy knows that Keli is usually very well prepared but wants to reinforce the expectation of preparation for supervision. Keli mentions another service user she wants to follow up and a request to attend a workshop. The agenda thus has three items and Keli wants to start with her meeting with Mary Anne.

Keli's task was to meet Mary Anne at the benefits office to support her to apply for a sole parent benefit and housing assistance. When she arrived at the waiting room she was surprised to see Mary Anne wearing dirty jeans, an old t-shirt and scuffed shoes. Mary Anne has always been immaculately dressed. Mary Anne sees Keli's shocked expression and says loudly, 'I thought I should look like I'm on the benefit. I was going to give myself a fake black eye as well but I thought that was going too far.' She laughs heartily and asks Keli 'I'm a single parent now, do I look the part?'

The Event

Having identified the item of top priority on the agenda, the student and placement educator begin to focus on this item. The task for this stage of the model is for the student and Nancy to identify the core issue or key question which the student wants to address in supervision about this agenda item.

Keli is invited to tell the full story. Ownership of the situation leads to responsibility for the subsequent intervention and assists the student to gain both confidence and competence (Ford and Jones 1987). It is *her* story and the act of retelling of the story enables Keli to re-experience the situation. In recounting it, she begins her process of making meaning from the encounter and it should be heard without interpretation at this stage, unless it is her own. It enables Nancy to hear the story from Keli's perspective and to hear what she emphasizes.

The task for Nancy is to encourage the Keli to tell enough of the story for both the student and Nancy to understand the context and issues but not, at this stage, to begin to address the issue. Ford and Jones (1987) suggest here that the field educator is framing the problem from two perspectives. The first is to get a clear understanding of the issue presented and the second is to hold the student and the problem in a broader context. What is the significance of this particular problem and what might it suggest about the student's stage of knowledge and competence?

The task for Nancy and the student in the Event stage is to explore the issue sufficiently in order to identify what it is that the student wants from supervision. What is Keli's understanding of the problem and what does she wish to take away from the session? Nancy encourages Keli to elaborate her story of the visit to the benefit's office but contains it within the context of *'Let us work out how best we can use supervision to help you with this situation. What do you want from supervision about this situation?'* Keli says she wants to know how she should have reacted to Mary Anne's remarks. Nancy knows Keli to be an enthusiastic student who is respectful of others and polite. She suspects her inexperience will not have prepared her for the embarrassing situation created by the service user.

The Exploration: Impact and Implications

The Exploration stage of this model is where the work of supervision occurs and where the issue is explored, understood and potential solutions identified. The stage is divided into two phases: impact and implications.

Impact

The Impact phase of the Exploration stage is the time where the student is encouraged to reflect on the issue and how it has impacted them and what meaning this event has in terms of current or previous experience. Learning is often unsettling and the student's world view will be impacting how they experience these interactions (Butler 1996, pp.274–275). How are they feeling about the issue? How have these feelings been addressed, accommodated and expressed? How have the feelings affected the work in hand? What ideas, thoughts, judgements and opinions has the student had about the situation? Are there any patterns to these ideas, feelings? Have they been experienced anywhere before? (See Chapter 5 for suggestions for supervisory questions.) The task for Nancy in this phase is to help the student to locate themselves in the event. What meaning does it have for her as a beginning social worker?

Implications

The second phase of Exploration, Implications, moves the student from a focus on themselves to a broader focus on the context of the 'Event' or issue. The presenting problem is considered here with reference to policy, legislation, treatment protocols and professional ethics and understandings of the social worlds of service users.

The stage allows Nancy to assess Keli's knowledge and awareness and is the phase of supervision where Nancy is most active and where she has an opportunity to teach, inform and prescribe. She can ask questions to promote critical reflection on power and authority issues in this situation (Brookfield 2009). She can jog Keli's understanding of critical theory and point out that the 'forces present in the wider society always intrude into our work with clients and colleagues' (Brookfield 2009, p.300). It is also a place for feedback, reassurance and affirmation.

During the Exploration stage of the model, the student and placement educator may move between impact and implication phases as questions of a more conceptual nature and reflection on feelings and patterns may be identified. The task of the Exploration stage is to reach some decision or understanding about the issue being discussed.

Impact and Implications

Nancy can see that Keli is still very upset about the incident and encourages her to talk about how she feels. Keli describes a range of feelings: anger, frustration, helplessness and embarrassment. She talks about all her enthusiasm for the visit and how she had looked forward to 'empowering Mary Anne at the benefits office'. She describes her feelings of surprise that Mary Anne could be so insensitive to the other people in the room – 'the worst thing was that I just said, "Oh, you didn't need to do that" and tried to change the subject but she then made a loud speech about people ripping off the taxpayer and that she was at least 'only getting back some of her taxes, because at least I paid some, unlike most of these scrubbers', and then it got really nasty. Two women in the waiting room had reacted angrily and made threatening remarks. Keli tells Nancy, 'I wimped out. I couldn't get her into the interview room fast enough. And I didn't say anything. I should have said something.' She has spent the weekend feeling conflicted over her lack of courage.

Nancy sympathizes with this experience and affirms Keli for her honesty and courage in owning her strong negative feelings. She observes that it is hard when service users treat others badly and wonders if Keli has ever experienced anything like this before. Keli is able to connect her feelings with a similar experience in a youth group she ran as a teenager and is encouraged by Nancy to recall how she handled that.

With support, Keli is able to examine her own position in the situation. She realizes that she wanted so badly to be helpful and yet Mary Anne had embarrassed her by making her a party, however unwillingly, to stereotypical and judgemental comments about single parents. How can she be a social worker if she's so lacking in courage?

Implications

Nancy asks Keli how she would have liked it to be. What was her goal in going to the benefits office? What was her role? Keli is clear that her goal was to support Mary Anne as she thought she might be vulnerable having to ask for help. Mary Anne's negative and discriminatory attitude to single parents strikes a discordant note in Keli's, up until now, positive regard for Mary Anne. Keli is unable to imagine what was happening for Mary Anne when she made those comments. Nancy recognizes this as an important teaching moment in supervision.

Brookfield (2009, p.295) points out that learning frequently begins with an event that highlights a 'discrepancy between assumptions and perspectives that explain the world satisfactorily and what happens in real life. Mezirow and other theorists of transformative learning call this a 'disorienting dilemma' (p.295). Bennett and Deal (2009) note that cognitively students tend to 'understand clients...in generalized, somewhat stereotypical terms... High anxiety and an underdeveloped ability to understand complex situations leads beginning students to engage in action oriented, concrete interventions', in this case moving on quickly when faced with a professionally challenging moment (p.106). Nancy reviews with Keli the purpose of attending and asks how she might have better prepared Mary Anne.

Is Keli able to hazard a guess at what might have been going through Mary Anne's mind as she dressed to go out that day? Keli is now able to make some thoughtful comments about how Mary Anne may have been responding to the stress of applying for a benefit and as she explores this she is able to recognize that her criticism of Mary Anne is lessening and her criticism of her own lack of preparation is increasing. Nancy applauds her for this shift and encourages her to focus, not on what she has done wrong, but on what she can learn from this situation. Nancy again asks what Keli could have done differently.

From her response, Nancy recognizes that Keli has not considered how anger and bitterness are emotions related to grief, loss and trauma. Before assumptions can be challenged, Brookfield asserts, 'they need to be identified clearly. This is the first discrete task of reflection. Assumptions are the understandings we hold about how the world works, or ought to work' (p.295). Nancy thus spends some time outlining some features of grief and gives Keli some relevant literature.

> Nancy checks out what Keli is thinking and how she is feeling about this situation now. Keli acknowledges her sense of helplessness and incompetence. She remembers the multi-faceted nature of individual values and beliefs. One formulation is that Mary Anne's self-image is not congruent with her current financial and emotional vulnerability. Keli understands more clearly the dynamics at play in the visit and how her newness and lack of preparation have compounded an already complex situation.
>
> Nancy asks Keli what she is going to do next. Keli appears a little startled at this and says she doesn't want to see Mary Anne again though she does understand her better. Nancy encourages her to plan a careful visit which will include an exploration of Mary Anne's emotional needs.

The Experimentation

It is our experience that the focus on an issue brought to supervision often ends when a solution has been chosen or when insight has been gained. The supervision session will then move on to the next item on the agenda. All too often in these situations, the plan or strategy identified by the supervisee is not put into effect or the insight is not integrated into practice or awareness. In the Reflective Learning Model, the Experimentation stage explicitly attends to how the student will move forwards with the issue. Is this the best plan? What are the limitations? What will happen if the plan fails? What resources are needed? Nancy is thus able to consider what extra support or resources the student may need to promote a successful outcome.

> Keli feels good about her plan and the decision to visit Mary Anne. Nancy asks when she is going to do this visit and asks her to imagine the steps. She suggests they role-play a possible conversation with Mary Anne. As they explore this conversation, Keli finds her own words to express what she wants to say and grows more confident in her delivery. Nancy affirms her development.

The Evaluation

> The Evaluation stage brings Nancy and Keli full circle to consider whether or not the agenda item has been successfully addressed.

Does Keli now have the knowledge and confidence to move forwards? What has she learned from the supervision session? On reflection, Keli says she is very happy with the outcome which is more than she had asked for and 'much better'. She has discovered a way to approach her next contact with Mary Anne and along the way has changed her perceptions.

Nancy also enquires what Keli has learned from talking about this experience. After some thought, Keli says that she realizes that she might have been able to identify in advance the nature of this meeting for Mary Anne. She also ventures, tentatively, that she is learning about the importance of learning from mistakes.

Ending

Bennett and Deal (2009) note that 'gradual cognitive change is expected to occur in students' development of complex, nuanced, differentiated understanding of clients, their situations, and the helping process itself' (p.106). Guided reflection, augmented with some teaching as demonstrated in Keli's supervision, supports this development.

When Nancy and Keli have addressed all of the items on the agenda or the supervision time is up, the supervision session ends. The ending of the session is important as it marks the conclusion of this period of learning. It is useful for Keli and Nancy to spend a moment reflecting on the placement challenges and progress. The spectre of assessment is ever-present and regular feedback can be reassuring.

> Keli and her supervisor Nancy have now addressed all three issues on the agenda and the supervision time is almost up. Nancy asks Keli how the session has been and asks if there are any themes Keli has noted. Keli is warm in her appreciation of the help she received in relation to the first issue. She still feels bad about having not considered all the issues for Mary Anne. Nancy reiterates that it is not the mistakes which are of concern but rather whether or not Keli has learned from them.
>
> She sets Keli two tasks for the next supervision session: to prepare an agenda, and to spend time thinking about her approach to 'preparation' for direct work with service users.
>
> Nancy rounds off the session with an affirming comment on Keli's progress to date and they confirm the time and place of the next meeting.

Conclusion

A reflective learning model applied within supervision is flexible enough to enable both teaching and the facilitation of reflection. Students need parameters, guidelines and information as well as some gentle challenges to their assumptions and expectations of themselves and others in order to begin to construct their own sense of mastery of the skills and interventions required by practice. This approach and the vignette provided support supervisors to find a middle ground between didactic teaching and reflection (Davys and Beddoe 2009).

Within this reflective framework, the personal, communicative, cognitive, social, emotional and cultural dimensions of learning in professional practice can be addressed, ideas teased out, and intellectual challenges separated from raw emotion and reaction and within a supportive environment put together again as meaning is made in the clinical placement.

CHAPTER 11

Supervision in Child Welfare

Work with at-risk children and young people and their families is one of the most challenging fields of practice in health and social care. This chapter will focus mainly on supervision of social workers, as it is the profession of social work on which the challenge of addressing child abuse and neglect largely rests, certainly in the public eye. While doctors, nurses and health visitors in some countries may have significant exposure to child protection issues and require supervision, the intensification of decision-making responsibility for child welfare in the public discourse is, nevertheless, with social work (Green Lister and Crisp 2005; Warner 2014).

This chapter will explore the contribution supervision can make to enhancing accountability, professional development and support of social workers in child protection. Traditional and contemporary models of supervision have emphasized the importance of balancing the administrative, support-oriented and educative aspects of supervision (Brown and Bourne 1996; Hughes and Pengelly 1997; Kadushin 1976). Ruch (2007b) found the traditional tripartite approach inadequate, not least in part due to the tensions between the quality assurance aspects of supervision, increasingly associated with surveillance, and the supportive and learning-focused aspects of supervision (Peach and Horner 2007; Beddoe 2010). We maintain our perspective that support is a core condition of supervision and this is very well supported by research on wellbeing and retention issues for child welfare workers.

Recent research on supervision in child protection

In the decade since our first edition of this book there has been a burst of activity in research on supervision. Much research has demonstrated that social work supervision in child welfare services isn't particularly reflective, rarely addresses the emotional effects of the work and is mostly about formal case direction, management (e.g., Turner-Daly and Jack 2014; Wilkins *et*

237

al. 2017). Several observational studies have been conducted designed to explore what really happens during supervision sessions in child and family practice (Wilkins 2017). Wilkins *et al.* (2017), for instance, provide a snapshot of supervision highlighting the discrepancy between what the supervisors expect to do in supervision sessions and what was observed on audio recording. This study consisted of two phases: conducting group interviews with managers concerning their perceptions of good supervision and analysing 34 recordings of supervision sessions provided by first line managers (Wilkins *et al.* 2017). Despite managers' perceptions that essential components of quality supervision were child focused, reflective, supportive and analytical, analysis of the recorded data showed that supervision sessions did not proceed as planned and were primarily aimed at managerial oversight. While managers checked in with supervisees about their general wellbeing, once the session focused on casework with particular families, 'emotional references were largely absent'. And while the social workers' feelings were sometimes sought, 'there was only limited consideration of why the social worker felt a particular way or how their feelings might be impacting on their behaviour and decision-making' (Wilkins *et al.* 2017 p.946).

Other recent studies demonstrate that where supervision is aligned with supporting a particular focused approach to practice, outcomes are better. A US-based study was conducted through an online survey of 427 frontline child welfare workers in the US (Julien-Chinn and Lietz 2015). This study noted a link between workers' self-efficacy in decision making and improved client outcomes in timely decisions for children placed in foster care when supervision was focused on supporting permanency. In an English study, Wilkins *et al.* (2018) report the presence of a 'golden thread between supervision (of a particular type), improved practice skills (measured in a certain way), and better parental engagement and goal agreement (within a specific context)' (p.501). The beginning of this 'golden thread' was practice-focused supervision which Wilkins *et al.* suggest aims to answer three important questions: 1) What is the social worker going to do next? 2) Why is the social worker going to do those things? 3) How is the social worker going to do these things? (Wilkins *et al.* 2018, p.501). Skilful, practice-focused supervision was also found associated with higher levels of parental engagement and goal agreement between parents and practitioners.

The child protection environment

It is well documented that child protection social work is practised in a climate characterized by risk-averse social service agencies, stringent regulation, prescribed practice and an ever-present fear of media scapegoating (Connolly

2017; Green 2007; Littlechild 2008; Parton 1998; Parton, Thorpe and Wattam 1997; Scourfield and Welsh 2003; Stanley 2007; Webb 2006). The essential conundrum for child protection is encapsulated in the pendulum of practice culture (and often public opinion) that oscillates between poles of supportive, prevention-focused family intervention on the one hand, and over-zealous child protection on the other (Driscoll 2009). The latter has often focused on technological approaches to surveillance of at-risk children and young people (Garrett 2005; Munro 2004a; Parton 2009). Child protection is indeed 'risky work' (Stanley 2007). Gillingham and Blomfield attribute 'the fear factor' in child protection to this conundrum:

> On the one hand it is the social construction of blame for the perceived lack of protection afforded by services to children who have died at the hands of their carers. On the other, it is also concerned with those who have been harmed through what is perceived to be over-intervention by child protection services. (Gillingham and Bromfield 2008, p.19)

A number of writers have explored the ways in which political criticism and public inquiries have also contributed to this 'culture of blame' in child protection, creating more risk-averse practices (Connolly and Doolan 2007; Keddell, 2017; Keddell & Hyslop, Munro 2004b).

There has been a fundamental change in the culture of social work practice in the past three decades, arising from the influence of a risk-management approach (Lonne *et al.* 2008). The impact of high-profile reviews, common to many countries, also generated a more prescriptive and procedure-focused response (Warner 2014, 2015). Chenot (2011) has described a vicious cycle of political, media and administrative responses to these high-profile cases: 'internally, [this] includes several concrete manifestations of collective anxiety, guilt, and the avoidance of blame during the backlash prompted by grievous events…internal investigations, a "heads will roll" mentality' (p.175). Lonne *et al.* assert that these political cycles, observed in many jurisdictions, have resulted in a 'case management culture, whereby professional discretion has been curtailed in favour of detailed and complex procedural guidance. Caring is replaced by a culture of surveillance' (Lonne *et al.* 2008, p.xii). Vigorous debate has questioned the prevailing forensic approach to child welfare dominated as it is by procedures and risk thinking (Featherstone, Morris and White 2014; Parton 2014). Analysis has led to an understanding that this approach is counterproductive and diminishes social workers' aspiration to provide a more positive engagement in strengthening families and to keep 'policing and coercive interventions to a minimum' (Parton 2009, p.716).

As noted earlier in this book, supervision has always been subject to wider influences and has reflected tensions between organizational and professional concerns, perhaps most vigorously in social work because of its links to child protection where supervision is an easy 'band aid' solution to very complex professional concerns. Jones described the reconciliation of these tensions in supervision as a 'trade-off' (Jones 2004, p.12) between the new public management ideologies and the professions, 'making it available for appropriation by competing interests' (Jones 2004, p.13). Noble and Irwin (2009) agree, suggesting that supervision frequently mirrors practice and, as social work is 'unsettled by the shifts and divergences that have marked the later part of the 20th century' (p.348), it is important 'that the supervisory relationship, like the helping relationship, is built on a trusting, confidential, caring, supportive and empathic experience, which sets the atmosphere for the professional work to be undertaken' (Noble and Irwin 2009, p.347). One major impact of this discourse is the increased focus on computer-mediated assessment 'technologies' and the manner in which knowledge is created and used in welfare systems. Parton (2009) draws on Howe (1996) in exploring how social workers have become driven by 'performativity' as 'the dominant criterion for knowledge evaluation' (Parton 2009, p.716). Risk thinking in practice is now considered to have had an impact on supervision (Beddoe 2010; Peach and Horner 2007). Significantly, in terms of supervision, in information-driven systems, the major child welfare role is to collect information in order to manage cases, judge risk and allocate resources. For Parton (2009) a consequence of this is that 'the emphasis on the relationship was thereby stripped of its social, cultural and professional significance. Knowledge was only relevant in so far as it aided the gathering, assessing, monitoring and exchange of information – which became the central focus of the work' (Parton 2009, p.717). In this conceptualization, there is a concomitant danger that supervision becomes surveillance of surveillance.

Supervision of child welfare practice thus can be stressful and ridden by anxiety and fear, or reduced to checklist approaches which mirror the proceduralized 'informational' approaches to work with families. Taylor, Beckett and McKeigue have noted the complex interaction between social workers' anxieties and those of the wider society and suggest that as such 'social workers are society's defences against anxieties about damage and delinquency' (Taylor *et al.* 2008, p.25). In a climate where there is a preoccupation with risk and low tolerance for public service failure, supervision can be captured by the potential for judgement of how effectively social work assesses and responds to risk. McLaughlin (2007) notes how these attempts to reduce uncertainty can be critiqued for leading to professionals' anxiety and lack of confidence in their abilities to assess and make decisions. 'Failure to follow the correct procedure can leave the worker vulnerable to disciplinary or judicial action if things go wrong' (McLaughlin 2007, p.1264). The proliferation of audits in health and social care was noted in Chapter 4. Audits and recorded data form 'the visible track record of social workers' attempts to assess and reduce risk – therefore, the social worker's job is less about the "right decision" and more about a defensible decision' (Pollack 2008, p.12). As Green (2007) asserts, 'apprehension about making a mistake, rather than achieving desired outcomes, leads to an increasing focus on the assessment and management of risk, perceived as the primary defence against poor outcomes for the organization as well as the client' (Green 2007, p.400).

Research by Taylor *et al.* (2008) identifies social workers as the 'prime candidates for the projection of society's anxiety in the form of criticism' and yet simultaneously social workers may be characterized as having less expertise in the complex inter-institutional arrangements for child protection. A social worker in Taylor *et al.*'s research said, 'I think the courts will look on the doctor, or the psychiatrist or the psychologist's report as having more weight…than the social worker's report. Because doctors are really professional aren't they, it's one of those careers your parents want you to go into whereas social workers…!' (Taylor *et al.* 2008, p.25).

Barry (2007) undertook a major literature review of risk assessment for the Scottish Executive Education Department. In this she notes that:

> supervision is one of the key avenues for practitioners to have the time and capacity to reflect on their practice and to identify, discuss and learn from mistakes. However, the culture of the organization needs to allow for such dialogue with confidence and trust on the part of both the supervisee and supervisor. (Barry 2007, p.34)

Barry (2007) cites Stanley's (2005) study of social workers in New Zealand where supervision assisted in the management of risk in child protection, 'but on the assumption that the organizational culture will be welcoming of sharing and learning in supervision, rather than being fearful of reprisals for admissions of failure' (Barry 2007, p.34). These tensions continue more than a decade later to create major challenges for supervision and the management of risk so that it is often regarded as a panacea for deeper professional, organizational and societal concerns.

The child protection system

The public perception of statutory organizations such as child protection agencies is that they are very powerful, although this power is viewed with some ambivalence. There are of course two kinds of professional power –

that in which acting is powerful and that in which not acting has major consequences. In many reviews of practice, inaction or declining to take action has had major consequences for the child protection agency at the centre, although the service staff were frequently not the only people to decline to act in a child protective way. There is a recurring theme of communication failures within and between organizations (Choate 2016; Stanley and Manthorpe 2004). Ironically though, as we have noted earlier, child protection social workers, while rightly seen as very powerful by services users, often feel powerless and undervalued in the public domain. As Taylor *et al.* have noted, there is also a perception that social workers are less well trained and there is constant challenge to their expertise: 'Medical knowledge is seen as specialized, while social workers' knowledge is in those areas where everybody considers themselves an expert – parenting and family life' (Taylor *et al.* 2008, p.25).

In any human enterprise where emotions, values and belief systems are in interaction with powerful institutions – the state, the courts, the police, the news media – there is inevitably tension, anxiety and potential conflict and a systemic approach is a prerequisite for understanding. In Chapter 9, we found that a systemic approach was useful to explore the demands of professional practice and the drain on personal emotional resources. A systems framework for child protection workers recognizes that there are four critical sets of relationships in which child protection workers operate: their relationships with the families with which they work; their relationships with colleagues and supervisors; their engagement within the organizational context and, lastly and significantly often under-emphasized, their relationships with other professionals and social systems within the community. Figure 11.1 illustrates this complex set of relationship and the key components within it.

Worker–family relationships

Foremost in the child protection system is the worker–family relationship and one of the difficulties for practitioners and supervisors is how to retain hope and positive regard when so often facing the most unpleasant circumstances and challenging conversations. The supervisor has a vital role in ensuring that practitioners bring a full account of their interactions to the table. In supervision and informal discussions, a number of questions can guide the supervisor:

- How is the practitioner presenting both the risk factors and strengths of the family?

- What cultural and social perspectives are present in the telling of this story?

- What evidence am I hearing about planning for collaborative approaches?

- What feelings and fears are stated and what might be ignored or minimized'?

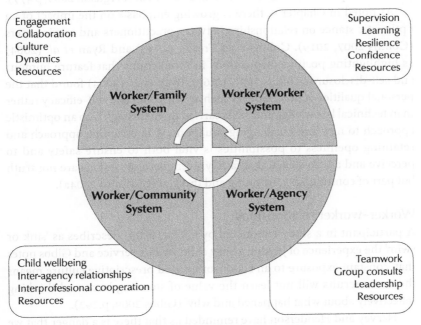

Figure 11.1: The child protection system

While it is important to seek positive engagement with families, despite fears and challenges, it is frequently unsafe to minimize unpleasant feelings and disturbing thoughts. A balance is needed. Ferguson (2009) notes that 'it is quite remarkable how little attention is given to the practitioner's perspective and experience of doing the work' of child protection when referring to the lived experience of child protection workers in conducting home visits (Ferguson 2009, p.473). Ferguson reminds us that practitioners face many challenges when they enter the private worlds of families they encounter. In the worst situations, they may have feelings of 'disgust and fears for their own bodily integrity and wellbeing' and notes from his study (2009) indicate that these feelings were not mentioned in supervision. The failure to properly discuss such feelings 'meant that they could not be worked through and gone beyond to reach more authentic engagement with the child's life and needs' and this may impact on adequate examination especially in highly neglectful conditions where practitioners may 'distance and detach themselves from abused children' (Ferguson 2009, p.476). The supervisor in such situations needs to encourage full description, for example, 'Tell me about the atmosphere and what reverberates within you about this child/adult/home/ family?'– trusting that, as we found in Chapter 8, feelings generated in practice can provide rich information in assessment (Ferguson 2009, p.477).

As noted in Chapter 9, there is growing emphasis on the impact of an optimistic stance on relationships between practitioners and service users (Collins 2007, 2019). Collins cites Trotter (1999) and Ryan *et al.* (2004) as highlighting positive dispositions in interactions that feature humour and self-disclosure (Collins 2007, p.265). Ryan *et al.* (2004) found that the personal qualities of practitioners such as self-belief and self-efficacy rather than technical knowledge and skills carried them through into an optimistic approach to new and challenging situations. A questioning approach and retaining openness to possibilities is vital both to ensure safety and to perceive and acknowledge that family strengths assessments are not truth but part of continuing questioning and theorizing (Munro 2004a).

Worker–worker relationships

A participant in a study conducted by Gibbs (2009) describes as 'sink or swim' the experience of joining a busy child welfare service and Gibbs notes that 'constant exposure to an action-orientated prescriptive culture means the new recruits will not learn the value of standing back and thinking reflectively about what happened and why' (Gibbs 2009, p.292).

Harvey and Henderson have reminded us that there is a danger that we can hold a dichotomous view of supervision 'where it is regarded as either nurturing or controlling; all about feelings or all about procedure' (2014, p.344). What we do know, as reported throughout this book, is that a strong supervisory relationship, providing both support and facilitation of reflection and learning, has considerable impact for child welfare workers. In particular, the impact of the supervisor through the supervision relationship includes:

- the provision of guidance (Scannapieco and Connell-Carrick 2007)

- challenge to over-reliance on paperwork and compliance as 'ways of avoiding the emotional challenges of working with dysfunctional and abusive families' (Gibbs 2009, p.293)

- navigation through the demands and responsibilities for child welfare practice (Ellett, Collins-Carmargo and Ellett 2007)

- delivering positive messages to improve worker's self-esteem and self-efficacy (Gibbs 2001)

- a bridge between executive management and frontline workers (Morrison 2001)

- instruction on how to strive for the most effective practice in the face of differing work activities, large volume of work, stress of the daily work and challenges faced in child welfare work (Ellett *et al.* 2006)

- creation of a definitive structure to allow the practice of new skills and encourage an environment of open discussion and support (Gibbs 2009; Yankeelov *et al.* 2009)

- protection against deleterious effects of stress and exposure to harm from professional practice (Mor Barak *et al.* 2009)

- an important association with job satisfaction, maintaining commitment to the organization and linked to employees' perceptions of the support they receive from their employer (Carpenter, Webb and Bostock 2013).

Yankeelov *et al.* (2009) highlights awareness that 'supervision is a multi-dimensional construct' and among the factors identified (cited in Yankeelov 2009, p.549) were: supervisors providing work opportunities to meet practitioners' skill development, modelling good practices, providing strong verbal support to motivate and providing affirming feedback to workers. Further on in this chapter we will examine the potential for group approaches to working with very complex situations. Supervisors may find that group supervision provides excellent, complementary opportunities to model good reasoning, open not closed assessment practices and recognition of the value of listening to feelings.

Revell and Burton (2015) note that just as the 'relationship has been placed at the core of the "practitioner–service user" interaction and intervention, relationship is also central to the formation of safe and confidential spaces to explore difficult emotions in both formal and informal supervision' (p.1592). As we have explored earlier, relationship building is essential for the promotion of deeply reflective discussions. Research undertaken by Turney and Ruch (2018) explored supervisory practice through facilitated reflective discussions. They found that both supervisors and supervisees often emphasized 'doing' over thinking or feeling. They noted a tendency to want to jump in to problem solving without listening' to what the supervisee wanted to tell them about an experience' (p.135). As in many studies, Turney and Ruch found that the day-to-day demands tend to render the supervision relationship to be more focused on targets, timescales and performance indicators, meaning that doing 'the "right" things (i.e., those that meet externally specified targets) takes precedence over making sure that the right kind of *thinking* is being supported' (2018, p.135).

Worker–agency relationships

Supervision is a central relationship within the organizational context. It can be multifaceted, including along with facilitation of reflection and support, advocacy, negotiation about resources and 'managing up' (Kaiser and Kuechler 2008, p.78) as noted in Chapter 4, especially in 'internal' supervision where administrative aspects of supervision are routine. A positive view of administration, conceptualizing it as assessing the need for resources, rather than mere compliance, can underpin both support and concern for quality.

Supervision is often allowed to languish in times of great pressure, despite good evidence of the effectiveness of supervision in relation to a number of key factors: retention of staff, mitigation of impact of stress (Mor Barak *et al.* 2009), and job satisfaction (Mor Barak *et al.* 2006; Stalker *et al.* 2007). Optimism can be generated about the potential for different approaches to supervision to add support for continuing competence, for example from: the strengths-based approaches (Presbury *et al.* 1999; Santa Rita 1998), positive psychology (Howard 2008) and relationship-based practice approaches (Ruch 2012).

Retention of employees in the child welfare services is an issue that receives international attention (Chen and Scannapieco 2009; DePanfilis and Zlotnik 2008; Nissly et al. 2005; Yankeelov et al. 2009). Research strongly supports the importance of supervision as a factor in retention in the child welfare workforce, especially when linked to worker confidence in their own abilities. Chen and Scannapieco (2009) have found that, consistent with findings of prior research, their study 'confirmed the importance of supervisors' support to workers' desire to stay, additionally, the study further identified the interaction between supervisors' support and workers' self-efficacy and found that the influence of supervisors' support was particularly important to low self-efficacy workers' (p.12). The results of an earlier study by Nissly *et al.* (2005) had demonstrated that 'embeddedness in a supportive network, consisting of co-workers as well as one's supervisor, can reduce employees' intentions to leave' (Nissly *et al.* 2005, p.96). Despite such clear support for supervision, recent research reports the limited training opportunities available for supervisors (Griffiths *et al.* 2019a) and high stress levels of supervisors (Griffiths *et al.* 2019b).

Worker–agency–community relationships

The child protection system is made up of many agencies and professionals and the anxiety generated by child abuse underpins much of the conflict and miscommunication. Cahn (2009) describes supervisors in child welfare settings as having a key role to 'gain resources, align vision and build stronger connections' (p.152) and 'coach workers to represent the agency mandate' and in the wider community to help practitioners 'to navigate the system…in interagency situations' (p.104). Reflecting the complexity of child protection work, Barry (2007) suggests that different groups represent three crucial sets of interests, intersecting at the point of intervention: 'the rights of the child, the integrity and rights of the family and the duties and powers of the state' (Barry 2007, p.27). Effective supervision can aid practitioners in navigating these complex relationships and dynamics.

Worker–community relationships: a learning vignette

The following example is provided in order to illustrate the complexity of interprofessional and inter-agency work for supervisors. Note: this example and the discussion is adapted from Beddoe and Davys (2008, pp.38–39) and used with the kind permission of the editors of *Social Work Now*, the practice journal of the New Zealand Child, Youth and Family Service. This is a problem-based scenario which is useful because it has highly emotional content, contains the seeds of interprofessional difference and conflict, and is highly realistic as the kind of 'worry' a clinical practitioner might bring to supervision, where clinical (in this case medical) knowledge is not the main dimension of the problem. This case example is fictional and it has been used in teaching settings on many occasions. The discussion which follows and the views expressed by the 'professionals' are fictionalized and a composite of many different discussions.

■ VIGNETTE: MELISSA

Timothy, a community health nurse, came to his supervisor with the following situation on the top of his agenda. He was providing post-operative wound care for Melissa (aged nine) who had multiple chronic health problems. The treatment plan had been provided by the surgical registrar at the hospital and Melissa was due to go back in for a check-up next week. Melissa's parents had also engaged the services of an alternative healer. The alternative healer did not support the medical treatment and the parents were following the healer's regime. The alternative treatment was very expensive and Timothy knew that the family was on a very limited budget and was already in huge debt.

He had had conversations with the parents and the healer to no avail. Timothy had talked to the family's GP who advised seeking an earlier check-up appointment if the family wouldn't bring Melissa in to her surgery. The alternative treatment was not working and the wound was now infected, and at the next home visit Melissa complained of considerable pain. The community health team social worker angrily told Timothy in the staff room that this was bordering on a child protection issue and he had to report it to the child protection agency. Timothy was feeling torn between his concern for Melissa and his desire to maintain a relationship with the parents.

Some questions arose in supervision which identifed the main issues for Timothy and his colleagues in the health agency:

- Where was the duty of care?
- What about family rights and empowering people?
- What about the paramount rights of the child...?
- What about the views of the rest of the family?
- Had anyone talked to Melissa?
- Did Timothy have to refer Melissa to the child protection agency?
- How do we maintain the relationship with a long-term family of the service?
- Melissa could die if she got blood poisoning. But the family loved her; surely, they were trying to do the right thing...?

What the vignette shows is that professional practitioners bring their own assumptions, reactions, disciplinary and theoretical orientation, emotional responses, and political perspectives to this one situation. It demonstrates how much is going on beneath the surface when different professionals encounter a situation. The critical question is whose views will prevail when all these differences are present in a real organizational context? Where is the power? Who has the mandate to decide action? What is the role of supervisors when dealing with complex situations where there are multiple, potentially contested perspectives and stakeholders' views to hold in balance?

Professional practitioners develop a cognitive map where personal characteristics and experience, values and beliefs determine some key aspect of their practice (Hall 2005, p.190). Professional values also emphasize different aspects of working with service users: for some professions science directs decision making and interaction with service users; for other professions, listening to client stories is what is valued. Language is often an important means of differentiation, and supervision questions like those above, which focus on specific aspects of the situation, often highlight the different ways of describing what we do. There has long been considerable support in the literature for improved collaboration among profession and sectors in health and social care to ensure the safety of children and vulnerable adults (Marsh 2006). Marsh suggested that key elements may include knowing about the other professionals' practice, being able to communicate well across disciplines, and directly working together. In these and other situations where conflict, role and boundary issues may put client and worker outcomes at risk, supervisors have a key role to play (Beddoe and Davys 2008, p.35). While only a small component of work in health and social care, an interprofessional approach to learning for supervision, leadership and management may provide rich opportunities for changing the culture. Learning to focus on relationships and mutuality rather than knowledge from and for specific clinical domains is potentially transformative.

■ VIGNETTE: MELISSA – THE REST OF THE STORY

On a home visit, Timothy found Melissa in pain and deteriorating, and following some heated discussion back in the office, and Timothy's strong opposition, child health nurse Mary called in the child protection team.

On receiving the referral, child protection social worker Rob, a new graduate, and his supervisor Kristy met with Melissa and her family, spoke to the health professionals and consulted the legal service. Two days later legal intervention was used to obtain orthodox treatment for Melissa. Timothy was very upset about this outcome and relationships were frayed among members of the professional system. Timothy was still visiting Melissa and her family but felt that trust had been eroded. Rob met with Timothy and Mary to work out a longer-term plan for teamwork with Melissa's family as she would have long-term needs. The meeting was tense and difficult. Timothy and Mary argued and Rob got frustrated and walked out. Rob went to supervision with Kristy and was visibly upset, 'What's the point of it all if even the workers can't get it together and put the child's needs first, instead of their own egos?' Kristy acknowledged Rob's feelings and drew out the issues, which they mapped on a whiteboard. Rob could see that the tensions were in part due to different ways of seeing the same situation, and that all did have the wellbeing of the family in mind. Rob was able to re-focus on

Melissa's needs and go back to his core role. They arranged another meeting and worked out how to ensure the plan was indeed developed. Rob and Kristy role-played the phone calls he needed to make and he left supervision feeling more resolved to get people working together and understanding that managing these professional relationships was part of the job.

As was noted in Chapter 9, Mor Barak *et al.*'s study identified three key supervisory dimensions which assisted child protection workers to remain focused and manage stress: task assistance, social and emotional support, and strong supervisory interpersonal interaction (Mor Barak *et al.* 2009, p.27). A key supervisory task is to promote mastery and independence. In the vignette, Kristy (supervisor) demonstrated all these: she was supportive and could contain Rob's strong emotions, she was able to assist him to work out a way forward and to facilitate his development, rather than stepping in and taking over his work. However, while she could take a supportive stance and empathize with his strong child advocacy stance, Kristy could also model a collaborative inter-agency stance. Some good explorative questions might include: 'What was going on for Timothy and Mary in this situation; what might they have been thinking?' Timothy's concern was underpinned by concern for the trust and rapport established with Melissa's family and the health professionals would have a long-term role protecting Melissa, so a good question might be: 'how could we work past this current conflict to support good outcomes for the family, and foster better inter-agency work?'

Effective supervision in child protection

There are three major threats to the effectiveness of supervision: the lack of skill to develop curiosity and lack of courage to challenge, the domination of 'blame and shame' tactics in contemporary human services, and the weakening of professional values 'in action' by a focus on bureaucratic practices that put targets, timescales and other performance indicators above relationship-based reflective supervision. Nowhere are these threats more overt than in the field of child protection.

Supervision was described as 'the cornerstone of good social work practice' in Lord Laming's report into the death of Victoria Climbié, (2003, p.12). Recommendation 45 of this report emphasized regular supervision of frontline children's social workers (p.376). Ruch (2007b) commented that if there was to be more than rhetoric about effective supervision then there was an urgent need to 'propose different and creative support forums for practitioners' (2007b, p.372). Lord Laming's review of progress (Laming

2009) found that inconsistent provision of supervision remained a persistent problem and recommended attention to improvement (Laming 2009 p.30). The Social Work Task Force (Department for Children, Schools and Families 2009b), established to respond to the Laming report, subsequently reported extensive feedback from frontline social workers about supervision. Practitioners noted that 'access to supervision was often threatened or put on hold due to staff shortages and mounting caseloads', and that there was insufficient time to reflect and learn as teams (Department for Children, Schools and Families 2009b, p.20). In addition, the task force noted that 'access to supervision can vary significantly between authorities but also within the same authority. In the eyes of frontline staff, supervision tended to be process driven and dominated by case management' (p.20), to the detriment of a supportive and reflective practice environment. Developing a strong commitment to better supervision in child welfare needs skills, training and support because it requires a balance over time of careful oversight of a form of practice in which, as has been explored above, there are both vulnerable children and vulnerable workers and a complex interplay of factors between these two. Of equal importance is the focus on the professional development of supervisees. Two key dimensions of professional development that need to be particularly strengthened in the supervision of child protection workers are use of self and critical reasoning.

Use of self

A clear task of supervision is to support the practitioner in relation to the emotional demands of the work. Increasingly this is understood as how to assist professionals to manage their exposure to trauma in the work (Knight 2018), as we have explored in Chapter 9. While more than a decade earlier, Mandell (2008, p.235–236) noted that the concept of 'use of self' has fallen out of favour in recent decades in social work, self-awareness has long been regarded in popular wisdom as a key attribute of social work. As supervision educators, the authors have often noted to students that our 'tools of trade' do not come in a box or a kit but are located in our person. Yip suggests that 'use of self', essential in reflective practice, happens across a number of dimensions in the person of the practitioner where 'self-recall, self-evaluation, self-observation and self-analysis take place within the social worker's mind' (Yip 2006, p.782). Yip argues that practitioners need to find or create time and space in which they can 'distance themselves, to stop and think, to deal with…uncomfortable feelings and to analyse and resolve discrepancies in practice' (Yip 2006, p.782).

Mandell suggests that writing on 'use of self' in 'the mainstream' has not considered how awareness might enhance critical practice (p.236); however, Davis (2002), noting the inherent ambiguity in child protection's dual role of both investigation and support, raised the importance of self-awareness in promoting strengths-based practice with families. Davis (2002) notes a number of factors that impede strengths-focused work with families: over-reliance on procedures, a 'shallow conceptual model for understanding the relationships between the families, themselves and the agency's mission' and 'over-reliance on personal intuition' (p.187). This latter factor, when 'combined with insufficient self-awareness', can create barriers to 'searching for families' strengths and lead to more punitive responses' (pp.187–188). More recently, the concept of trauma-informed practice has been extended to understand the impact of work such as child protection on professionals, and the concomitant need to be mindful of trauma exposure in supervision (Knight 2018).

Kondrat (1999), in a seminal article, assists us to sort through the many conceptualizations of 'use of self'. She identifies three conceptualizations of self in practice: simple conscious awareness, reflective self-awareness and reflexive self-awareness (p.452) and describes them as follows:

Simple conscious awareness	'Becoming awake to present realities, noticing one's surroundings, and being able to name perceptions, feelings, and nuances of behavior'. The self can recognize what it is experiencing (p.453).
Reflective self-awareness	Reflective self-awareness turns attention to a self who 'has' the experience. The self's behaviors, affect, cognitive content and accomplishments become objects of reflection.
	A 'metaphor of distance' is often used 'the self steps back to observe and consider its own performance' (pp.453–454).
Reflexive self-awareness	Self-knowledge becomes possible not by creating distance and otherness but by reducing the 'distance' and relying on sameness between 'knower and known' (pp.456–457).
	Important here is the notion that the self is a 'construct that is continuously emerging within specific social contexts (pp.459–460).

Kondrat (1999) notes that postmodernist thinking challenges the notion of a 'self-contained self' able to stand back from experience and observe from a neutral 'uncontaminated perspective, because our "knowledge" is constructed in our broad context and thus when considering self-knowledge the problem is intensified by our inescapable insider' status (p.456). The work of child protection poses many challenges for the 'critical' practitioner. Not least is the need to remain strongly in tune with the values and commitments that led practitioners to the work in the first place (Rankine *et al.* 2018).

There is a potential for a focus on the risks of exposure to abuse and the need for self-care to individualize practice and isolate workers rather than build a collective sense of commitment based in teamwork. Profitt (2008) reminds us that much of the literature that addresses self-care and compassion fatigue focuses on psychological and individual explanations of these problems. She points to the social context of much of what traumatizes people, 'the witnessing of social phenomena such as gender violence, hunger and poverty' and the relocation of this to 'the realm of private injury' (Profitt 2008, p.160). Good supervisory questions might include: how do we participate in collaborative opportunities to consider the impact of the work? What do we process at work and what seeps into our personal lives? How can we keep each other safe? What do you need to retain perspective, hope and an understanding of the social inequalities that underpin so much violence and distress? To avoid such questions risks the depersonalization and distancing we noted in Chapter 9.

Critical reasoning in child protection social work

Failures in practice may often be failures of deep thinking and critical reasoning. Ruch (2007b) attributes this to the enormous pressure on social workers 'to do something'. 'Concrete manifestations of this emphasis on "doing" social work abound in the burgeoning of procedures and audit requirements that represent an increasingly technical–rational understanding of practice' (Ruch 2007b, p.371). Such responses reflect reduced confidence in the skills of the profession and are exacerbated by the diminishing professional autonomy within professional practice in public services (Karvinen-Niinikoski *et al.* 2019).

Through processes which develop 'reflective self-awareness', Kondrat (1999) has suggested students and new practitioners can be urged to become aware of the potential impact in practice of their personal values, needs and biases in order that they may work consciously and objectively. Prescriptions for increasing objectivity in self-reflection include scrutiny of practice, eliciting feedback from service users, using reflective tools such as audio and video recording, engaging in group supervision, an examination of the 'cognitive products of the self such as reasoning and judgment, and attending to the practice knowledge assumed to be implicit' in everyday practice (p.455). A challenge for social work in particular is that much practice focuses on the 'everyday' of human life – relationships, families, parenting, sex, religious and political beliefs, values and so forth. There is an assumption that there are truths about all these things that are self-evident and therefore formal knowledge is of questionable value. This is often evident in the belittling of social science by proponents of 'tough love' approaches to social problems. In the course of professional practice, it is always apparent that what we learn in our own formative experiences about the intimate aspects of family life and relationships shapes our thinking (and seeing) but sometimes in ways that are not always helpful to the families we work with (Kondrat 1999). Effective practice requires a theoretical base for practice, the ability to critically analyse the information which underpins decisions as well as a good grasp of the evidence-informed 'best practices'. As Munro (2008) has noted, the novice practitioner 'has to learn to use formal knowledge as well as their pre-existing wisdom…as they become more experienced their use of formal theories becomes absorbed into their intuitive approach' (Munro 2008, p.5).

Maintaining hope

As we saw in Chapter 9, resilient practitioners maintain hopefulness and optimism, and Koenig and Spano (2007) suggest that conscious attention to the fostering of these qualities can be a focus of supervision. Child welfare supervision has a major role to play in safeguarding the supportive engagement of staff, assisting them to manage uncertainty and address the risks at the intersection of the personal and professional experience. These intersections are often where 'dangerousness' may be a fear. Stanford (2007) studied social workers' reflections on their interventions and her work supports supervision as providing a place for rekindling of hopefulness:

> Recognition of hope and the possibility of change, alongside a commitment to care therefore need to become directives, as opposed to incidentals, of practice. Supervision is a site in which this orienting framework could be mutually explored and supported by managers and practitioners. Critical reflections of interventions could be used to support this process. (Stanford 2007, p.257)

To retain critically reflective practice, exploration of practitioners' understanding of risk and uncertainty in practice needs to be given a central space in supervision. Moral reasoning and a more nuanced exploration of risk stories can strengthen supervision practice. Profitt (2008) notes that neither intellectual work (critical analysis) nor the containment of deep feelings alone can 'assuage pervasive feelings such as deep sadness…While sorting out internal boundaries as an act of self care and survival can protect helpers, without a mentor or group of trustworthy colleagues, how do workers protect their human sensibility…?'(p.161). Conrad and Kellar-Guenther (2006) studied the relationship between compassion fatigue (distress experienced by the helper), burnout, and 'compassion satisfaction' (fulfilment from helping others and positive relationships with colleagues) for child welfare workers. They found that child welfare workers with high satisfaction had lower levels of compassion fatigue and lower levels of burnout. They suggest that strong social support from colleagues and supervisors may be crucial in buffering workers from their emotionally draining daily work. Shared work builds understanding, draws on different perspectives and knowledge and encourages positive, open and honest team communication, where challenging questions can be asked. Hopefulness requires nurturing to maintain the belief in possibilities.

This highlights the need to develop opportunities to share experience, to explore ideas for action and to grow confidence in collaborative decision making, and points to group supervision which is structured to meet the particular demands of child protection practice. This need not be uni-professional; indeed, it seems likely that well-designed group processes involving several disciplines could enhance interprofessional understanding and respect.

Bringing it all together: collaborative decision making

In the seminal work *Communities of Practice*, Wenger argued that 'learning is the engine of practice and practice is the history of that learning' (Wenger 1998, p.96.) The 'history of learning' is practice wisdom that develops when there is support and time to learn from success as well as practice mistakes. If thinking space is a scarce resource and absent at the frontline, where is this history formed? Laming (2009) regards supervision as critical, as is the provision of 'routine opportunities for peer-learning and discussion. Currently, not enough time is dedicated to this' (Laming 2009, p.32). While individual supervision is a vital component in supporting and developing individual child protection workers, regardless of their profession, there is growing support for a revitalization of group supervision. This could be in new forms, to address the complex dimensions of assessment and decision making in a field where there are so many challenges at personal, interpersonal, interprofessional, team, organizational and inter-institutional levels. Some questioning of supervision and a re-shaping of its application particularly in child welfare services (Lietz 2009; Strand and Badger 2007) led to a greater focus on critical reasoning and shared decision making (Jones, Washington and Steppe 2007; Munro 2008). Lietz (2009) argues that approaches to decision making have been dominated by two styles: the 'practice experience' model and the 'empirically based decision making' model. The former highly values the autonomy of the individual worker to develop expertise and rejects rigid rules and prescriptions for practice (Lietz

2009, pp.192–194). The latter is premised on a critique of the former, where lack of formal guidelines for practice means that decision making can be idiosyncratic and inconsistent. The problem with empirically based models is that they assume a level of competence in locating and utilizing research findings which may be illusory.

Shared decision making

A process in which decision making can be shared (Stevenson 2005) and many minds applied to the development of plans and processes seems to offer much to advance child welfare goals. Supervisors and practitioners are accountable to the agency, their professions and to the public. Shared decision making confirms commitment to legal, ethical, safe and transparent practice within the framework that has been mandated for the safety of children. Shared decision making in group supervision or a group consultation process can incorporate many safeguards and benefits. Space does not allow a full examination of these but the following points provide a summary, with suggestions of relevant material for further exploration:

- Peer review of professional decisions, drawing on both analytical skills (the application of theory in practice and utilization of empirical evidence) and intuitive capacity (practice wisdom) leading to an improved focus on critical reasoning (Keddell 2016; Munro 2008).

- Encouragement of a climate where practitioners' voices are heard questioning, challenging, and being open about their decision-making process (O'Connor and Leonard 2013), committed to taking shared responsibility for decisions (Lietz 2009) and which creates a reflective space where practitioners are prepared to challenge each other in the interests of the children and families (Jones and Gallop 2003; Saltiel 2016).

- Protection of human rights. Open discussion contributes to clarity of purpose in making legal interventions and ensuring that no service user's rights are adversely affected (e.g., coming into care) without scrutiny of that decision (Connolly and Ward 2008) and ensures that the perspectives of children, parents and carers have been sought and considered and the most respectful relationships forged (Duffy 2011; Gupta and Blumhardt 2017; Morris and Burford 2017).

- Protection of service users. It ensures that children and young people are not left in unacceptable risk situations on the basis of a single practitioner's assessment or choices, or unchallenged assumptions (Gibbs 2009).

- Protection of staff. It ensures that practitioners are not put into a position where situations may exceed their knowledge, skills or experience or where they have to manage very stressful emotional or potentially traumatic situations on their own (Davis 2002; Ferguson 2009).

- Maintenance and development of an optimistic stance, professional commitment and compassion that preserve hopefulness and morale (Collins 2007, 2019; Koenig and Spano 2007).

Group processes can 'provide the conditions in which Laming's "respectful uncertainty" and "healthy scepticism" might flourish' (Ruch 2007b, p.373). Wenger's notion of a 'community of practice' is useful to consider in this context (Wenger 1998). The concept recognizes the social nature of learning in everyday life, how human beings understand their roles and practices in family, school, community and work, negotiating meaning, identity and power in all the relationships they encounter. Wenger sees learning within all of these communities and alerts us to the complexity of learning within organizations. 'Organizations are social design directed at practice… Communities of practice are thus key to an organization's competence and to the evolution of that competence' (Wenger 1998, p.241). Wenger notes, however, that communities of practice differ from organizations in that 'they arise, evolve and dissolve according to their own learning', though they may do so in respect to institutional events and they shape their own boundaries though these may at times may be congruent with institutional boundaries (Wenger 1998, p.241). Most importantly, communities of practice are the location of the real work, where 'the official meets the everyday' (p.243) and of course where things are inclined to go wrong. As he points out, policies and procedures can be designed but 'in the end it is practice that produces results', not policies and processes (p.243). The challenge for health and social care practice, especially in high-risk services, is to support 'the knowledgeability of practice' while allowing sufficient structure to hold the organization together as over-emphasis on proceduralism is not helpful, serving to support the apparatus, rather than the practice (Wenger 1998, pp.243–244).

Collaborative approaches to supervision in child protection can offer a solution to the problem of how to organize effective supervision to ensure balanced attention to education, support and administrative aspects. The administrative aspect can be reconceptualized as shared decision making that is not procedure driven but reflective and evidence informed. Educational aspects can be addressed by utilization of practice frameworks (Connolly 2007) and through engagement in informed critical reflection (Fook and Gardner 2007). Ruch (2007b) explored how practitioners understood and carried out reflection and found that teams were crucial in facilitating reflective practice. Significantly, practices designed to improve communication and collaborative work, such as co-work, consultation forums and case discussions, were found to create vital 'spaces where practitioners could stop "doing" and think about their practice' (Ruch 2007b, p.373). Supervision and support for peer-based reflective learning, if well designed and facilitated, can create the spaces to stop and think.

Afterword

Ten years after the publication of *Best Practice in Professional Supervision* we have taken another look at what we have described as 'that complex process called supervision'. This second edition presents an overview of our own experiences, shares our subsequent research, our ponderings and our developing ideas and questions about supervision. Again, we pay tribute to, and acknowledge, the ideas and work of others which continue to challenge and inspire us in our practice, research and teaching of professional supervision.

The core models of supervision of such authors as Hawkins and Shohet (1989, 2000, 2006, 2012), Hughes and Pengelly (1997), Inskipp and Proctor (1993) and Morrison (2001) continue to provide the base from which we consider professional supervision but onto these frameworks are crafted the challenges, ideas and opportunities offered by so many others through the supervision literature and research. The past ten years have been particularly rich in this regard.

The framework established by the triangle of functions (Chapter 2) continues to provide, in our opinion, the best definition of the territory of supervision. Whatever approach or model is used in supervision this triangle links supervision practice to its mandate and its, at times conflicting, accountabilities. At its centre stands the supervision relationship (Chapter 3). It is here that the nurture, replenishment and what is sometimes called the 'magic' of supervision occur. In this edition, we have emphasized that supervision is a collaborative relationship and have offered some additional considerations for supervisees.

The importance of the overarching culture of the organization on supervision practice is explored in Chapter 4 and our central belief that supervision is the forum for learning and development is reflected in the Reflective Learning Model described in Chapter 5. Recent research and critique have reinforced our belief that this is a very transportable model which can be used in a variety of contexts. Our commitment to providing supervisors with a map for their own journey is highlighted in Chapter 6 where we consider the development of supervisory competence. Chapters 7 and 8 present the 'doing' of supervision, skills and interactions and the role of supervision to respect and work with the emotions generated through the workplace. This is expanded in Chapter 9 where professional resilience is explored and we examine the role of supervision as a central resource to assist with the stress and distress encountered in the workplace. Our belief that the supervision of students is a parallel, but separate, process is explored in Chapter 10 and, finally, Chapter 11 addresses the role of supervision in care and protection of children.

Our journey with supervision continues to delight and challenge. In 2010, we noted the increased acknowledgement from organizations and regulatory bodies of the heavy emotional toll exacted on practitioners at the interface between professional 'people' practitioners and the people themselves. We hoped that practices like supervision would be mandated and resourced to provide effective focus and support for these practitioners. We were disappointed by the pragmatic responses which provided inadequate resources and a compliance-directed form of supervision. This is a situation which has, for a number of practitioners, continued and in some cases worsened with supervision driven through computer monitoring demands for reports on actions, timeframes and targets (Wilkins, Forrester and Grant 2017). However, we have been heartened and inspired by more recent research and reported supervision practice which has described inclusion, diversity and interprofessionality. Supervision is increasingly recognized as a form of professional practice which is differently understood across geographic and professional boundaries, where it accommodates a range of definitions and parameters. Nevertheless, rather than being considered as barriers, these differences are being noticed, discussed and debated, and accepted. Conversations about supervision are considering the richness, rather than the constraints, of diversity. At the individual practice level we continue to witness the resilience of professional practitioners from all disciplines who have understood and actualized the potential for supervision to be a truly sustaining practice which provides safety for all.

In 2010, we acknowledged the areas which were not covered in this book and in 2016 were pleased that the publication of *Challenges in Professional Supervision: Current Themes and Models for Practice* (Beddoe and Davys) gave us the opportunity to expand on our ideas and to explore topics not covered in the earlier book. That being said, we are clear that supervision is a steadily growing practice which generates more questions than can be addressed in any one forum. We reiterate our views from 2010 that 'the quest for learning and knowing has no destination, only a journey, and it is the quality of that journey which holds the magic, the creativity, the playfulness and the passion of supervision' (p.239).

Research continues in supervision and, as each practitioner, supervisor, manager and researcher contributes to the body of knowledge, understanding and possibility increase.

Supervision remains for us a vital, sustaining and necessary practice within which we have both delighted in witnessing the growth and development of others and have valued how this has added to our own growth and development. We know the depths of possible exploration of ourselves in supervision and the humility which comes from accompanying another in this journey.

We hope then that this second edition continues to offer some of our learning and convey our passion.

References

Adams, R. E., Figley, C. R. and Boscarino, J. A. (2008) 'The compassion fatigue scale: Its use with social workers following urban disaster.' *Research on Social Work Practice*, 18(3), 238–250.

Adamson, C. (1999) 'Towards a social work knowledge base for traumatic events.' *Social Work Review*, 11(1), 29–34.

Adamson, C. (2001) 'The Role of Supervision in the Management of Critical Incidents and Traumatic Events.' In L. Beddoe and J. Worrall (eds), *Supervision from Rhetoric to Reality. Conference Proceedings* (pp.33–43). Auckland College of Education, Auckland.

Adamson, C. (2011) 'Supervision is not politically innocent.' *Australian Social Work*, 65(2), 185–196. doi:10.1080/0312407x.2011.618544.

Adamson, C., Beddoe, L. and Davys, A. (2012) 'Building resilient practitioners: Definitions and practitioner understandings.' *British Journal of Social Work*, 44(3), 522–541. doi:10.1093/bjsw/bcs142.

Alaszewski, A. and Coxon, K. (2009) 'Uncertainty in everyday life: Risk, worry and trust.' *Health, Risk & Society*, 11(3), 201–207.

Alonso, A. (1985) *The Quiet Profession: Supervisors of Psychotherapy*. New York, NY: Macmillan.

Andersson, L., King, R. and Lalande, L. (2010) 'Dialogical mindfulness in supervision role-play.' *Counselling and Psychotherapy Research*, 10(4), 287–294. doi:10.1080/14733141003599500.

Antczak, H. B., Mackrill, T., Steensbæk, S. and Ebsen, F. (2019) 'What works in video-based youth statutory caseworker supervision – caseworker and supervisor perspectives.' *Social Work Education*, 1–16. doi:10.1080/02615479.2019.1611757.

Argyris, C. (1991) 'Teaching smart people how to learn.' *Harvard Business Review*, 69(3), 99–109.

Argyris, C. and Schön, D. (1974) *Theory in Practice: Increasing Professional Effectiveness*. San Francisco, CA: Jossey-Bass.

Argyris, C. and Schön, D. (1978) *Organizational Learning*. Reading, MA: Addison Wesley.

Arkin, N. (1999) 'Culturally sensitive student supervision: Difficulties and challenges.' *The Clinical Supervisor*, 18 (2), 1–16.

Arndt, J., King, S., Suter, E., Mazonde, J., Taylor, E. and Arthur, N. (2009) 'Socialization in health education: Encouraging an integrated interprofessional socialization process.' *Journal of Allied Health*, 38(1), 18.

Austin, J. and Hopkins, K. M. (eds) (2004) *Supervision as Collaboration in the Human Services: Building a Learning Culture*. Thousand Oaks, CA: Sage.

Baer, R. (2006) *Mindfulness-Based Treatment Approaches: Clinician's Guide to Evidence Base and Applications*. San Diego, CA: Elsevier Academic Press.

Bagnall, R. (1998) 'Professional Codes of Conduct: A Critique with Implications for Continuing Professional Education.' In D. Dymock (ed.) *CPE 98 Meeting the Challenge of Change* (pp.81–91). Queensland: University of New England.

Baines, D. (2010) '"If we don't get back to where we were before": Working in the restructured non-profit social services.' *British Journal of Social Work*, 40(3), 928–945. doi:10.1093/bjsw/bcn176.

Baines, D., Charlesworth, S., Turner, D. and O'Neill, L. (2014) 'Lean social care and worker identity: The role of outcomes, supervision and mission.' *Critical Social Policy*, 34(4), 433–453. doi:10.1177/0261018314538799.

Banks, S. (2008) 'Critical commentary: Social work ethics.' *British Journal of Social Work*, 38(6), 1238–1249.

Barretti, M. A. (2009) 'Ranking desirable field instructor characteristics: Viewing student preferences in context with field and class experience.' *The Clinical Supervisor*, 28(1), 47–71.

Barry, M. (2007) *Effective Approaches to Risk Assessment in Social Work: An International Literature Review*. Edinburgh: Education Information and Analytical Services, Scottish Executive.

Baxter, P. (2007) 'The CCARE model of clinical supervision: bridging the theory – practice gap… (Communication, collaboration, application, reflection, evaluation).' *Nurse Education in Practice*, 7(2), 103–111.

Bay, U. and Macfarlane, S. (2011) 'Teaching critical reflection: A tool for transformative learning in social work?' *Social Work Education*, 30(7), 745–758. doi:10.1080/02615479.2010.516429.

Beck, U. (1992) *Risk Society: Towards a New Modernity*. London: Sage.

Beddoe, L. (2000) 'The Supervisory Relationship.' In L. Cooper and L. Briggs (ed.), *Fieldwork in the Human Services* (pp.41–54). Sydney: Allen & Unwin.

Beddoe, L. (2003) 'Danger and disdain: Truth or dare in social work education.' *Women in Welfare Education (Australia)*, 6, 13–25.

Beddoe, L. (2009) 'Creating continuous conversation: Social workers and learning organizations.' *Social Work Education*, 28(7), 722–736

Beddoe, L. (2010) 'Surveillance or reflection: Professional supervision in "the risk society".' *British Journal of Social Work*, 40(4), 1279–1296. doi:10.1093/bjsw/bcq018.

Beddoe, L. (2011) 'External supervision in social work: Power, space, risk, and the search for safety.' *Australian Social Work*, 65(2), 197–213. doi:10.1080/0312407x.2011.591187.

Beddoe, L. (2013) 'Starting Out in Supervision.' In K. E. Stagnitti, A. Schoo and D. Welch (eds), *Clinical and Fieldwork Placement in the Health Professions* (second edition) (pp.368–381). Melbourne: Oxford University Press.

Beddoe, L. (2015a) 'Supervision and developing the profession: One supervision or many?' *China Journal of Social Work*, 8(2), 150–163. doi:10.1080/17525098.2015.1039173.

Beddoe, L. (2015b) 'Social Work Supervision for Changing Contexts.' In L. Beddoe and J. Maidment (eds), *Supervision in Social Work: Contemporary Issues* (pp.82–95). London: Routledge.

Beddoe, L. (2017) 'Harmful supervision: A commentary.' *The Clinical Supervisor*, 36(1), 88–101. doi:10.1080/07325223.2017.1295894.

Beddoe, L. and Davys, A. (1994) 'The status of supervision: Reflections from a training perspective.' *Social Work Review*, 6 (5/6), 16–21.

Beddoe, L. and Davys, A. (2008) 'Revitalizing supervision education through stories of confirmation and difference: The case for interprofessional learning.' *Social Work Now*, 40, 34–41.

Beddoe, L. and Davys, A. (2016) *Challenges in Professional Supervision: Current Themes and Models for Practice*. London: Jessica Kingsley Publishers.

Beddoe, L., Davys, A. M. and Adamson, C. (2014) 'Never trust anybody who says "I don't need supervision": Practitioners' beliefs about social worker resilience.' *Practice*, 26(2), 113–130. doi:10.1080/09503153.2014.896888.

Beddoe, L. and Egan, R. (2009) 'Social Work Supervision.' In M. Connolly and L. Harms (eds), *Social Work: Contexts and Practice* (second edition) (pp.410–422). Melbourne: Oxford University Press.

Beddoe, L. and Howard, F. (2012) 'Interprofessional supervision in social work and psychology: Mandates and (inter) professional relationships.' *The Clinical Supervisor*, 31(2), 178–202. doi:10.1080/07325223.2013.730471.

Beddoe, L., Karvinen-Niinikoski, S., Ruch, G. and Tsui, M.-s. (2016) 'Towards an international consensus on a research agenda for social work supervision: Report on the first survey of a Delphi study.' *British Journal of Social Work*, 46(6), 1568–1586. doi:10.1093/bjsw/bcv110.

Beddoe, L. and Maidment, J. (2009) *Mapping Knowledge for Social Work Practice: Critical Intersections*. Melbourne: Cengage.

Beddoe, L. and Maidment, J. (eds) (2015) *Supervision in Social Work: Contemporary Issues*. London: Routledge.

Beinart, H., and Clohessy, S. (2017) *Effective Supervisory Relationships: Best Evidence and Practice*. Chichester: John Wiley and Sons.

Bennett, S. and Deal, K. H. (2009) 'Beginnings and endings in social work supervision: The interaction between attachment and developmental processes.' *Journal of Teaching in Social Work* 29(1), 101–117.

Benton, A. D., Dill, K. and Williams, A. E. (2017) 'Sacred time: Ensuring the provision of excellent supervision.' *Journal of Workplace Behavioral Health*, 32(4), 290–305. doi:10.1080/15555240.2017.1408416

Berger, R. and Quiros, L. (2016) 'Best practices for training trauma-informed practitioners: Supervisors' voice.' *Traumatology*, 22, 145–154. doi:10.1037/trm0000076.

Bernard, J. M. (2005) 'Tracing the development of clinical supervision.' *The Clinical Supervisor*, 24(1), 3–21.

Bernard, J. M. (2006) 'Tracing the development of clinical supervision.' *The Clinical Supervisor*, 24(1), 3–21. doi:10.1300/J001v24n01_02.

Bernard, J. M. and Goodyear, R. K. (2009) *Fundamentals of Clinical Supervision* (fourth edition). Upper Saddle River: NJ: Pearson.

Bernard, J. M. and Goodyear, R. K. (2014) *Fundamentals of Clinical Supervision* (fifth edition). Boston, MA: Pearson.

Berne, E. (1974) *What Do You Say After You Say Hello?* London: Transworld Publishers.

Bernler, G. and Johnsson, L. (1985) *Handledning i psykosocialt arbete*. Stockholm: Natur ochKultur.

Bierema, L. L. and Eraut, M. (2004) 'Workplace-focused learning: Perspectives on continuing professional education and human resource development.' *Advances in Developing Human Resources*, 6(1), 52–68.

Birnbaum, L. (2005) 'Connecting to inner guidance: Mindfulness meditation and transformation of professional self-concept in social work students.' *Critical Social Work* 6:2 Available at: www.criticalsocialwork.com, accessed 13 September 2009.

Black, P. E. and Plowright, D. (2010) 'A multi-dimensional model of reflective learning for professional development.' *Reflective Practice*, 11(2), 245–258. doi:10.1080/14623941003665810.

Bogo, M. and Dill, K. (2008) 'Walking the tightrope: Using power and authority in child welfare supervision.' *Child Welfare*, 87(6), 141–157.

Bogo, M., Paterson, J., Tufford, L. and King, R. (2011) 'Interprofessional clinical supervision in mental health and addiction: Toward identifying common elements.' *The Clinical Supervisor*, 30(1), 124–140. doi: 10.1080/07325223.2011.564961.

Bolton, R. (1979) *People Skills: How to Assert Yourself, Listen to Others, and Resolve Conflicts*. New York, NY: Prentice-Hall.

Bond, M. and Holland, S. (1998) *Skills of Clinical Supervision for Nurses*. Buckingham: Open University Press.

Bond, M. and Holland, M. (2010) *Skills of Clinical Supervision for Nurses* (second edition). Maidenhead: Open University Press.

Borders, L. D. (2010) 'Principles of Best Practices for Clinical Supervision Training Programs.' In J. R. Culbreth and L. L. Brown (eds), *State of the Art in Clinical Supervision* (pp.127–150). New York, NY: Routledge.

Bottrell, D. (2009) 'Understanding "marginal" perspectives: Towards a social theory of resilience.' *Qualitative Social Work*, 8(3), 321–339.

Boud, D., Keogh, R. and Walker, D. (eds) (1985) *Reflection: Turning Experience into Learning*. London: Kogan Page.

Bower, S. A. and Bower, G. H. (1991) *Asserting Yourself: A Practical Guide for Positive Change*. Cambridge, MA: Peresus Books.

Bradley, G. and Hojer, S. (2009) 'Supervision reviewed: Reflections on two different social work models in England and Sweden.' *European Journal of Social Work*, 12(1), 71–85.

Brookfield, S. (1995) *Becoming a Critically Reflective Teacher*. San Francisco, CA: Jossey-Bass.

Brookfield, S. (2009) 'The concept of critical reflection: Promises and contradictions.' *European Journal of Social Work*, 12(3), 293–304.

Brown, A. and Bourne, I. (1996) *The Social Work Supervisor*. Buckingham: Open University Press.

Burke, R. J. (2001) 'Workaholism in organizations: the role of organizational values.' *Personnel Review*, 30(5/6), 637.

Busse, S. (2009) 'Supervision between critical reflection and practical action.' *Journal of Social Work Practice: Psychotherapeutic Approaches in Health, Welfare and the Community*, 23(2), 159–173.

Butler, J. (1996) 'Professional development: Practice as text, reflection as process, and self as locus.' *Australian Journal of Education*, 40(3), 265–283.

Butterworth, T. (1994) 'Preparing to take on clinical supervision.' *Nursing Standard*, (8), 32–34.

Butterworth, T., Bell, L., Jackson, C. and Pajnkihar, M. (2008) 'Wicked spell or magic bullet? A review of the clinical supervision literature 2001–2007.' *Nurse Education Today*, 28(3), 264–272.

Cahn, K. (2009) 'The World Beyond the Unit.' In C. C. Potter and C.R. Brittain (eds), *Child Welfare Supervision: A Practical Guide for Supervisors, Managers and Administrators* (pp.146–176). New York, NY: Oxford University Press.

Calvert, I. (2014). 'Support for midwives – A model of professional supervision based on the recertification programme for midwives in New Zealand.' *Women and Birth, 27*, 2, 145–150.

Carpenter, J., Webb, C. M. and Bostock, L. (2013) 'The surprisingly weak evidence base for supervision: Findings from a systematic review of research in child welfare practice (2000–2012).' *Children & Youth Services Review*, 35(11), 1843–1853. doi: http://dx.doi.org/10.1016/j.childyouth.2013.08.014.

Carroll, M. (2007) 'One more time: what is supervision?' *Psychotherapy in Australia*, 13(3), 34–40.

Carroll, M. (2009) 'Supervision: critical reflection for transformational learning, part one.' *The Clinical Supervisor*, 28(2), 210–220.

Carroll, M. (2010) 'Supervision: critical reflection for transformational learning, part two.' *The Clinical Supervisor*, 29(1), 1–19.

Carroll, M. (2014) *Effective Supervision for the Helping Professions* (second edition). London: Sage Publications.

Carroll, M. and Gilbert, M. (2011) *On Being a Supervisee: Creating Learning Partnerships* (second edition). Australia: Psychoz.

Carroll, M. and Shaw, E. (2013) *Ethical Maturity in the Helping Professions: Making Difficult Life and Work Decisions*. London: Jessica Kingsley Publishers.

Carver, C., Scheier, M. and Weintraub, J. (1989) 'Assessing coping strategies: A theoretically based approach.' *Journal of Personality and Social Psychology*, 56, pp. 267–83.

Casey, C. (2003) 'The learning worker, organizations and democracy.' *International Journal of Lifelong Education*, 22(6), 620–634.

Chang, C. Y., Hays, D. G. and Milliken, T. F. (2009) 'Addressing social justice issues in supervision: a call for client and professional advocacy.' *The Clinical Supervisor*, 28(1), 20–35.

Chen, S.-Y. and Scannapieco, M. (2009) 'The influence of job satisfaction on child welfare worker's desire to stay: An examination on the interaction effect of self-efficacy and supportive supervision.' *Children & Youth Services Review*. doi:10.1016/j.childyouth.2009.10.014.

Chenot, D. (2011) 'The vicious cycle: Recurrent interactions among the media, politicians, the public, and child welfare services organizations.' *Journal of Public Child Welfare*, 5(2–3), 167–184. doi:10.1 080/15548732.2011.566752.

Chiller, P. and Crisp, B. R. (2012) 'Professional supervision: A workforce retention strategy for social work?' *Australian Social Work*, 65(2), 232–242. doi:10.1080/0312407x.2011.625036.

Chinnery, S. A., Appleton, C. and Marlowe, J. M. (2019) 'Cultivating students' reflective capacity through group-based mindfulness instruction.' *Social Work with Groups*, 1–17. doi:10.1080/01609513.2019 .1571760.

Choate, P. (2016) 'Child Protection Inquiries: What Are They Teaching Us? A Canadian Perspective.' In H. Montgomery, D. Badry, D. Fuchs and D. Kikulwe (eds), *Transforming Child Welfare: Interdisciplinary Practices, Field Education, and Research* (pp.61–85). Regina, SK: University of Regina Press.

Clare, B. (2007) 'Promoting deep learning: a teaching, learning and assessment endeavour.' *Social Work Education*, 26(5), 433–446.

Clare, M. (2001) 'Operationalising professional supervision in this age of accountabilities.' *Australian Social Work*, 54(2), 69–79.

Clarke, N. (2006) 'Developing emotional intelligence through workplace learning: Findings from a case study in healthcare.' *Human Resource Development International*, 9(4), 447–465.

Claxton, G. (2005) 'Mindfulness, learning and the brain.' *Journal of Rational-Emotive and Cognitive-Behavior Therapy*, 23(4), 301–314.

Clouder, L. and Sellars, J. (2004) 'Reflective practice and clinical supervision: An interprofessional perspective.' *Journal of Advanced Nursing*, 46(3), 262–269.

Cole, B. and Wessel, J. (2008) 'How clinical instructors can enhance the learning experience of physical therapy students in an introductory clinical placement.' *Advances in Health Sciences Education*, 13(2) 163–179.

Collins, S. (2007) 'Social workers, resilience, positive emotions and optimism.' *Practice*, 19(4), 255–269.

Collins, S. (2008) 'Statutory social workers: stress, job satisfaction, coping, social support and individual differences.' *British Journal of Social Work*, 38(6), 1173–1193.

Collins, S. (2019) *The Positive Social Worker*. London: Routledge

Connolly, M. (ed.) (2017) *Beyond the Risk Paradigm in Child Protection*. London: Palgrave.

Connolly, M. (2007) 'Practice frameworks: conceptual maps to guide interventions in child welfare.' *British Journal of Social Work*, 37(5), 825–837.

Connolly, M. and Doolan, M. (2007) *Lives Cut Short: Child Death by Maltreatment*. Wellington, New Zealand: Dunmore Press.

Connolly, M. and Ward, T. (2008) *Morals, Rights and Practice in the Human Services: Effective and Fair Decision-Making in Health, Social Care and Criminal Justice*. London, Philadelphia, PA: Jessica Kingsley Publishers.

Conrad, D. and Kellar-Guenther, Y. (2006) 'Compassion fatigue, burnout, and compassion satisfaction among Colorado child protection workers.' *Child Abuse & Neglect*, 30(10), 1071–1080.

Cooper, A. (2001) 'The state of mind we're in: Social anxiety, governance and the audit society.' *Psychoanalytic Studies*, 3(3–4), 349–362.

Cooper, L. (2000) 'Organizational Changes and Social Work Supervision: Analysis and Reconstruction.' In L. Beddoe and J. Worrall (eds), *Supervision: From Rhetoric to Reality* (pp.21–32). Auckland: Auckland College of Education.

Cooper, L. (2006) 'Clinical supervision: Private arrangement or managed process?' *Social Work Review*, 18(3), 21–30.

Cooper, L. and Anglem, J. (2003) *Clinical Supervision in Mental Health*. Adelaide: Australian Centre for Community Services Research (ACCSR).

Cornelius, H. and Faire, S. (2006) *Everyone Can Win: Responding to Conflict Constructively* (second edition). Sydney: Simon & Schuster.

Danso, R. (2016) 'Cultural competence and cultural humility: A critical reflection on key cultural diversity concepts.' *Journal of Social Work*, 18(4), 410–430. doi:10.1177/1468017316654341.

Davies, E. J., Tennant, A., Ferguson, E. and Jones, L. F. (2004) 'Developing models and a framework for multiprofessional clinical supervision.' *British Journal of Forensic Practice*, 6 (3) 36–42.

Davis, B. (2002) 'Group supervision as a learning laboratory for the purposeful use of self in child protection work.' *Journal of Teaching in Social Work*, 22(1), 183–198.

Davys, A. (2001) 'A Reflective Learning Process for Supervision.' In L. Beddoe and J. Worrall (eds), *Supervision: From Rhetoric to Reality* (pp.87–98). Auckland: Auckland College of Education.

Davys, A. (2002) *Perceptions through a Prism: Three Accounts of Good Supervision*. Master's thesis, Massey University, Palmerston North. Retrieved from http://hdl.handle.net/10179/5754.

Davys, A. (2005a) 'At the heart of the matter: Culture as a function of supervision.' *Social Work Review*, 17(1), 3–12.

Davys, A. (2005b) 'Supervision: Is what we want what we need?' In L. Beddoe, J. Worrall and F. Howard. (eds.) *Weaving Together the Strands of Supervision: 2004 Conference Proceedings*. (pp.15–24). Auckland: University of Auckland.

Davys, A. (2017) 'Interprofessional supervision: A matter of difference.' *Aotearoa New Zealand Social Work*, 29(3), 79–94. doi:10.11157/anzswj-vol29iss3id278.

Davys, A. (2019) *Interprofessional Supervision: Mapping the Interface between Professional Knowledge, Practice Imperatives and Difference*. PhD thesis, University of Auckland, Auckland, New Zealand. Retrieved from http://hdl.handle.net/2292/48860.

Davys, A. and L. Beddoe (2008) 'Interprofessional learning for supervision: Taking the blinkers off.' *Learning in Health and Social Care*, 8(1), 58–69.

Davys, A. M. and L. Beddoe (2009) 'The Reflective Learning Model: Supervision of social work students.' *Social Work Education*, 28(8), 919–993.

Davys, A. and Beddoe, L. (2000) 'Supervision of students : A map and a model for the decade to come.' *Social Work Education*, 19(5), 438–449.

Davys, A. and Beddoe, L. (2010) *Best Practice in Professional Supervision: A Guide for the Helping Professions*. London: Jessica Kingsley Publishers.

Davys, A. and Beddoe, L. (2016) 'Interprofessional Supervision: Opportunities and Challenges.' In L. Bostock (ed.), *Interprofessional Staff Supervision in Adult Health and Social Care Services* (Vol. 1, pp.37–41). Brighton: Pavilion.

Davys, A., May, J., Burns, B. and O'Connell, M. (2017) 'Evaluating social work supervision.' *Aotearoa New Zealand Social Work*, 29(3), 108–121. doi:http://dx.doi.org/10.11157/anzswj-vol29iss3id314.

Davys, A., O'Connell, M., May, J. and Burns, B. (2016) 'Evaluation of professional supervision in Aotearoa/New Zealand: An interprofessional study.' *International Journal of Mental Health Nursing.* doi:10.1111/inm.12254.

de Shazer, S. (1985) *Keys to Solution in Brief Therapy.* New York, NY: Norton.

Deal, K. H. (2004) 'The relationship between critical thinking and interpersonal skills.' *The Clinical Supervisor*, 22(2), 3–19.

Deal, K. H. and Pittman, J. (2009) 'Examining predictors of social work students' critical thinking skills.' *Advances in Social Work*, 10(1), 87–102.

Dekel, R. and Baum, N. (2009) 'Intervention in a shared traumatic reality: A new challenge for social workers.' *British Journal of Social Work*, 40(6), 1927–1944. doi:10.1093/bjsw/bcp137.

Delgado, C., Upton, D., Ranse, K., Furness, T. and Foster, K. (2017) 'Nurses' resilience and the emotional labour of nursing work: An integrative review of empirical literature.' *International Journal of Nursing Studies*, 70, 7–88.

DePanfilis, D. and Zlotnik, J. L. (2008) 'Retention of front-line staff in child welfare: A systematic review of research.' *Children and Youth Services Review*, 30(9), 995–1008.

Department for Children, Schools and Families (2009b) *Facing up to the Task – The Interim Report of the Social Work Task Force.* London: HM Stationery Office.

Dewey, J. (1998) 'Analysis of Reflective Thinking. How We Think (1933).' In L. A. Hickman and T. M. Alexandra (eds), *The Essential Dewey, Volume 2: Ethics, Logic, Psychology.* Bloomington, IN: Indiana University Press.

Dirkx, J. M., Gilley, J. W. and Gilley, A. M. (2004) 'Change theory in CPE and HRD: Towards a holistic view of learning and change in work.' *Advances in Developing Human Resources*, 6(1), 35–51.

Dolgoff, R. (2005) *An Introduction to Supervisory Practice in Human Services.* Boston, MA: Pearson Education.

Driscoll J (1994) 'Reflective practice for practise – a framework of structured reflection for clinical areas.' *Senior Nurse*, 14 (1), 47–50.

Driscoll, J. J. (2009) 'Prevalence, people and processes: A consideration of the implications of Lord Laming's progress report on the protection of children in England.' *Child Abuse Review*, 18(5), 333–345.

Ducat, W., Martin, P., Kumar, S., Burge, V. and Abernathy, L. (2016) 'Oceans apart, yet connected: Findings from a qualitative study on professional supervision in rural and remote allied health services.' *Australian Journal of Rural Health*, 24(1), 29–35.

Duffy, J. (2011) 'Explicit argumentation as a supervisory tool for decision making in child protection cases involving human rights issues.' *Practice: Social Work in Action*, 23(1), 31–44.

Duggleby, W., Cooper, D. and Penz, K. (2009) 'Hope, self-efficacy, spiritual wellbeing and job satisfaction.' *Journal of Advanced Nursing*, 65(11), 2376–2385.

Dwyer, S. (2007) 'The emotional impact of social work practice.' *Journal of Social Work Practice*, 21(1), 49–60.

Edwards, J. K. (2012) *Strengths-Based Supervision in Clinical Practice.* Thousand Oaks, CA: Sage Publications.

Edwards, J. K. and Chen, M. W. (1999) 'Strength-based supervision: Frameworks, current practice and future directions.' *Family Journal: Counselling and Therapy for Couples and Families*, 7(4), 349–357.

Ellett, A. J., Collins-Camargo, C. and Ellett, C. D. (2006) 'Personal and organizational correlates of child outcomes in child welfare: Implications for supervision and continuing professional development.' *Professional Development: The International Journal of Continuing Social Work Education*, 9(2/3): 44–53.

Ellis, M. V., Berger, L., Hanus, A. E., Ayala, E. E., Swords, B. A. and Siembor, M. (2014) 'Inadequate and harmful clinical supervision: Testing a revised framework and assessing occurrence.' *The Counseling Psychologist*, 42(4), 434–472. doi:10.1177/0011000013508656.

Ellis, M. V., Creaner, M., Hutman, H. B. and Timulak, L. (2015) 'A comparative study of clinical supervision in the Republic of Ireland and the US.' *Journal of Counseling Psychology*, 62, 621–631.

Elston, M., Gabe, J. and O'Beirne, M. (2006) 'A "Risk of the Job"? Violence Against Nurses from Patients and the Public as an Emerging Policy Issue.' In P. Godin (ed.), *Risk and Nursing Practice.* Basingstoke: Palgrave Macmillan.

Enlow, P. T., McWhorter, L. G., Genuario, K. and Davis, A. (2019) 'Supervisor-supervisee interactions: The importance of the supervisory working alliance.' *Training and Education in Professional Psychology,* 13(3), 206–211. doi: org/10.1037/tep0000243.

Eraut, M. (1994) *Developing Professional Knowledge and Competence.* London: Falmer.

Eraut, M. (2004) 'Sharing practice: Problems and possibilities.' *Learning in Health and Social Care,* 3(4), 171–178.

Eraut, M. (2006) 'Editorial.' *Learning in Health and Social Care,* 5(3) 111–118.

Eruera, M. (2007) 'He Korero Korari.' In D. Wepa (ed.), *Clinical Supervision in Aotearoa/New Zealand: A Health Perspective* (pp.141–152). Auckland: Pearson Education.

Evetts, J. (2009) 'New professionalism and new public management: Changes, continuities and consequences.' *Comparative Sociology,* 8(2), 247–266. doi:10.1163/156913309X421655.

Facione, R. A. (1998) *Critical Thinking: What It Is and Why It Counts.* Millbrae, CA: California Academic Press.

Facione, P.A (2013) *Critical thinking: What it is and why it counts.* Palm Beach. CA. Measured Reasons LLC & Insight Assessment.

Falender, C. A. and Shafranske, E. P. (2014). 'Clinical supervision in the era of competence.' In: W. B. Johnson and N. Kaslow (Eds), *Oxford Handbook of Education and Training in Professional Psychology* (pp. 291–313). New York: Oxford University Press.

Falender, C. A., Shafranske, E. P. and Falicov, C. J. (eds) (2014) *Multiculturalism and Diversity in Clinical Supervision: A Competency-Based Approach.* Washington DC: American Psychological Association.

Farmer, S. S. (1988) 'Communication competence in clinical education/supervision: Critical notes.' *The Clinical Supervisor,* 6(2), 29–46.

Fawcett, B. (2009) 'Vulnerability: Questioning the certainties in social work and health.' *International Social Work,* 52(4), 473–484.

Featherstone, B., Morris, K. and White, S. (2014) *Re-imagining Child Protection: Towards Humane Social Work with Families.* Bristol: Policy Press.

Ferguson, H. (2009) 'Performing child protection: Home visiting, movement and the struggle to reach the abused child.' *Child & Family Social Work,* 14(4), 471–480.

Ferguson, H. (2018) 'How social workers reflect in action and when and why they don't: The possibilities and limits to reflective practice in social work.' *Social Work Education,* 37(4), 415–427. doi:10.1080 /02615479.2017.1413083.

Ferguson, K. (2005) 'Professional Supervision.' In M. Rose and D. Best (eds), *Transforming Practice through Clinical Education, Professional Supervision and Mentoring* (pp.293–307). Edinburgh: Elsevier Churchill Livingstone.

Feudtner, C., Santucci G., Feinstein J.A., Snyder C.R., O'Rourke M.T. and Kang T.I. (2007) 'Hopeful thinking and level of comfort regarding providing pediatric palliative care: A survey of hospital nurses.' *Pediatrics,* 119(1), e186–e192.

Fook, J. and Askeland, G. A. (2007) 'Challenges of critical reflection: Nothing ventured, nothing gained.' *Social Work Education,* 26(5), 520–533.

Fook, J. and Gardner, F. (2007) *Practising Critical Reflection: A Resource Handbook.* Maidenhead: Open University Press.

Ford, K. and Jones, A. (1987) *Student Supervision.* London: BASW Macmillan.

Foster, K., Roche, M., Delgado, C., Castillo, C., Giandinoto, J.-A. and Furness, T. (2019) 'Resilience and mental health nursing: An integrative review of international literature.' *International Journal of Mental Health Nursing,* 28(1), 71–85. doi:10.1111/inm.12548.

Fox, R. (1989) 'Relationship: The cornerstone of clinical supervision.' *Social Casework,* 70(3), 146–152.

Franks, V. (2004) 'Evidence-based uncertainty in mental health nursing.' *Journal of Psychiatric & Mental Health Nursing,* 11(1), 99–105.

Freeth, D., Hammick, M., Reeves, S., Koppel, I. and Barr, H. (2006) *Effective Interprofessional Education Development.* Oxford: CAIPE and Blackwell.

Froggett, L. (2000) 'Staff supervision and dependency culture: a case study.' *Journal of Social Work Practice,* 14(1), 27–35.

Gabe, J. and Elston, M. (2008) '"We don't have to take this": Zero tolerance of violence against health care workers in a time of insecurity.' *Social Policy & Administration,* 42(6), 691–709.

Galpin, D., Maksymluk, A. and Whiteford, A. (2019) 'Social workers are being blamed for their own stress and burnout.' *The Guardian*, 31 July 2019. Available at www.theguardian.com/society/2019/jul/31/social-workers-stress-burnout-resilience, accessed 31 March 2020.

Gardiner, D. (1989) *The Anatomy of Supervision: Developing Learning and Professional Competence for Social Work Students*. Milton Keynes: Society for Research on Higher Education and Open University Press.

Gardner, F. (2009) 'Affirming values: using critical reflection to explore meaning and professional practice.' *Reflective Practice: International and Multidisciplinary Perspectives*, 10(2), 179–190.

Garrett, K. J. and Barretta Herman, A. (1995) 'Moving from supervision to professional development.' *The Clinical Supervisor*, 13(2), 97–110.

Garrett, P. M. (2005) 'Social work's "electronic turn": Notes on the deployment of information and communication technologies in social work with children and families.' *Critical Social Policy*, 25(4), 529–553.

Gazzola, N. and Theriault, A. (2007) 'Super- (and not-so-super) vision of counsellors-in-training: Supervisee perspectives on broadening and narrowing processes.' *British Journal of Guidance & Counselling*, 35(2), 189–204.

Gelman, C. R. and Baum, N. (2010) 'Social work students' pre-placement anxiety: An international comparison.' *Social Work Education: The International Journal*, 29(4), 427–440.

Gibbs, J. (2001) 'Maintaining front-line workers in child protection: A case for refocusing supervision.' *Child Abuse Review*, 10(5), 323–335.

Gibbs, J. (2009) 'Changing the cultural story in child protection: learning from the insider's experience.' *Child & Family Social Work*, 14(3), 289–299.

Giddens, A. (1999) 'Risk and responsibility.' *Modern Law Review*, 62(1), 1–10.

Gilbert, T. (2001) 'Reflective practice and clinical supervision: meticulous rituals of the confessional.' *Journal of Advanced Nursing*, 36(2), 199–205.

Gillig, P. M. and Barr, A. (1999) 'A model for multidisciplinary peer review and supervision of behavioral health clinicians.' *Community Mental Health Journal*, 35(4), 361–365.

Gillingham, P. and Bromfield, L. (2008) 'Child protection, risk assessment and blame ideology.' *Children Australia*, 33(1), 18–24.

Glisson, C. (2000) 'Understanding Organizational Climate and Culture.' In R. J. Patti (ed.), *The Handbook of Social Welfare Management* (pp.195–218). Thousand Oaks, CA: Sage Publications.

Goddard, C. and Tucci, J. (1991) 'Child protection and the need for the appraisal of the social worker-client relationship.' *Australian Social Work*, 44(2), 3–10.

Goleman, D. (2005) *Emotional Intelligence* (tenth anniversary edition). New York, NY: Bantam Books.

Gordon, P. K. (2012) 'Ten steps to cognitive behavioural supervision.' *The Cognitive Behaviour Therapist*, 5(4), 71–82.

Gould, N. and M. Baldwin (eds) (2004) *Social Work, Critical Reflection and the Learning Organization*. Aldershot: Ashgate.

Gould, N. and Harris, N. (1996) 'Student imagery of practice in social work and teacher education: A comparative research approach.' *British Journal of Social Work*, 26, 223–237.

Gould, N. and Taylor, I. (eds) (1996) *Reflective Learning for Social Work – Research, Theory and Practice*. Aldershot: Arena Ashgate.

Grant, L. and Kinman, G. (2014) 'Emotional resilience in the helping professions and how it can be enhanced.' *Health and Social Care Education*. doi: 10.11120/hsce.2014.00040.

Grauel, T. (2002) 'Professional Oversight: The Neglected Histories of Supervision.' In M. McMahon and W. Patton (eds), *Supervision in the Helping Professions: A Practical Approach* (pp.261–271). Frenchs Forest, NSW: Prentice Hall.

Gray, M. (2011) 'Back to basics: A critique of the strengths perspective in social work.' *Families in Society: The Journal of Contemporary Social Services*, 92(1), 5–11.

Green, D. (2007) 'Risk and social work practice.' *Australian Social Work*, 60(4), 395–409.

Green Lister, P. and Crisp, B. R. (2005) 'Clinical supervision in child protection for community nurses.' *Child Abuse Review*, 14(1), 57–72.

Greenberg, I. A. (1974) *Psychodrama: Theory and Therapy*. New York, NY: Behavioral Publishing Company.

Griffiths, A., Harper, W., Desrosiers, P., Murphy, A. and Royse, D. (2019a) '"The stress is indescribable": Self-reported health implications from child welfare supervisors.' *The Clinical Supervisor*, 1–19. doi :10.1080/07325223.2019.1643433.

Griffiths, A., Desrosiers, P., Gabbard, J., Royse, D. and Piescher, K. (2019b) 'Retention of child welfare caseworkers: The wisdom of supervisors.' *Child Welfare*, 97(3), 61–83.

Gupta, A. and Blumhardt, H. (2017) 'Poverty, exclusion and child protection practice: the contribution of "the politics of recognition & respect".' *European Journal of Social Work*, 21(2), 247–259.

Hair, H. J. (2013) 'The purpose and duration of supervision, and the training and discipline of supervisors: What social workers say they need to provide effective services.' *British Journal of Social Work*, 43(8), 1562–1588. doi:10.1093/bjsw/bcs071.

Hair, H. J. (2014) 'Power relations in supervision: Preferred practices according to social workers.' *Families in Society: The Journal of Contemporary Social Services*, 95(2), 107–114.

Hair, H. J. and O'Donoghue, K. (2009) 'Culturally relevant, socially just social work supervision: Becoming visible through a social constructionist lens.' *Journal of Ethnic and Cultural Diversity in Social Work*, 18(1), 70–88.

Hall, P. (2005) 'Interprofessional teamwork: Professional cultures as barriers.' *Journal of Interprofessional Care*, 19(s1), 188–196.

Harvey, A. and Henderson, F. (2014) 'Reflective supervision for child protection practice – reaching beneath the surface.' *Journal of Social Work Practice*, 28(3), 343–356. doi:10.1080/02650533.2014 .925862.

Hawkins, P. and Shohet, R. (1989) *Supervision in the Helping Professions*. Maidenhead: Open University Press.

Hawkins, P. and Shohet, R. (2000) *Supervision in the Helping Professions* (second edition). Maidenhead: Open University Press.

Hawkins, P. and Shohet, R. (2006) *Supervision in the Helping Professions* (third edition). Maidenhead: Open University Press.

Hawkins, P., and Shohet, R. (2012) *Supervision in the Helping Professions* (fourth edition). London: Open University Press McGraw-Hill.

Hawkins, P. and Smith, N. (2006) *Coaching, Mentoring and Organizational Consultancy: Supervision and Development*. Maidenhead: Open University Press.

Hay, K., Maidment, J., Ballantyne, N., Beddoe, L., and Walker, S. (2019). 'Feeling lucky: The serendipitous nature of field education.' *Clinical Social Work Journal, 47*, 1, 23–31.

Healy, K. and Meagher, G. (2004) 'The reprofessionalization of social work: Collaborative approaches for achieving professional recognition.' *British Journal of Social Work*, 34(2), 243–260.

Healy, K., Meagher, G. and Cullin, J. (2009) 'Retaining novices to become expert child protection practitioners: Creating career pathways in direct practice.' *British Journal of Social Work*, 39(2), 299–317.

Heath, H. and Freshwater, D. (2000) 'Clinical supervision as an emancipatory process: avoiding inappropriate intent.' *Journal of Advanced Nursing*, 32(5), 1298–1306.

Heid, L. (1997) 'Supervisor development across the professional lifespan.' *The Clinical Supervisor*, 16(2), 139–152.

Hernández, P. and McDowell, T. (2010) 'Intersectionality, power, and relational safety in context: Key concepts in clinical supervision.' *Training and Education in Professional Psychology*, 4(1), 29–35. doi:10.1037/a0017064.

Heron, J. (2001) *Helping the Client: A Creative Practical Guide*. London: Sage Publications.

Hess, A. K. (1986) 'Growth in Supervision: Stages of Supervisee and Supervisor Development.' In F. W. Kaslow (ed.), *Supervision and Training: Models, Dilemmas and Challenges* (pp.51–67). New York, NY: Haworth.

Hewson, D. and Carroll, M. (2016) *Reflective Practice in Supervision: Companion Volume to The Reflective Practice Toolkit*. Hazelbrook NSW: MoshPit.

Hingley-Jones, H. and Ruch, G. (2016) '"Stumbling through?" Relationship-based social work practice in austere times.' *Journal of Social Work Practice*, 30(3), 235–248.

Hirst, V. M. (2001) 'Professional supervision for managers: An effective organizational development intervention: An inquiry based on the perceptions and experiences of managers of social work.' Unpublished Master's thesis. University of Auckland, Auckland, New Zealand.

Howard, F. (1997) 'Supervision.' In H. Love and W. Whittaker (eds), *Practice Issues for Clinical and Applied Psychologists in New Zealand*. Wellington: The New Zealand Psychological Society.

Howard, F. (2008) 'Managing stress or enhancing wellbeing? Positive psychology's contributions to clinical supervision.' *Australian Psychologist*, 43(2), 105–113.

Howe, D. (1996) 'Surface and depth in social-work practice.' In N. Parton (ed.), *Social Theory, Social Change and Social Work* (pp.77–97). London: Routledge.

Howe, D. (2008) *The Emotionally Intelligent Social Worker*. Basingstoke: Palgrave.

Hughes, L. and Pengelly, P. (1997) *Staff Supervision in a Turbulent Environment – Managing Process and Task in Front-Line Services*. London: Jessica Kingsley Publishers.

Hunt, S., Goddard, C., Cooper, J., Littlechild, B. and Wild, J. (2015) '"If I feel like this, how does the child feel?" Child protection workers, supervision, management and organisational responses to parental violence.' *Journal of Social Work Practice*, 30(1) 5–24. doi:10.1080/02650533.2015.1073145.

Hunter, M. (2009) 'Poor supervision continues to hinder child protection practice.' *Community Care*. Available at: www.communitycare.co.uk/Articles/2009/04/22/111327/poor-supervision-continues-to-hinder-child-protection.html, accessed 16 April 2010.

Hunter, B. and Warren, L. (2013) *Investigating Resilience in Midwifery*. Cardiff: Cardiff University for Royal College of Midwives.

Hutchings, J., Cooper, L. and O'Donoghue, K. (2014) 'Cross-disciplinary supervision among social workers in Aotearoa New Zealand.' *Aotearoa New Zealand Social Work*, 26(4), 53–64.

Hutchison, J. S. (2015) 'Anti-oppressive practice and reflexive lifeworld-led approaches to care: A framework for teaching nurses about social justice.' *Nursing Research and Practice*, 2015, 5. doi:10.1155/2015/187508.

Ingram, R. (2012) 'Emotions, social work practice and supervision: an uneasy alliance?' *Journal of Social Work Practice*, 27(1), 5–19. doi:10.1080/02650533.2012.745842.

Inman, A. G., Hutman, H., Pendse, A., Devdas, L., Luu, L. and Ellis, M. V. (2014) 'Current Trends Concerning Supervisors, Supervisees, and Clients in Clinical Supervision.' In C. E. Watkins and D. L. Milne (eds), *Wiley International Handbook of Clinical Supervision* (pp.61–102). Chichester: Wiley.

Inskipp, F. and B. Proctor (1993) *Making the Most of Supervision: A Professional Development Resource for Counsellors, Supervisors and Trainees*. Twickenham: Cascade.

Johns, C. (2001) 'Depending on the intent and emphasis of the supervisor, clinical supervision can be a different experience.' *Journal of Nursing Management*, 9(3), 139–145.

Johns, C. (2005) 'Expanding the Gates of Perception.' In C. Johns and D. Freshwater (eds) *Transforming Nursing Through Reflective Practice* (second edition). Oxford: Blackwell Publishing.

Johns, C. and Freshwater, D. (eds) (2005) *Transforming Nursing through Reflective Practice*. Oxford: Blackwell Publishing.

Jones, A. (2006) 'Clinical supervision: what do we know and what do we need to know? A review and commentary.' *Journal of Nursing Management*, 14(8), 577–585.

Jones, A. (2008) 'Clinical supervision is important to the quality of health-care provision.' *International Journal of Mental Health Nursing*, 17, 379–380.

Jones, J. and Gallop, L. (2003) 'No time to think: Protecting the reflective space in children's services.' *Child Abuse Review*, 12(2), 101–106.

Jones, J. L., Washington, G. and Steppe, S. (2007) 'The role of supervisors in developing clinical decision-making skills in Child Protective Service (CPS).' *Journal of Evidence-Based Social Work*, 4(3/4), 103–116.

Jones, M. (2004) 'Supervision, Learning and Transformative Practices.' In N. Gould and M. Baldwin (eds), *Social Work, Critical Reflection and the Learning Organization* (pp.11–22). Aldershot: Ashgate.

Jones, S. and Joss, R. (1995) 'Models of Professionalism.' In M. Yelloly and M. Henkel (eds), *Learning and Teaching in Social Work: Towards Reflective Practice* (pp.15–33). London: Jessica Kingsley Publishers.

Juhnke, G. A. (1996) 'Solution focused supervision: Promoting supervisee skills and confidence through successful solutions.' *Counsellor Education and Supervision*, 36, Sept, 48–57.

Julien-Chinn, F. J. and Lietz, C. A. (2015) 'Permanency-focused supervision and workers' self-efficacy: Exploring the link.' *Social Work*, 61(1), 37–44.

Kadushin, A. (1976) *Supervision in Social Work*. New York, NY: Columbia University Press.

Kadushin, A. and Harkness, D. (2002) *Supervision in Social Work* (fourth edition). New York, NY: Columbia University Press.

Kaiser, T. L. and Kuechler, C. F. (2008) 'Training supervisors of practitioners: Analysis of efficacy.' *The Clinical Supervisor*, 27(1), 76–96.

Kalliath, T. and Beck, A. (2001) 'Is the path to burnout and turnover paved by a lack of supervisory support? A structural equations test.' *New Zealand Journal of Psychology*, 30 (2) 72–78.

Kalliath, P., Hughes, M. and Newcombe, P. (2011) 'When work and family are in conflict: Impact on psychological strain experienced by social workers in Australia.' *Australian Social Work*, 65(3), 355–371. doi:10.1080/0312407X.2011.625035.

Kane, R. (2001) 'Supervision in New Zealand Social Work.' In M. Connolly (ed.), *New Zealand Social Work: Contexts and Practice*. Auckland: Oxford University Press.

Karpman, S. (1968) 'Fairy tales and script drama analysis.' *Transactional Analysis Bulletin*, 7(26), 39–44.

Karpman, S. B. (2007) The New Drama Triangles: USATAA/ITAA Conference lecture, August 11, 2007. Available at https://karpmandramatriangle.com/pdf/thenewdramatriangles.pdf, accessed on 5 February 2020.

Karvinen-Niinikoski, S., Beddoe, L., Ruch, G. and Tsui, M.-s. (2019) 'Professional supervision and professional autonomy.' *Aotearoa New Zealand Social Work*, 31(3), 10. doi:10.11157/anzswj-vol31iss3id650.

Keddell, E. (2016) 'Interpreting children's best interests: Needs, attachment and decision-making.' *Journal of Social Work*, 17(3), 324–342. doi:10.1177/1468017316644694.

Keddell, E. (2017). 'Comparing Risk-Averse and Risk-Friendly Practitioners in Child Welfare Decision-Making: A Mixed Methods Study.' *Journal of Social Work Practice*, 31, 4, 411–429.

Keddell, E., and Hyslop, I. (2018). 'Role type, risk perceptions and judgements in child welfare: A mixed methods vignette study.' *Children and Youth Services Review*, 87, 130–139.

Kelly, S. and Green, T. (2019) 'Seeing more, better sight: Using an interprofessional model of supervision to support reflective child protection practice within the health setting.' *British Journal of Social Work*. doi:10.1093/bjsw/bcz030.

Kerlinger, F. N. (1986) *Foundations of Behavioral Research* (third edition). New York, NY: Holt, Rinehart & Winston.

Kilminster, S. M. and Jolly, B. C. (2000) 'Effective supervision in clinical practice settings: A literature review.' *Medical Education*, 34(10), 827–840.

King, L., M., Jackson, M., T., Gallagher, A., Wainwright, P. and Lindsay, J. (2009) 'Towards a model of the expert practice educator – interpreting multi-professional perspectives in the literature.' *Learning in Health and Social Care*, 8(2), 135–144.

Knight, C. (2018) 'Trauma-informed supervision: Historical antecedents, current practice, and future directions.' *The Clinical Supervisor*, 1–31. doi:10.1080/07325223.2017.1413607.

Koenig, T. and Spano, R. (2007) 'The cultivation of social workers' hope in personal life and professional practice.' *Journal of Religion and Spirituality in Social Work: Social Thought*, 26(3), 45–61.

Kofman, F. and Senge, P. (1993) 'Communities of commitment: The heart of learning organizations.' *Organizational Dynamics*, 22(2), 5–23.

Koivu, A., Saarinen, P. I. and Hyrkas, K. (2012) 'Who benefits from clinical supervision and how? The association between clinical supervision and the work-related wellbeing of female hospital nurses.' *Journal of Clinical Nursing*, 21(17–18), 2567–2578. doi:10.1111/j.1365-2702.2011.04041.x.

Kolb, D. (1984) *Experiential Learning as the Source of Learning and Development*. Englewood Cliffs, NJ: Prentice Hall.

Kondrat, M. E. (1992) 'Reclaiming the practical: Formal and substantive rationality in social work practice.' *Social Service Review* (June 1992), 237–255.

Kondrat, M. E. (1999) 'Who is the "self" in self-aware: Professional self-awareness from a critical theory perspective.' *Social Service Review*, 73(4), 451–477.

Koppes, L. L. (2008) 'Facilitating an organization to embrace a work-life effectiveness culture: A practical approach.' *Psychologist-Manager Journal*, 11(1), 163–184.

Krause, A. and Allen, G.J. (1988) 'Perceptions of counsellor supervision: An examination of Stoltenberg's model from the perspective of supervisor and supervisee.' *Journal of Counseling Psychology*, 35: 77–80.

Ladany, N., Ellis, M. V. and Friedlander, M. L. (1999) 'The supervisory working alliance, trainee self-efficacy, and satisfaction.' *Journal of Counseling and Development*, 77(4), 447–455.

Ladany, N., Mori, Y. and Mehr, K. E. (2013) 'Effective and ineffective supervision.' *The Counseling Psychologist*, 41, 28–47. https://doi.org/10.1177/0011000012442648.

Laming, W.H. (2003) *The Victoria Climbié Inquiry: Report of an Inquiry by Lord Laming.* (Cm. 5730) London: The Stationery Office.

Laming, W.H (2009) *The Protection of Children in England: A Progress Report.* London: The Stationery Office.

Lau, M., Bishop, S., Segal, Z., Buis, T. *et al.* (2006) 'The Toronto mindfulness scale: Development and validation.' *Journal of Clinical Psychology,* 62(12), 1445–1467.

Lave, J. and Wenger, E. (1991) *Situated Learning: Legitimate Peripheral Participation.* Cambridge: Cambridge University Press.

Lay, K. and McGuire, L. (2010) 'Building a lens for critical reflection and reflexivity in social work education.' *Social Work Education,* 29(5), 539–550. doi:10.1080/02615470903159125.

Leavy, P. (2017) 'Introduction to Privilege Through the Looking-Glass.' In P. Leavy (ed.), *Privilege Through the Looking-Glass* (pp.1–6). Rotterdam: Sense Publishers.

Leggat, S., Phillips, B., Pearce, P., Dawson, M., Schulz, D. and Smith, J. (2016) 'Clinical supervision for allied health staff: Necessary but not sufficient.' *Australian Health Review,* 40, 431–437. doi:org/10.1071/AH15080.

Le Maistre, C., Boudreau, S. and Pare, A. (2006) 'Mentor or evaluator? Assisting and assessing newcomers to the professions.' *The Journal of Workplace Learning,* 18(6), 344–354.

Leonard, K. and Weinstein, J. (2009) 'Interprofessional Practice Education and Learning.' In M. Doel and S. Shardlow (eds), *Educating Professionals: Practice Learning in Health and Social Care* (pp.215–231). Farnham: Ashgate.

Lewis, P. (2005) 'Suppression or expression: An exploration of emotion management in a special care baby unit.' *Work, Employment and Society,* 19(3), 565–581. doi:10.1177/0950017005055673.

Lietz, C. A. (2009) 'Critical theory as a framework for child welfare decision-making: Some possibilities.' *Journal of Public Child Welfare,* 3(2), 190–206.

Lietz, C. A. (2010) 'Critical thinking in child welfare supervision.' *Administration in Social Work,* 34(1), 68–78.

Lietz, C. A. and Julien-Chinn, F. J. (2017) 'Do the components of strengths-based supervision enhance child welfare workers' satisfaction with supervision?' *Families in Society: The Journal of Contemporary Social Services,* 98(2), 146–155.

Littlechild, B. (2008) 'Child protection social work: Risks of fears and fears of risks – impossible tasks from impossible goals?' *Social Policy and Administration,* 42(6), 662–675.

Lizzio, A., Stokes, L. and Wilson, K. (2005) 'Approaches to learning in professional supervision: Supervisee perceptions of processes and outcome.' *Studies in Continuing Education,* 27(3), 239–256.

Lizzio, A. and Wilson, K. (2002) 'The Domain of Learning Goals in Professional Supervision.' In M. McMahon and W. Patton (eds), *Supervision in the Helping Professions: A Practical Approach* (pp.27–41). Frenchs Forest, NSW: Pearson Education.

Lizzio, A., Wilson, K. and Que, J. (2009) 'Relationship dimensions in the professional supervision of psychology graduates: supervisee perceptions of processes and outcome.' *Studies in Continuing Education,* 31(2) 127–140.

Loganbill, C., Hardy, E. and Delworth, U. (1982) 'Supervision: A conceptual model.' *The Counseling Psychologist,* 10(1), 3–42.

Lombardo, C., Milne, D. and Proctor, R. (2009) 'Getting to the heart of clinical supervision: A theoretical review of the role of emotions in professional development.' *Behavioural and Cognitive Psychotherapy,* 37(02), 207–219.

Lonne, B., Parton, N., Thomson, J. and Harries, M. (2008) *Reforming Child Protection.* Routledge: London.

Low, H. and Weinstein, J. (2000) 'Interprofessional Education.' In R. Pierce and J. Weinstein (eds), *Innovative Education and Training for Care Professionals* (pp.205–220). London: Jessica Kingsley Publishers.

Luthans, F. (2002) 'The need for and meaning of positive organizational behavior.' *Journal of Organizational Behavior,* 23(6), 695–706.

Luthans, F., Avolio, B.J., Avey, J. B. and Norman, S. M. (2007a) 'Positive psychological capital: Measurement and relationship with performance and satisfaction.' *Personnel Psychology,* 60, 541–572.

Luthans, F., Youssef, C. M. and Avolio, B. J. (2007b) *Psychological Capital.* New York, NY: Oxford University Press.

Luthar, S. and Cicchetti, D. (2000) 'The construct of resilience: Implications for interventions and social policies.' *Development and Psychopathology,* 12(4), 857–885.

Lynch, L., Hancox, K., Happell, B. and Parker, J. (2008) *Clinical Supervision for Nurses*. Chichester: Wiley Blackwell.

Mafile'o, T., and Su'a-Hawkins, A. (2005) 'A Case for Cultural Supervision: Reflections on Experiences of Pasifika Cultural Supervision.' In *Weaving Together the Strands of Supervision: Proceedings of the 2004 Conference, Auckland New Zealand* (pp.119–123). Auckland: Faculty of Education, University of Auckland.

Maidment, J. and Crisp, B. R. (2010) 'The impact of emotions on practicum learning.' *Social Work Education*, 30(04), 408–421. doi:10.1080/02615479.2010.501859.

Maidment, J. and Beddoe, L. (2012) 'Is social work supervision in "Good Heart"? A critical commentary.' *Australian Social Work*, 65(2), 163–170. doi:10.1080/0312407x.2012.680426.

Mandell, D. (2008) 'Power, care and vulnerability: Considering use of self in child welfare work.' *Journal of Social Work Practice*, 22(2), 235–248.

Mänttäri-van der Kuip, M. (2014) 'The deteriorating work-related wellbeing among statutory social workers in a rigorous economic context.' *European Journal of Social Work*, 17(5), 672–688. doi:10.1080/13691457.2014.913006.

Marlowe, J. M., Appleton, C., Chinnery, S.-A. and Van Stratum, S. (2015) 'The integration of personal and professional selves: Developing students' critical awareness in social work practice.' *Social Work Education*, 34(1), 60–73. doi:10.1080/02615479.2014.949230.

Marris, P. (1974) *Loss and Change*. London: Routledge & Kegan Paul.

Marsh, P. (2006). 'Promoting Children's Welfare by Inter-professional Practice and Learning in Social Work and Primary Care.' *Social Work Education, 25*, 2, 148–160.

Marshall, T. (2019) 'The concept of reflection: A systematic review and thematic synthesis across professional contexts.' *Reflective Practice*, 20(3), 396–415. doi:10.1080/14623943.2019.1622520.

Maslach, C. (1978) 'Job burnout: How people cope.' *Public Welfare*, 36, 56–58.

McCann, D. (2000) 'From Here to Eternity and Back Again: Developing a Supervisory Relationship with Training Family Therapists.' In G. G. Barnes, G. Down and D. McCann (eds), *Systemic Supervision – A Portable Guide for Supervision Training* (pp.41–52). London: Jessica Kingsley Publishers.

McDonald, G., Jackson, D., Wilkes, L. and Vickers, M. H. (2012) 'A work-based educational intervention to support the development of personal resilience in nurses and midwives.' *Nurse Education Today*, 32(4), 378–384. doi:10.1016/j.nedt.2011.04.012.

McFadden, P. (2018) 'Two sides of one coin? Relationships build resilience or contribute to burnout in child protection social work: Shared perspectives from Leavers and Stayers in Northern Ireland.' *International Social Work*, 1(13), 1–13. doi:10.1177/0020872818788393.

McFadden, P., Campbell, A. and Taylor, B. (2014) 'Resilience and burnout in child protection social work: Individual and organizational themes from a systematic literature review.' *British Journal of Social Work*, 45(5), 1546–1563. doi:10.1093/bjsw/bct210.

McLaughlin, K. (2007) 'Regulation and risk in social work: The General Social Care Council and the Social Care Register in context.' *British Journal of Social Work*, 37(7), 1263–1277.

McNamara, Y., Lawley, M. and Towler, J. (2007) 'Supervision in the context of youth and community work training.' *Youth and Policy*, 97/98, 73–90.

McMahon, A. (2014) 'Four guiding principles for the supervisory relationship.' *Reflective Practice*, 15(3), 333–346. doi:10.1080/14623943.2014.900010.

McNamara, M. L., Kangos, K. A., Corp, D. A., Ellis, M. V. and Taylor, E. J. (2017) 'Narratives of harmful clinical supervision: Synthesis and recommendations.' *The Clinical Supervisor*, 36(1), 124–144. doi:10.1080/07325223.2017.1298488.

Mezirow, J. (1981) 'A critical theory of adult learning and education.' *Adult Education*, 32(1, Fall), 3–24.

Middleman, R. and Rhodes, G. (1980) 'Teaching the practice of supervision.' *Journal of Education for Social Work*, 16, 51–59.

Miller, W. R. and Rollnick, S. (2013) *Motivational Interviewing: Helping People Change* (third edition). New York, NY: Guilford Press.

Milne, D., Aylott, H., Fitzpatrick, H. and Ellis, M. V. (2008) 'How does clinical supervision work? Using a "best evidence synthesis" approach to construct a basic model of supervision.' *The Clinical Supervisor*, 27(2), 170–190.

Moffatt, K. (1996) 'Teaching Social Work as a Reflective Practice.' In N. Gould and I. Taylor (eds), *Reflective Learning for Social Work – Research, Theory and Practice*. Aldershot: Arena Ashgate.

Moorhead, B., Manthorpe, J. and Baginsky, M. (2019) 'An examination of support and development mechanisms for newly qualified social workers across the UK: Implications for Australian social work.' *Practice*, 1–15. doi:10.1080/09503153.2019.1660314.

Mor Barak, M. E., Levin, A., Nissly, J. A. and Lane, C. J. (2006) 'Why do they leave? Modeling child welfare workers' turnover intentions.' *Children & Youth Services Review*, 28(5), 548–577.

Mor Barak, M. E., Travis, Dnika, J., Pyun, H. and Xie, B. (2009) 'The impact of supervision on worker outcomes: A meta-analysis.' *Social Service Review*, 83(1), 3–32.

Moreno, J. L. (1946, revised and enlarged in 1964) *Psychodrama, Vol. 1.* New York, NY: Beacon.

Morris, K. and Burford, G. (2017) 'Engaging Families and Managing Risk in Practice.' In M. Connolly (ed.), *Beyond the Risk Paradigm in Child Protection* (pp.91–108). London: Palgrave.

Morrison, T. (1997) 'Emotionally Competent Child Protection Organizations: Fallacy, Fiction or Necessity.' In J. Bates, R. Pugh and N. Thompson (eds), *Protecting Children: Challenges and Changes*. Aldershot: Arena.

Morrison, T. (2001) *Staff Supervision in Social Care: Making a Real Difference for Staff and Service Users.* Brighton: Pavilion.

Morrison, T. (1993) *Staff Supervision in Social Care: An Action Learning Approach.* Brighton: Pavilion.

Morrison, T. (2007) 'Emotional intelligence, emotion and social work: Context, characteristics, complications and contribution.' *British Journal of Social Work*, 37(2), 245–263.

Mullarkey, K., Keeley, P. and Playle, J. F. (2001) 'Multiprofessional clinical supervision: Challenges for mental health nurses.' *Journal of Psychiatric and Mental Health Nursing*, 8(3), 205–211.

Munro, E. (2004a) 'A simpler way to understand the results of risk assessment instruments.' *Children & Youth Services Review*, 26: 873–883.

Munro, E. (2004b) 'The Impact of Child Abuse Inquiries since 1990.' In N. Stanley and J. Manthorpe (eds), *The Age of the Inquiry: Learning and Blaming in Health and Social Care* (pp.75–91). London: Routledge.

Marton, F. and Saljo, R. (1976) 'On qualitative difference in learning: outcome and process.' *British Journal of Educational Psychology*, 46(1), 4–11.

Munro, E. (2008) 'Improving reasoning in supervision.' *Social Work Now*, 40, 3–10.

Munson, C. E. (1993) *Clinical Social Work Supervision* (second edition). New York, NY: Haworth Press.

Neukrug, E. (2008) *Theory, Practice and Trends in the Human Services: An Introduction* (fourth edition). Melbourne, Australia: Thomson/Brooks/Cole.

Nissly, A., Mor Barak, M. and Levin, A. (2005) 'Stress, social support, and workers' intentions to leave their jobs in public child welfare.' *Administration in Social Work*, 29 (1), 79–100.

Noble, C. and Irwin, J. (2009) 'Social work supervision: An exploration of the current challenges in a rapidly changing social, economic and political environment.' *Journal of Social Work*, 9(3), 345–358.

Noble, C., Gray, M. and Johnston, L. (2016) *Critical Supervision for the Human Services.* London: Jessica Kingsley Publishers.

Nordentoft, H. M. (2008) 'Changes in emotion work at interdisciplinary conferences following clinical supervision in a palliative outpatient ward.' *Qualitative Health Research*, 18(7), 913–927.

Northcott, N. (2000) 'Clinical Supervision: Professional Development or Management Control.' In J. Spouse and L. Redfern (eds), *Successful Supervision in Health Care Practice* (pp.10–29). London: Blackwell Science.

Nye, C. (2007) 'Dependence and independence in clinical supervision: An application of Vygotsky's developmental learning theory.' *The Clinical Supervisor*, 26(1), 81–98.

Oates, F. (2019) 'You are not allowed to tell: Organizational culture as a barrier for child protection workers seeking assistance for traumatic stress symptomology.' *Children Australia*, 1–7. doi:10.1017/cha.2019.12.

O'Connor, L. and Leonard, K. (2013) 'Decision making in children and families social work: The practitioner's voice.' *British Journal of Social Work*, 44(7), 1805–1822. doi:10.1093/bjsw/bct051.

O'Donoghue, K. (2003) *Re-Storying Social Work Supervision.* Palmerston North: Dunmore Press.

O'Donoghue, K. (2015) 'Issues and challenges facing social work supervision in the twenty-first century.' *China Journal of Social Work*, 8(2), 136–149. doi:10.1080/17525098.2015.1039172.

O'Donoghue, K. and Tsui, M.-s. (2012) 'Towards a professional supervision culture: The development of social work supervision in Aotearoa New Zealand.' *International Social Work*, 55(1), 5–28. doi:10.1177/0020872810396109.

O'Neill, O. (2002) *A Question of Trust: Lecture One 'Spreading Suspicion'*. Paper presented at the 2002 Reith Lecture Series, BBC. Available at: www.bbc.co.uk/radio4/reith2002/lecture1.shtml accessed 31 March 2020.

Owen, D. (2008) 'The Ah-Ha Moment: Passionate Supervision as a Tool for Transformation and Metamorphosis.' In R. Shohet (ed.), *Passionate Supervision* (pp.50–68). London: Jessica Kingsley Publishers.

Owen, D. and Shohet, R. (Eds.). (2012). *Clinical Supervision in the Medical Profession: Structured Reflective Practice*. Maidenhead McGraw Hill, Open University Press.

Pack, M. (2009a) 'Clinical supervision: An interdisciplinary review of literature with implications for reflective practice in social work.' *Reflective Practice: International and Multidisciplinary Perspectives*, 10(5), 657–668.

Pack, M. (2009b) 'Supervision as a liminal space: Towards a dialogic relationship.' *Gestalt Journal of Australia and New Zealand*, 5(2): 60–78.

Page, S. and Wosket, V. (2015) *Supervising the Counsellor and Psychotherapist*. Hove, East Sussex: Routledge.

Papell, C. P. (1996) 'Reflections on Issues in Social Work Education.' In N. Gould and I. Taylor (eds), *Reflective Learning for Social Work: Research, Theory and Practice*. Aldershot: Ashgate.

Parton, N. (ed.) (1996) *Social Theory, Social Change and Social Work*. London: Routledge.

Parton, N. (1998) 'Risk, advanced liberalism and child welfare: The need to rediscover uncertainty and ambiguity.' *British Journal of Social Work*, 28(1), 5–27.

Parton, N. (2009) 'Challenges to practice and knowledge in child welfare social work: From the "social" to the "informational"?' *Children and Youth Services Review*, 31(7), 715–721.

Parton, N. (2014) 'Social work, child protection and politics: Some critical and constructive reflections.' *British Journal of Social Work*, 44(7), 2042–2056. doi:10.1093/bjsw/bcu091.

Parton, N., Thorpe, D. and Wattam, C. (1997) *Child Protection: Risk and the Moral Order*. Basingstoke: Macmillan.

Patton, M. J. and Kivlighan, D. M. (1997) 'Relevance of the supervisory alliance to the counseling alliance and to treatment adherence in counselor training.' *Journal of Counseling Psychology*, 44(1), 108–115.

Payne, M. (1994) 'Personal Supervision in Social Work.' In A. Connor and S. E. Black (eds), *Performance Review and Quality in Social Care* (pp.43–58). London: Jessica Kingsley Publishers.

Peach, J. and Horner, N. (2007) 'Using Supervision: Support or Surveillance.' In M. Lymbery and K. Postle (eds), *Social Work: A Companion to Learning* (pp.228–239). London: Sage Publications.

Pettes, D. E. (1967) *Supervision in Social Work: A Method of Student Training and Staff Development (Vol. 10)*. London: Allen & Unwin.

Plath, D. (2013) 'Organizational processes supporting evidence-based practice.' *Administration in Social Work*, 37(2), 171–188. doi:10.1080/03643107.2012.672946.

Pollack, S. (2008) 'Labelling clients "risky": Social work and the neo-liberal welfare state.' *British Journal of Social Work*, 40(4), 1263–1278. doi:10.1093/bjsw/bcn079.

Presbury, J., Echterling, L. G. and McKee, J. E. (1999) 'Supervision for inner vision: Solution-focused strategies.' *Counsellor Education and Supervision*, 39(2), 146–156.

Proctor, B. (2001) 'Training for the Supervision Alliance Attitude, Skills and Intention.' In J. R. Cutcliffe, T. Butterworth and B. Proctor, *Fundamental Themes in Clinical Supervision* (pp.25–46). New York, NY: Routledge.

Profitt, N. J. (2008) 'Who cares about us? Opening paths to a critical, collective notion of self-care.' *Canadian Social Work Review*, 25(2), 146–167.

Rankine, M., Beddoe, L., O'Brien, M., and Fouché, C. (2018). 'What's your agenda? Reflective supervision in community-based child welfare services.' *European Journal of Social Work, 21*, 3, 428–440.

Rast, K. A., Herman, D. J., Rousmaniere, T. G., Whipple, J. L. and Swift, J. K. (2017) 'Perceived impact on client outcomes: The perspectives of practicing supervisors and supervisees.' *SAGE Open*, 7(1), 2158244017698729.

Redmond, B. (2004) *Reflection in Action: Developing Reflective Practice in Health and Social Services*. Aldershot: Ashgate.

Research in Practice (2019) 'Resources and tools for practice supervisors.' Available at: https://practice-supervisors.rip.org.uk, accessed 31 March 2020.

Revell, L. and Burton, V. (2015) 'Supervision and the dynamics of collusion: A rule of optimism?' *British Journal of Social Work*, 46(6), 1587–1601. doi:10.1093/bjsw/bcv095.

Richards, K. (2000) 'Counsellor supervision in Zimbabwe: A new direction.' *International Journal for the Advancement of Counselling*, 22(2), 143–155.

Richmond, D. (2009) 'Using multi-layered supervision methods to develop creative practice.' *Reflective Practice: International and Multidisciplinary Perspectives*, 10(4), 543–557.

Rieck, T., Callahan, J. L. and Watkins Jr, C. E. (2015) 'Clinical supervision: An exploration of possible mechanisms of action.' *Training and Education in Professional Psychology*, 9(2),187.

Robinson, V. P. (1949) *Dynamics of Supervision Under Functional Controls: A Professional Process in Social Casework*. Philadelphia, PA: University of Pennsylvania Press.

Roche, A. M., Todd, C. L. and O'Connor, J. (2007) 'Clinical supervision in the alcohol and other drugs field: An imperative or an option?' *Drug & Alcohol Review*, 26(3), 241–249.

Ruch, G. (2002) 'From triangle to spiral: Reflective practice in social work education, practice and research.' *Social Work Education*, 21(2), 199–216.

Ruch, G. (2007a) 'Reflective practice in contemporary child-care social work: The role of containment.' *British Journal of Social Work*, 37, 659–680.

Ruch, G. (2007b) '"Thoughtful" practice: Child care social work and the role of case discussion.' *Child and Family Social Work*, 12, 370–379.

Ruch, G. (2009) 'Identifying "the critical" in a relationship-based model of reflection.' *European Journal of Social Work*, 12(3), 349–362.

Ruch, G. (2012) 'Where have all the feelings gone? Developing reflective and relationship-based management in child-care social work.' *British Journal of Social Work*, 42(7), 1315–1332. doi:10.1093/bjsw/bcr134.

Ryan, M., Merighi, J., Healy, B. and Renouf, N. (2004) 'Belief, optimism and caring: Findings from a cross national study of expertise in mental health social work.' *Qualitative Social Work*, 3(4): 411–429.

Ryan, S. (2004) *Vital Practice: Stories from the Healing Arts: The Homeopathic and Supervisory Way*. Portland: Sea Change.

Saltiel, D. (2016) 'Supervision: A contested space for learning and decision making.' *Qualitative Social Work*, 16(4), 533–549. doi:10.1177/1473325016633445.

Santa Rita, E. (1998) 'Solution-focused supervision.' *The Clinical Supervisor*, 17(2) 127–139.

Satymurti, C. (1981) *Occupational Survival*. Oxford: Pergamon.

Scaife, J. (2001) *Supervision in Mental Health Professions*. Hove, East Essex: Brunner Routledge.

Scaife, J. (2009) *Supervision in Clinical Practice: A Practitioner's Guide* (second edition). London: Routledge.

Scaife, J. (2010) *Supervising the Reflective Practitioner: An Essential Guide to Theory and Practice*. London: Routledge.

Scammell, J. (2016) '"Prioritise people": The importance of anti-oppressive practice.' *British Journal of Nursing*, 25(4), 226–226. doi:10.12968/bjon.2016.25.4.226.

Scannapieco, M. and Connell-Carrick, K. (2007) 'Child welfare workplace: The state of the workforce and strategies to improve retention.' *Child Welfare*, 86(6), 31–52.

Schein, E. H. (1996) 'Three cultures of management: The key to organizational learning.' *Sloan Management Review*, 38(1), 9–20.

Schindler, N. J. and Talen, M. R. (1996) 'Supervision 101: The basic elements for teaching beginning supervisors.' *The Clinical Supervisor*, 14(2), 109–120.

Schmidt, G. and Kariuki, A. (2019) 'Pathways to social work supervision.' *Journal of Human Behavior in the Social Environment*, 29(3), 321–332. doi:10.1080/10911359.2018.1530160.

Schön, D. (1983) *The Reflective Practitioner*. London: Temple Smith.

Schön, D. (1987) *Educating the Reflective Practitioner*. San Francisco, CA: Jossey-Bass.

Schutte, N. S., Malouff, J. M., Bobik, C., Coston, T. D. *et al.* (2001) 'Emotional intelligence and interpersonal relations.' *Journal of Social Psychology*, 141(4), 523–536.

Scourfield, J. and Welsh, I. (2003). 'Risk, reflexivity and social control in child protection: new times or same old story?' *Critical Social Policy*, 23, 3, 398–420.

Senge, P. (1990) *The Fifth Discipline: The Art and Practice of the Learning Organization*. New York, NY: Doubleday.

Sewell, K. M. (2018) 'Social work supervision of staff: A primer and scoping review (2013–2017).' *Clinical Social Work Journal*, 46(4), 252–265. doi:10.1007/s10615-018-0679-0.

Skills For Care and Children's Workforce Development Council (2007) *Providing Effective Supervision*. London: Skills for Care.

Sloan, G. (2006) *Clinical Supervision in Mental Health Nursing*. Chichester: Wiley.

Sloan, G. and Grant, A. (2012) 'A rationale for a clinical supervision database for mental health nursing in the UK.' *Journal of Psychiatric and Mental Health Nursing*, 19(5), 466–473. doi:10.1111/j.1365-2850.2012.01894.x.

Smith, M. (2000) 'Supervision of fear in social work: A re-evaluation of reassurance.' *Journal of Social Work Practice*, 14(1), 17–26.

Smith, M. (2006). 'Too little fear can kill you: Staying alive as a social worker.' Journal of *Social Work Practice, 20,*1, 69–81.

Smith, M. (2017) 'Looking into the seeds of time: Visual imagery in Macbeth and its relevance to social work practice, supervision and research.' *Journal of Social Work Practice*, 31(2), 121–133. doi:10.1080/02650533.2017.1298577.

Smith, R. and Anderson, L. (2008) 'Interprofessional learning: Aspiration or achievement?' *Social Work Education: The International Journal*, 27(7), 759–776.

Smythe, E. A., MacCulloch, T. and Charmley, R. (2009) 'Professional supervision: Trusting the wisdom that "comes".' *British Journal of Guidance & Counselling*, 37(1), 17–25.

Snyder, C. R. (2000) *Handbook of Hope: Theory, Measures & Applications*. San Diego, CA: Academic Press.

Sprengel, A. and Job, L. (2004) 'Reducing student anxiety by using clinical peer mentoring with beginning nursing students.' *Nurse Educator*, 29(6), 246–250.

Stagnitti, K. E., Schoo, A. and Welch, D. (eds) (2013) *Clinical and Fieldwork Placement in the Health Professions* (second edition). Melbourne: Oxford University Press.

Stalker, C. A., Mandell, D., Frensch, K. M., Harvey, C. and Wright, M. (2007) 'Child welfare workers who are exhausted yet satisfied with their jobs: How do they do it?' *Child & Family Social Work*, 12(2), 182–191.

Stanford, S. (2007) 'The Operations of Risk: The Meaning, Emotion and Morality of Risk Identities in Social Work Practice.' Unpublished PhD thesis, University of Tasmania, Launceston.

Stanley, J. and Goddard, C. (2002) *In the Firing Line: Violence and Power in Child Protection Work*. Chichester; New York, NY: John Wiley and Sons.

Stanley, N. and Manthorpe, J. (eds) (2004) *The Age of the Inquiry: Learning and Blaming in Health and Social Care*. London: Routledge.

Stanley, T. (2007) 'Risky work: Child protection practice.' *Social Policy Journal of New Zealand*, 30, 163–177.

Stevenson, J. (2005) *Professional Supervision in Social Work*. Unison, City of Edinburgh Branch. Available at: www.unison-edinburgh.org.uk/oldsite/socialwork/supervision.html, accessed 31 March 2020.

Stoltenberg, C. D., Bailey, K. C., Cruzan, C. B., Hart, J. T. and Ukuku, U. (2014) 'The Integrative Developmental Model of Supervision.' In C. E. Watkins and D. L. Milne (eds), *The Wiley International Handbook of Clinical Supervision* (pp.576–597). Chichester: John Wiley & Sons.

Strand, V. and Badger, L. (2007) 'A clinical consultation model for child welfare supervisors.' *Child Welfare*, 86(1), 79–96.

Sue, D. W. and Sue, D. (1999) *Counseling the Culturally Different: Theory and Practice* (third edition). Hoboken, NJ: John Wiley & Sons.

Tai, J. H. M., Canny, B. J., Haines, T. P. and Molloy, E. K. (2017) 'Implementing peer learning in clinical education: A framework to address challenges in the "real world".' *Teaching and Learning in Medicine*, 29(2), 162–172. doi:10.1080/10401334.2016.1247000.

Taylor, H., Beckett, C. and McKeigue, B. (2008) 'Judgements of Solomon: Anxieties and defences of social workers involved in care proceedings.' *Child & Family Social Work*, 13(1), 23–31.

The Institute for Research and Innovation in Social Services (2019) *Improving understanding about supervision*. Available at: www.iriss.org.uk/news/news/2019/11/27/improving-understanding-about-supervision, accessed 31 March 2020.

Thomas, C. and Davis, S. (2005) 'Bicultural Strengths Based Supervision.' In M. Nash, R. Munford and K. O'Donoghue (eds), *Social Work Theories in Action* (pp.189–204). London: Jessica Kingsley Publishers.

Thomas, T., Dickson, D., Broadbridge, J., Hopper, L. *et al.* (2007) 'Benefits and challenges of supervising occupational therapy fieldwork students: Supervisors' perspectives.' *Australian Occupational Therapy Journal*, 54(s1), S2–S12.

Thompson, N. (2009) 'Stress.' In N. Thompson and J. Bates (eds), *Promoting Workplace Well-Being* (pp.3–15). London: Palgrave Macmillan.

Toasland, J. (2007) 'Containing the container: An exploration of the containing role of management in a social work context.' *Journal of Social Work Practice*, 21(2), 197–202.

Trotter, C. (1999) *Working with Involuntary Clients: A Guide to Practice*. Sydney: Sage.

Tsong, Y. and Goodyear, R. (2014) 'Assessing supervision's clinical and multicultural impacts: The Supervision Outcome Scale's psychometric properties.' *Training & Education in Professional Psychology*, 8(3), 189–195.

Tsui, M.-S. (1997) 'The roots of social work supervision.' *The Clinical Supervisor*, 15(2), 191–198. doi:10.1300/J001v15n02_14.

Tsui, M.-S. and Ho, W.-S. (1998) 'In search of a comprehensive model of social work supervision.' *The Clinical Supervisor*, 16(2), 181–205. doi:10.1300/J001v16n02_12.

Tsui, M.-S., O'Donoghue, K. and Ng, A. K. T. (2014) 'Culturally Competent and Diversity-Sensitive Clinical Supervision.' In C. E. Watkins and D. L. Milne (eds), *The Wiley International Handbook of Clinical Supervision* (pp.238–254). Chichester: John Wiley & Sons.

Tugade, M. and B. Frederickson. (2004) 'Resilient individuals use positive emotions to bounce back from negative emotional experiences.' *Journal of Personality and Social Psychology*, 86(2), 320–333.

Turner-Daly, B. and Jack, G. (2014) 'Rhetoric vs. reality in social work supervision: The experiences of a group of child care social workers in England.' *Child & Family Social Work*, 22(1), 36–46. doi:10.1111/cfs.12191.

Turney, D. and Ruch, G. (2016) 'Thinking about thinking after Munro: The contribution of cognitive interviewing to child-care social work supervision and decision-making practices.' *British Journal of Social Work*, 46(3), 669–685.

Turney, D. and Ruch, G. (2018) 'What makes it so hard to look and to listen? Exploring the use of the Cognitive and Affective Supervisory Approach with children's social work managers.' *Journal of Social Work Practice*, 32(2), 125–138. doi:10.1080/02650533.2018.1439460.

Ungar, M. (2006) 'Practicing as a postmodern supervisor.' *Journal of Marital and Family Therapy*, 32(1), 59–71.

Urdang, E. (1999) 'Becoming a field instructor: A key experience in professional development.' *The Clinical Supervisor*, 18(1), 85–103.

Valkeavaara, T. (1999) 'Sailing in calm waters doesn't teach: Constructing expertise through problems in work.' *Studies in Continuing Education*, 21(2), 177–196.

van Heugten, K. (2009) 'Bullying of social workers: Outcomes of a grounded study into impacts and interventions.' *British Journal of Social Work*, bcp003. doi:10.1093/bjsw/bcp003.

Van Kessel, K. and Haan, D. (1993) 'The Dutch concept of supervision: Its essential characteristics as a conceptual framework.' *The Clinical Supervisor*, 11(1), 5–27.

Vec, T., Rupnik Vec, T. and Žorga, S. (2014) 'Understanding How Supervision Works and What It Can Achieve.' In C. E Watkins. and D. Milne (eds), *The Wiley International Handbook of Clinical Supervision*. New York, NY: John Wiley and Sons.

Wallace, E. (2019) 'Ngā aroro and social work supervision.' *Aotearoa New Zealand Social Work*, 31(3), 12.

Warner, J. (2014) '"Heads must roll?" Emotional politics, the press and the death of Baby P.' *British Journal of Social Work*, 44(6), 1637–1653. doi:10.1093/bjsw/bct039.

Warner, J. (2015) *The Emotional Politics of Social Work and Child Protection*. Bristol: Policy Press.

Watkins, C. E. (1990) 'Development of the psychotherapy supervisor.' *Psychotherapy*, 27, 553–560.

Watkins, C. E. (1997) 'The ineffective psychotherapy supervisor: Some reflections about bad behaviours, poor process and offensive outcomes.' *The Clinical Supervisior*, 16(1), 163–180.

Watkins, C. E. (2011) 'Does psychotherapy supervision contribute to patient outcomes? Considering thirty years of research.' *The Clinical Supervisor*, 30(2), 235–256. doi:10.1080/07325223.2011.619417.

Watkins, C. E. (2014a) 'Clinical supervision in the 21st century: Revisiting pressing needs and impressing possibilities.' *American Journal of Psychotherapy*, 68(2), 251–272.

Watkins, C. E. (2014b) 'The supervisory alliance: A half century of theory, practice, and research in critical perspective.' *American Journal of Psychotherapy*, 68(1), 19–55

Watkins Jr., C. E. (2017) 'Convergence in psychotherapy supervision: A common factors, common processes, common practices perspective.' *Journal of Psychotherapy Integration*, 27(2), 140.

Watkins Jr., C. E. (2019) 'What do clinical supervision research reviews tell us? Surveying the last 25 years.' *Counselling and Psychotherapy Research*. Early view. doi:10.1002/capr.12287.

Watkins, C. E. and Milne, D. (eds) (2014) *The Wiley International Handbook of Clinical Supervision*. New York, NY: John Wiley and Sons.

Watkins, C. E., Hook, J. N., Mosher, D. K. and Callahan, J. L. (2018) 'Humility in clinical supervision: Fundamental, foundational, and transformational.' *The Clinical Supervisor*, 1–21. doi:10.1080/073 25223.2018.1487355.

Watkins, C. E., Callahan, J. L. and Vîşcu, L. (2019) 'The common process of supervision process: The Supervision Session Pyramid as a teaching tool in the beginning supervision seminar.' *Journal of Contemporary Psychotherapy*, 50, 15–20. doi:10.1007/s10879-019-09436-5.

Watkins, C. E. and Wang, C. D. C. (2014) 'On the Education of Clinical Supervisors.' In C. Watkins and D. Milne (eds), *The Wiley International Handbook of Clinical Supervision* (pp.177–203). Chichester: Wiley.

Webb, S. A. (2006) *Social Work in a Risk Society: Social and Political Perspectives.* New York, NY: Palgrave Macmillan.

Webber-Dreadon, E. (1999) 'He Taonga Mo o Matou Tipuna (A gift handed down by our ancestors): An indigenous approach to social work supervision.' *Te Komako III Social Work Review*, 11(4), 7–11.

Wenger, E. (1998) *Communities of Practice: Learning, Meaning and Identity.* Cambridge: Cambridge University Press.

Wheeler, S. and Barkham, M. (2014) 'A Core Evaluation Battery for Supervision.' In C. Watkins and D. Milne (eds), *The Wiley International Handbook of Clinical Supervision* (pp.367–385). New York, NY: John Wiley and Sons.

White, E., Butterworth, T., Bishop, V., Carson, J., Jeacock, J. and Clements, A. (1998) 'Clinical supervision: Insider reports of a private world.' *Journal of Advanced Nursing*, 28(1) 185–192.

Wilkins, D. (2017) 'How is supervision recorded in child and family social work? An analysis of 244 written records of formal supervision.' *Child and Family Social Work*, 22(3), 1130–1140. https://doi.org/10.1111/cfs.12330.

Wilkins, D., Forrester, D. and Grant, L. (2017) 'What happens in child and family social work supervision?' *Child & Family Social Work*, 22(2), 942–951. doi:10.1111/cfs.12314.

Wilkins, D., Khan, M., Stabler, L., Newlands, F. and Mcdonnell, J. (2018) 'Evaluating the quality of social work supervision in UK children's services: Comparing self-report and independent observations.' *Clinical Social Work Journal*, 46, 350–360. doi:10.1007/s10615-018-0680-7.

Wilson, R. (2015) *The Perceived Effectiveness of a Reflective Learning Model of Supervision for Maori and Pasifika Supervisees.* Master's thesis. University of Auckland. Auckland.

Williams, L. and Irvine, F. (2009) 'How can the clinical supervisor role be facilitated in nursing: A phenomenological exploration.' *Journal of Nursing Management*, 17(4), 474–483.

Williams, M. E., Joyner, K., Matic, T. and Lakatos, P. P. (2019) 'Reflective supervision: A qualitative program evaluation of a training program for infant and early childhood mental health supervisors AU.' *The Clinical Supervisor*, 1–24. doi:10.1080/07325223.2019.1568942.

Winter, K., Morrison, F., Cree, V., Ruch, G., Hadfield, M. and Hallett, S. (2019) 'Emotional labour in social workers' encounters with children and their families.' *British Journal of Social Work*, 49(1), 217–233. doi:10.1093/bjsw/bcy016.

Worthington, E. L. (1987) 'Changes in supervision as counselors and supervisors gain experience: A Review.' *Professional Psychology: Research and Practice*, 18, 189–208.

Wright, T. A. and Quick, J. C. (2009) 'The emerging positive agenda in organizations: Greater than a trickle, but not yet a deluge.' *Journal of Organizational Behavior*, 30(2), 147–159.

Yankeelov, P. A., Barbee, A. P., Sullivan, D. and Antle, B. F. (2009) 'Individual and organizational factors in job retention in Kentucky's child welfare agency.' *Children and Youth Services Review*, 31(5), 547–554.

Yegdich, T. (1999) 'Lost in the crucible of supportive clinical supervision: Supervision is not therapy.' *Journal of Advanced Nursing*, 29(5), 1265–1275.

Yegdich, T. and Cushing, A. (1998) 'An historical perspective on clinical supervision in nursing.' *Australian & New Zealand Journal of Mental Health Nursing*, 7(1), 3.

Yip, K.-S. (2006) 'Self-reflection in reflective practice: A note of caution.' *British Journal of Social Work*, 36(5), 777–788.

Subject Index

Author Index

285